What Difference Did the War M

THEMES IN CONTEMPORARY BRITISH HISTORY

What Difference Did the War Make?

Edited by Brian Brivati and Harriet Jones

LEICESTER UNIVERSITY PRESS
London and New York

Distributed in the USA by St. Martin's Press Inc.

LEICESTER UNIVERSITY PRESS
A Cassell imprint
Wellington House, 125 Strand, London, WC2R 0BB, England

First published 1993
Paperback edition first published 1995

Distributed exclusively in the USA by St. Martin's Press, Inc., Room 400, 175 Fifth Avenue, New York, NY 10010, USA

British Library Cataloguing in Publication Data

A CIP catalogue record for this book is available fromThe British Library

ISBN 0 7185 2263 X

Library of Congress Cataloging-in-Publication Data

A CIP catalog record for this book is available from the Library of Congres

Typeset by Florencetype Ltd, Kewstoke, Avon
Printed and bound in Great Britain by Biddles Ltd of Guildford and King's Lynn

Contents

List of contributors

John Barnes lectures in Government and Politics at the London School of Economics and Political Science.

Brian Brivati is Deputy Director of the Institute of Contemporary British History.

Mark Cornwall lectures in History at the University of Dundee.

Mary Evans lectures in the Faculty of Social Sciences, Darwin College, University of Kent.

Peter Hennessy is Professor of Contemporary British History at Queen Mary and Westfield College, University of London.

Eric Hobsbawm is Emeritus Professor of History at Birkbeck College, University of London.

Harriet Jones is a Research Fellow at the Institute of Contemporary British History and lectures in History at the University of London.

Keith Middlemas is Professor of History at the University of Sussex.

David Morgan is Senior Lecturer in Sociology, Keynes College, University of Kent.

Bill Osgerby teaches at the University of Sussex. He has completed a doctoral thesis on youth culture in Brighton since the war.

Nicholas Owen is a research student at Christ Church, Oxford. He is completing a doctoral thesis on the Labour Party and the end of British rule in India.

E.G.H. Pedaliu lectures in History at the London School of Economics and Political Science.

J. Enoch Powell, former Conservative politician, is a retired Member of Parliament.

Malcolm Smith lectures in History at St. David's University College, University of Wales.

Penny Summerfield is Lecturer in the History of Education at the University of Lancaster.

Geoffrey Warner is Visiting Fellow in the Department of Politics and International Studies, University of Birmingham.

Preface

What difference did the war make?

This volume is the third in a series drawn from the annual Summer Schools organised by the Institute of Contemporary British History (ICBH) and the Department of Government of the London School of Economics. The theme of this, the fourth Summer School held in July 1991, was 'Continuity or Change, Britain 1929–1959'. The selection of papers included here reflect that theme by addressing the question, 'What difference did the war make?'.

The ICBH has always considered one of its primary tasks to be the bringing together of academics and researchers from a wide variety of disciplines. The Summer School therefore included papers on the political, economic, social, defence and foreign policy implications of the war for Britain. This multidisciplinary approach is reflected in the organisation of this book, which is divided into three sections.

The first, 'What difference did the war make to politics and economics?', includes papers by Professor Peter Hennessy and Professor Eric Hobsbawm. Professor Hennessy opens the volume with a powerful defence of 'Mr Attlee's Settlement' against the 'new orthodoxy' represented in the writing of Correlli Barnett. Professor Hobsbawm reviews the comparative economic performance of Britain in the post-war period. Both papers return to the critique expounded by Professor David Marquand in his book, *The Unprincipled Society*, that the central failure of post-war government in Britain has been the lack of a 'developmental state'. This widens the debate explored in the first volume of this series by Marquand himself.[1]

Commentaries on these papers by Professor Keith Middlemas, the Rt. Hon. Enoch Powell and Mr John Barnes reflect the variety of sometimes controversial views these issues raise. Mr Powell's well-known views are included in this volume because they represent an important strain of 'Little Englandism' which is part of the historical debate. The editors would like to stress that the views expressed by the commentators are their personal opinion and do not reflect the views of the ICBH.

The second section, 'What difference did the war make to society and the citizen?', begins with a historiographical assessment of the impact of the war on the British state by Dr Malcolm Smith. His views, as a political historian, on the evolution of the relationships between the citizen and the state are taken up from a very different perspective by Dr David Morgan and Dr Mary Evans. Their sociological consideration of the impact of the war on the definition of citizenship focuses on the writing of George Orwell and his fears that the interventionist state, while providing material well-being, would destroy or undermine political freedom. Moreover, they point to the paradox of a state which during the war was encouraging a new and more dynamic image of the 'citizen housewife' but which returned to a white patriarchal model of citizenship after 1945. Dr Penny Summerfield addresses this latter point in her survey of the current state of research into the difference that the war made to women's lives. In the final paper in this section, Bill Osgerby addresses the neglected field of youth culture and the advent of the 'teenager' in the 1950s. He explores the continuity between pre-war youth cultures and thereby challenges the idea that the teenager of the 1950s was a new social phenomenon. He particularly questions the notion that the social dislocation of a childhood in the war years led to teenage delinquency in the 1950s and re-examines the extent to which youth affluence was a uniquely post-war development.

The final section, 'What difference did the war make to Britain's role in the world?', begins with an overview of the impact of the Second World War on Britain's world position by Professor Geoffrey Warner. This general paper lays the framework for three case studies. Nick Owen examines the imperial dimension by analysing the difference that the war made to the British government's policy on India. This is followed by two European case studies, one from either side of the Iron Curtain. Dr Mark Cornwall takes the fascinating case of Czechoslovakia and explores what difference appeasement and war had on Anglo-Czech relations. Finally, Effie Pedaliu looks at Anglo-Italian relations and highlights the extent to which the 'great power fixation' referred to in the opening paper by Professor Hennessy was exposed by Britain's inability to compete with the Americans in influencing the development of the post-war Italian state.

As with previous volumes in this series, we hope that this collection of essays encourages discussion and debate, and reconfirms the importance of studying contemporary history.

The work of the ICBH depends upon the effort and enthusiasm of the many people who give their time and effort to the promotion of the study of contemporary British history. We would like to pay tribute here to the other organisers of the 1991 Summer School: Helen Mercer, Richard Aldrich, Michael Hopkins and C.J. Morris. We would also like to thank Dr Paul Addison for chairing the opening sessions and giving such useful advice; and Peter Hennessy for his good-humoured support. Stephanie Maggin very kindly took time off from her other work to help, and has also supplied us with a striking cover photograph. Finally, we thank Dr Peter Catterall, the Director of the ICBH, and Virginia Preston, Executive Director, who painstakingly transcribed the proceedings of the conference. This volume is dedicated to the retiring chairman of the Board of Management of the ICBH, Sir Frank Cooper. Sir Frank has been a constant source of help since the founding of the Institute and a critical part of its continuing success.

Brian Brivati
ICBH, April 1992   *Harriet Jones*

Notes

[1] See T. Gorst, L. Johnman and W.S. Lucas (1989), *Postwar Britain, 1945–64: Themes and Perspectives*, London, Pinter Publishers.

I
What difference did the war make to politics and economics?

1 Never again

Peter Hennessy

I think it is time to revisit mid-century Britain, for two reasons. First of all because I have just finished a book about it (Hennessy, 1992). But also, and rather more important, because those years have become a battleground of contemporary politics—very much so in the period from which we are only now emerging, the period of polarisation between the two major parties and to a large extent within the two major parties, as partisans of right, left and centre fought over the remains of those early post-war years and the significance to our predicament today, or otherwise, of what has become known as 'Mr Attlee's Settlement'.

Let me begin with an intriguing curiosity, a Central Intelligence Agency assessment of Britain in mid-1949, Britain's condition and Britain's prospects, prepared for President Truman (CIA, 1949). In proper Washington bureaucratic style, it summarises its gist at the beginning in a couple of paragraphs which it later fleshes out in more detail. This is what Truman was told, shortly before the pound sterling was devalued, a month and a half after NATO was formed.

> The basic security interests of the US and UK are practically identical. A tacit understanding has tended to grow up whereby a common strategic position is maintained. The ability of the UK to play its part is considered to be directly related to the state of its national economy; it is considered that the UK with respect to the reorganisation of its national economy has completed the first phase of its postwar history. Its success in doing so appears to have come from a tremendous productive effort, which created a surplus for export. It is now considered that the peak of this effort may have passed, and that although production remains high, the capacity of the world market to absorb the exportable surplus may be diminishing. If so, it will be increasingly difficult for the UK to maintain the economic strength needed to support its own policies and to carry out its responsibilities in the pattern of US/UK security. An unfavourable economic condition will lead to the problem of shifting more and more responsibility for maintaining a common strategic position from the UK to the US.

The body of the report focused on the impact of the Second World War on the United Kingdom and the permanent infirmity caused by our last great throw as a superpower—that is my phrase, not the CIA's. I am going to dip into it a bit more.

> The relative weakness of the UK at the end of the war, instead of being merely a condition caused by the war and corrected by the recovery of 1947–8, may be the

result of long term trends that were only momentarily halted. If so the weakness at the start of 1947 may increase and total US responsibility may develop progressively and call for progressively major adjustments on the part of the US. It is now reasonably certain that the UK is approaching the end of the first phase of its postwar history. This phase could be described in retrospect as the reorganising of the national economy in relation to the concept of the welfare state and the national potential in relation to profound changes in the international sphere. The adjustments called for were essentially political and economic. A large measure of democratic socialism has quietly revolutionised the national life of Great Britain.

Already this is faintly surprising, isn't it? If they had had such things in the modern form, this could have been a party political broadcast in the 1950 general election, a Labour one.

The Commonwealth and the Empire have undergone major political alterations of a realistic kind, without any suggestion of collapse. The national economy has with tremendous effort been momentarily adapted to the demands of the welfare state. The speed and success of these adjustments have been an undeniable factor in the development of the more favourable security position in which the US now stands. But it is also reasonably certain that the UK is now moving into the second phase of its postwar history. The basic problems that will be encountered in this phase, though different in character, will perhaps be even more critical in the long run than those that have already been dealt with. They will in any event require more comprehensive solutions than any that have yet been devised.

The central problems can be stated as follows: the maintenance of foreign trade at the high level required to sustain the demands on the national economy of the standards of British life and the welfare commitments of democratic socialism; and the international commitments of UK, Commonwealth and imperial policy. If this proves impossible, as it may very well do in view of developing trends in the world economy, the development of alternative ways, other than by a reduction in population, of sustaining the national economy will have to be found. Since income from British overseas investments is no longer an important item, the UK international account can be balanced only by the production and sale of exportable surplus. A sense of crisis in conjunction with government controls over domestic consumption, and the full use of manpower, gradually pushed up the volume of exports until in March 1949 they reached 106 per cent of 1938 and resulted in a momentary balance of payments. But even this unprecedented volume provides no cushion against the future.

The CIA goes on to say that the signs were now accumulating that suggested that Britain had already peaked by mid-1949 in its post-war life. These signs included overseas markets that were being increasingly satisfied by restored domestic industries and Britain's competitors. Japanese industry revived to reduce US occupation costs implied future serious competition; German industry, similarly revived but with its pre-war outlets in Eastern Europe still blocked, suggested even more severe competition. Demand in the United States had perceptively receded and there was no evidence of its early revival. The approach of these difficulties had been recognised—I question this, but I will come to that later—proposals for meeting them had been under consideration for some time. The proposals consisted of a devaluation of sterling, the reduction of production costs, the adjustment of sources of imports to avoid dollar costs, and the development of new economic resources, particularly in the dependent Empire. Some of these proposals called for time and capital investment on a scale then unavailable. Others would create new problems for the old ones solved. It is highly improbable that a complete solution could be found along these lines.

Now to me this is a remarkable document for many reasons. At this point, having praised it, I should point out that I am not now, nor ever have been, an officer of the Central Intelligence Agency, an agent, a client or in any other way related to its people, its offices or its practices. Having said that, I praise it again: it is quite a remarkably prescient piece of work. I can only surmise, for I don't know who wrote it, that it was someone who worked closely with us in the war in the Office of Strategic Services, and who, as so often with CIA men in London, had gone native on us. This is an utterly, without exception, favourable view of our post-war performance, and a realistic one of our prospects.

The sympathy shown for the Attlee government is very surprising because there is no trace here of the standard American line in certain right-wing circles in those years, that their dollars were paying for our hospitals and our welfare state and our nationalisation. There is praise, too, for the political skill with which the first great post-war imperial disposals had been handled. What is especially interesting, I think, then and now, is Washington's appreciation of our long-term predicament. It acknowledges, rightly, the successful nature of our immediate post-war reconstruction but watch out, it says, for our underlying economic strength and the implications for our competitiveness and balance of payments once Germany and Japan reappear on the world market. Note, too, the CIA analyst's appreciation of how problematic this would make any pretensions to a truly great power role.

One can also detect in this document many of the preoccupations of our current historiography. There is a complete absence of any Correlli Barnett-like suggestions that soft New Jerusalemers in high places were, through delusory and costly schemes, soaping the staircase for our rapid fall as a trading and a military nation (Barnett, 1986). I mustn't sound too sour about revisionism on the road from 1945, because any orthodoxy requires challenge, that's our business, and almost from the moment Paul Addison had published a book on the post-war consensus (*The Road to 1945* in 1975), the more comforting views of our post-war achievements were ruthlessly called into question, not least because Mr Attlee's settlement was crumbling before our very eyes, the victim of stagflation, made all the more acute by a quadrupling of the world oil price and all the industrial strife and political turmoil which came with it (Addison, 1975).

You could say that—even without the mind-concentrating events associated with the winter crises, the miners' strikes and the fall of Ted Heath— '1945' was an orthodoxy just waiting to be mugged, though another decade was to pass before Barnett, to the continuing rage of many, so thoroughly put the boot in. And remember the alacrity with which the then possessors of power seized upon his *Audit of War* in 1986. Sir Keith Joseph spoke publicly about its influence on him, it was read in No. 10 (Joseph, 1987). The more literate end of the business class would quote it uncritically and continually.

Why this intense desire to rubbish what, according to folk memory, was our last great collective achievement as a nation (by which I mean the 1940s as a whole, not just the post-war period)? It was because collectivism, of a mild British kind admittedly, had been the spur, the motivation. But, by this time, it had become despised and called 'corporatism'. And it had become the first of the usual suspects to be rounded up in the routine raids of the new right when they were searching for the guilty men and the guilty nostra. It was because, I suspect, these people had grown up in the shadow of 1945. The first post-war Conservative generation, by and large, had embraced nearly all of that settlement, as much as their Labour counterparts. The Macmillans, the Butlers and the Heaths were motivated by a never-again impulse. Never again would there be mass unemployment, never again would there be meagre, or nil, health care for ordinary people, never again would there be slums, never again would there be total war if the combination of collective security and nuclear weapons could be so arranged as to prevent it.

For those who were uneasy, perhaps guilty, about the long reach of the shadow of 1945, Correlli Barnett was pure catharsis. He gave them ammunition, they thought, to demolish its essentials, to mock the achievements, to claim that, in the end, they were ruinous, both of economic performance and social health—all public ownership, monopoly trade unions, corporate fudge and mudge, and dependency culture.

Can you remember the first Conservative party political broadcast after the 1983 election, in which Mrs Thatcher almost got as many seats in her majority as Clem had in 1945? It was the rubbishing of the Attlee years. No Conservative government to my knowledge, so directly, so publicly, or so visually in this form, had taken on 1945. In her moment of triumph, this was the artefact that had to fall. It did not work, but that is another discussion. This was the very first broadcast and she took Clem on, saintly Attlee, directly, and made the claims that I have just summarised.

Can you remember Nigel Lawson's lecture to the Centre for Policy Studies called 'The Tide of Ideas' in 1988? It was all about the two great political themes, viewpoints, that have dominated the post-war years. Until the late 1970s, Mr Attlee's Settlement, said Nigel Lawson, had swept all before it. Only with the advent of Mrs Thatcher had it been questioned and later toppled. The degree to which the shadow of 1945 affected, and still does to some extent, our current political debate is quite remarkable. Mrs Thatcher used to claim in private right from the beginning that she needed three parliaments to undo the work of the first six post-war years, which I always used to think was the greatest of backhanded compliments to the Attlee government that could be devised.

For these reasons, I think it is high time to revisit mid-century Britain, to ask if the new orthodoxy (although perhaps it is too early to say that Correlli Barnett & Co. are the new orthodoxy) might not be as flawed as the old one with which many of us grew up, to see what other factors, impulses, traditions, economic or political actions might or might not hold the key to a better (not a complete but a better) understanding both of the times and the legacy to the post-war period.

The first question that has to be asked is, are we right to be so obsessed, even now, with the period 1945–51? Yes, we are. To borrow Dean Acheson's phrase, those who lived through those years were 'present at the creation'. For 1945–51, when taken with the war years before which so powerfully shaped them, *did* set the context in which we operated as a fading world power, a shaky political economy and a welfare state, right up to the crisis of the mid-1970s which so shook up our politicians, our mandarins and our thinking classes. Britain-watchers abroad, too, were shaken by it, and our newspaper columnists and our professional historians even now constantly refer to those years.

The choices made, or funked, during the first six years after the war, were genuinely formative. Those that were later reversed—by our going into Europe instead of keeping out, by our dropping the full employment pledge as the political and social aspiration, shedding universality of welfare provision, the health service apart, as the principle of welfare across the board—each of these benchmarks when crossed proved both difficult and painful, as the still protracted and ever-raging arguments around them demonstrate.

Before going back properly to those years, let me declare my own interests (it's only fair), the inclinations and biases that I bring to the post-war years. Even now, I revisit them with sympathy, and a measure of admiration for their social purpose, their sense of equity. Delving among the documents, I still warm to the lack of defeatism on the part of ministers and civil servants, who thought and behaved, in those years, as though a better and a fairer country could be constructed out of the wreckage of the early 1940s. To the extent, in Paul Addison's phrase, that the solidarity of home-front Britain could be sustained and run on into the first post-war years, it was a sensible, and in some respects a highly successful strategy, although obviously the war dividend, as you might call it, was a fast-wasting asset by the time the Attlee government fell. The generosity of spirit, the optimism of those years, strike at least one middle-aged man in 1991, still reeling from the polarised politics of the 1970s and 1980s to which I was never reconciled. They still strike me, and cause me to be a little moved by the nobility of it all.

I do not mean to eulogise Major Attlee. It is very much out of this carrying-on-the-home-front-by-another-means that the basis of my critical piece arises. Restoring those export markets, pushing forward that reconstruction which so impressed the CIA, was achieved, like the tremendous surge of war production itself, by running existing plant and machinery and people flat out. What was lacking was the planning and investment for a sustained, long-term, economic and industrial performance of a higher order than before, once the rebuilding was over. This to me is the essential difference between the nation to which we are most comparable in those years, France.

Lord Plowden and his Central Economic Planning Staff now appear to be more management consultants to the existing way of doing business and organising our political economy when compared to Monnet's plan for the re-equipment and modernisation of France. Lord Plowden would say, I am sure, that it was quite impossible, given our political structure, for him to be the British Monnet. We had a Chancellor of the Exchequer called Stafford Cripps, we had a whole relationship between ministers and civil servants which meant that technocrats simply could not take over. I know all that. But the mystery that remains for me as I think it does for Eric Hobsbawm too, of the Attlee governments, is why the first British government devoted to planning, that proclaimed planning and used planning to distinguish itself from all other competitors in the political field, did so little to implement real planning of almost any kind that you can notice in those early post-war years, despite having a remarkable apparatus of control at its disposal under the wartime legislation. And this was carried over, and the nation was used to responding, at that stage, not any more, to central schemes of virtually all kinds nationally implemented.

For example, I cannot read the bundle of fascinating diaries that we have come our way over the last five years without constantly reflecting on this—, James Meade's (Howson and Muggeridge, 1990) and above all Robert Hall's (Cairncross, 1989). Robert Hall would go to Lord Plowden's Planning Board meetings and wonder what it was all for. He, like Lord Plowden, worried about the fact that they as civil servants were talking to businessmen and trade unionists about things which ministers either hadn't been told of or had yet to approve. It was, to use that overworked cliché, but in this case it is justified, a mere talking shop. Yet it was the great delight of Attlee and Morrison to make statements in parliament about the new uniquely British way of democratic socialist economic planning that enabled us to organise ourselves efficiently without losing individual liberty. It makes painful and almost absurd reading to look at *Hansard* for the spring of 1947 when Lord Plowden was appointed, and Cripps and Morrison in their different ways laid out to parliament how it was going to be. It was neither one thing nor the other. And it still baffles me that people, who in some ways had got where they were in 1947 on the back of these notions, Morrison in particular (but remember Attlee's one contribution to democratic socialist thought had been about the machinery of government) (Attlee, 1937), could be so casual about the piecemeal institution building in which they indulged in those early post-war years.

Now for me, this, and not soft-centred Keynesianism in high places, is the issue. I am not arguing that if we had by some miracle been able to do the modernisation and re-equipment plan here, it would have made necessarily all the difference for ever. There are certain other quite big factors which I will come to in a moment. But the fact that there was no real attempt to do it, even in the British circumstances, even within the British political and bureaucratic tradition, is still to me amazing. Talking of soft-centred Keynesianism in high places, I think we have got to beware a consensus here which didn't exist. It is quite plain, isn't it, in those documents as well as the diaries, that Keynes's *General Theory* was not carrying all before it in late-1940s Whitehall. There are constant complaints in Robert Hall's diaries that Sir Wilfred Eady and others not only didn't understand it but thought it was quite wrong and alien. In Meade's diaries too, there is the difficulty of getting the Treasury to get the basic statistics needed for the national income assessments and so on. There was a constant battle—it wasn't as if, from Kingsley Wood's 1941 budget (which is always cited) onwards, in the war years, that the new Keynesian orthodoxy swung into place with scarcely a squeak. The rearguard action was continuous and was where it mattered in day-to-day meetings inside Whitehall.

Even where the new orthodoxy had won hearts and minds, there was a running row of a fairly fundamental sort, about methods. Take, for example, the all too short diaries of 'Otto' Clarke[1] which stop just before the convertibility crisis in 1947. Before they stop you can see in them the constant row he had with Meade and others about planning, even in the way it was conceived. Meade dismissed Clarke and the other economic planners, who wanted physical controls used rather more vigorously, as 'Gosplan' people. This row was never resolved, even though it was put to Morrison on several occasions. Do we actually take the commanding heights of nationalised industry and think that will do most of the trick, and then carry out Keynesian fine-tuning using the budget to do the rest? Or do we actually try and run something approaching a centrally planned economy in conditions of acute scarcity? And Clarke would come home and rage in his diary, because ministers would do neither one thing nor the other. And even as late as 1950 Robert Hall is raging in his diaries because at some particular meeting of the Economic Policy Committee of the Cabinet they still didn't know which way to go on these issues. Fundamental differences of approach were there throughout.

And there was no real resolution of this at Cabinet level, on any of the big issues, as far as I can see, even during the chancellorship of that supremely organised man, the highest-placed management consultant in British political life until Heseltine, I suppose, Sir Stafford Cripps. And yet a great deal of ministerial energy was wasted on the public–private divide. I think Ken Morgan is right constantly to remind us how soon nationalisation went off the boil (Morgan, 1984). They had gone off it in a big way by 1948, as we all know, and iron and steel caused an immense problem. Certainly the legacy of those public ownerships lasted another forty years, but actually to behave, as some historians do, as if the impulse to public ownership of the standard Morrisonian sort carried on for generation after generation is quite absurd. But a great deal of time and energy was wasted on that, the precise organisation of this one or that one, who was going to chair it and so on.

For the book that I have just finished, going through the documents and diaries, I was struck continually by the relevance of David Marquand's thesis in his *The Unprincipled Society*, that perhaps apart from the first of our post-war incomes policies—the very successful wage freeze of 1948–50 (Cripps's one), which within a year had reduced the rate of wage rises by more than half—apart from that, and that was dependent on old impulses, the Bevin–Deakin axis, the hangover from the Second World War (they had certain things going for them)—apart from that there was no real attempt to introduce an institutional infrastructure of the kind needed to run a mixed economy/welfare state. Another huge gap right at the centre where, by and large, certain things can be done if ministers want them to be. Whitehall is not like the rest of the country. This is their bailiwick, and even here there was almost a complete failure to realise that the British state needed to be modernised.

Commander Geoffrey Cooper wrote to Attlee in 1946 (Labour MP for

Middlesbrough West, he was a businessman, one of the few Labour business-men who came in in 1945), saying, don't you think before you try and produce your transformation that you should do what Roosevelt did in 1933–4 when he looked at the federal bureaucracy – look at the instrument, see if it is capable of handling the new state that you are creating with these nationalisation statutes and the National Health Service. Attlee passed it on to Bridges, and Bridges as Head of the Civil Service had two meetings on it and, apart from Lord Franks (Oliver Franks, an outsider who had run the Ministry of Supply), they all said, we do not need to do this, we can go back to the way it happened in the 1930s; the businessmen were useful in the war, but we do not need them now, and the methods that have served us so well in the early part of this century will be adequate. Two meetings, two Saturdays in early 1946, they considered the need to modernise the British state and they said no, thank you (Hennessy, 1989, pp. 121–6).

And what is amazing to me is that Attlee, Dalton and, above all, Cripps, who, remember, had run a Royal Ordnance factory in the First World War, who was supremely interested in management, who set up the British Institute of Management, who was keen on management consultancy, did not bother to counteract Bridges or seriously to question the collective wisdom of the permanent secretaries. They treated the senior civil service as if it was a self-regulating profession, not something that was crucial to political social and economic outcomes, and their own electoral fortunes. It is extraordinary to me how that can be so.

I think we were the poorer for that, because what Cooper was after and what Franks was talking about in those meetings was what I suppose we could call now prototype Raynerism, quite simply a better-managed state. Not revolution by any means, but just the importation of a management impulse of the kind you were going to need if state activity, by one means or another, albeit at arm's length quite often in the nationalised industries, was going to remain at that level for the foreseeable future, which it quite patently was in 1946, with those nationalisation statutes, the National Health Service bill, rolling through the production process in the House of Commons.

You see this extraordinary management gap, not just in the public corpor-ations, but in the National Health Service too. Nye Bevan's achievement was quite remarkable, sorting out the rows about the voluntary hospitals and so on, simply by saying nationalise the lot, but the degree to which there was almost no discussion of how you would manage this vast enterprise was very surprising indeed. There was almost no contemplation of how you would actually get the thing to run once you had brought it all together.

In short, and this is the Marquand thesis and I am quite sure it fits, we simply lacked the institutional infrastructure for the modern state. And above all, with one or two exceptions, people lacked even the beginnings of an appreciation of its shortcomings. I have never been persuaded, you see, that in the mixed economy/welfare state, *welfare* was the problem. It seems to me that that is ideologues picking out the kind of suspect that they want to charge and demolish. Now why is that? There is one concession that I think we have to make to the thesis that the welfare state 'did for us' progressively in the post-war period, and that is that Germany did not actually get around to having a far more generous welfare state than ours was, or ever became, until 1955. For the first ten years after the war they by and large were in no position to do that, for obvious reasons. They didn't have a state until 1949, and the really generous, basic welfare state was not put into place until the mid-1950s. But if you read Douglas Ashford and others on France, they were putting together a kind of Christian Democratic welfare state of a fairly generous and fairly universal kind. It was not done with the fanfare that accompanied it in this country, because their governments were disorganised, and they did not have a Beveridge to put up on some sort of sacred pedestal either. It was not made the totem pole of those post-war governments in France in the way that it was of the Attlee government here. But they were doing it as well. If you look at the proportion of GDP going to welfare in the advanced western countries in the first ten years after the Second World War, we are not the odd nation out by any means. It is a common factor, by and large, with one or two exceptions.

It seems to me as well, while remaining on the central thrust of the Barnett case, that in that political climate you could not have spun an economic miracle out of the rubble without actually doing something about basic welfare provision. It was simply politically not on. All right, if there had been a Churchill government after August 1945, the National Health Service might have been the previous model, the 1944 green paper model, but there would have been a health service, free at the point of delivery for the poorer end of society. There would not have been public ownership—nationalised industries—of course not. But in terms of public welfare, the difference would have been one of degree, not a huge absolute difference. The politics of early post-war Britain were quite rightly and inevitably welfare-minded.

Now as you can see I do have problems of a personal sort in arguing against the Barnett thesis, because every time he drives down the M11 from Cambridge on his JCB, I always feel it is my own much-loved early post-war 'prefab' that he is about to push over. So I have to declare my interest again. The lost years for me, however, are the 1930s which (as well as the destruction of the Second World War) meant that there was scope, huge scope, which needed desperately to be utilised, for a kinder, gentler Britain. And you could say, even now, even with hindsight, even amidst the ruins of that settlement, that this was the greatest single achievement of the Attlee governments. If you take the Rowntree figures for York in 1950 and compare them with the same set of data for the same people in York in 1936—and I know that statistics have got far more sophisticated since then and the definitions of poverty have changed at least five times—but if you look at those figures, the transformation in life chances for those at the bottom of the heap was quite dramatic. Just take that one chart that Rowntree produced in his survey between 1936 and 1950: the number of working-class households living in poverty fell from 31.1 per cent to 2.77 per cent, and but for those wartime and post-war welfare measures it would have fallen to only 22.18 per cent.

That definition of poverty was not general, we must remember, but that is a remarkable achievement by any standards for any government in any advanced country at any time. It is all too easy to lose sight of the degree to which that comforted people in the early years of the loss of power after 1951. Sam Watson had made perhaps inflated claims at the 1950 party conference, saying that nobody goes hungry, nobody goes ill-clad, anybody can have a place at school and so on—the natural inflated language of party conferences. There was something measurable to show that Sam Watson was not simply crying at the moon and it is well to remember it. It was a prize worth having even if much of it depended indirectly on the billion dollars a year of American aid from 1946 onwards which Robert Hall, again in one of his more cathartic diary entries, reminded himself we had been living on since 1946 (Cairncross, 1989).

We did, however, suffer from the problem of overload. It wasn't just welfare overload, it was overload of a very deep and overarching kind. That said, I have always reckoned, since I have thought about it, that the industrial base we had in 1945 was very promising if you strip away hindsight. It should have been enough to take care of 46 million of us as we then were, our immediate material wants, with enough of a surplus to invest seed corn for the future. Sidney Pollard has always taken this line when he has gone through the areas in which we still had a lead and the new technologies in which we were very advanced compared to almost any one except the United States, and sometimes even compared to them, in 1945 (Pollard, 1982).

I was fascinated to dig out the paper that Keynes[2] sent to the War Cabinet in the last days of the war in Europe. It is mainly quoted by historians because of its overseas finance side, the IMF stuff. But if you look at the whole thing there are some fascinating asides in there, and one of them is his contention that the tragedy is that the Luftwaffe is no longer available to secure our economic future, he says, maybe the US Air Force could actually make a benign mistake and do it for us, but what we need are virtually all the factories and the staple industries in the North West and North East of England to be bombed, when preferably only the boards of directors are in residence. He went on to say that it was because wherever we had started from scratch, whether it was the Mosquito bombers or radar we could beat the world, on cost, on quality, on anything. But when it comes to making a steel billet or a cotton shirt we are hopeless, absolutely hopeless. Now, of course, he was known for his genius in touching up Cabinet papers in a way which nobody else before or since dared to do, and it was oversimplified. But there is something in that, if you actually strip away hindsight and go across the industrial base in 1945–6, it is immensely promising, intrinsically so, not just because the competitors were rubble. There were lots of sunrises in there, not just sunset industries, and that is all too easily forgotten. Change-and-decay merchants can get out of hand.

If I were in the business of scapegoating, which I am not, because the ICBH does not allow it, I would not round up the usual suspects in the National Insurance Offices, and the National Health Service Boards and the housing departments of the local authorities, or inside the allegedly bleeding hearts of that guilt-ridden generation of public schoolboys in high places. If I was rounding up suspects the one I would put in the dock is the great power fixation. In that same paper that Keynes put to the War Cabinet he says it is over a year now since the Middle East was cleared of Germans—in fact it was

18 months—and yet the war infrastructure there, the number of people of high rank is still immense; I fear the problem of the Major-Generals in Cairo is chronic, he said. Then he did some figures which suggested that our likely overseas deficit in the first post-war years would almost entirely match that of our overseas commitments.

Yet, having said that, it is all too easy to forget what 1945 looked like to those who were there and sat in offices. The best antidote to this that I have discovered is the chapter in the life of Bevin, Alan Bullock's one, which simply says 'August 1945'. And he goes, in meticulous detail, into the problems which passed over Bevin's desk in the first month of peace. It is overwhelming, absolutely overwhelming. And for anybody like me just to assume that we could have turned ourselves into a Scandinavia within a matter of years is absurd. I know that, and I understand that.

I do not sympathise, however, at the risk of upsetting Mr Powell, with Bevin's fury with Attlee for setting a deadline for withdrawal from India, 'I can't bear the shame of a scuttle without plan or dignity'—you remember that amazing letter he wrote to Attlee in 1947? I cannot entirely sympathise either with Bevin's determination to be the Sheikh of Araby for evermore. Nor can I—again I understand the reasons at the time, when it looked as though the Red Army might be about to march—understand why so much national treasure was thrown away in the rearmament post-Korea; even now I cannot understand it. There is one person in the room, Lord Croham, who as a young official in the Treasury argued against it, and there were others. So you see I am ambivalent. It is quite easy to see why the old drumbeats, the threnody went on so loud in those early post-war years. But the degree to which it went on and the length of time is a problem. Even the bomb, even now I would say that was a very arguable decision. To our generation Sir Henry Tissard's plea which upset everyone so much in 1949, that only if we cease to pretend to be a great power can we be sure of surviving as a great nation (Gowing, 1984, pp. 229–30), strikes us as good sense. But, having said all that, to sit in that Cabinet Room, in that Cabinet committee in January 1947, pre-NATO, the United States virtually completely withdrawn from Europe, with all the problems in that grim winter, even now I can understand why the decision to make a British atomic bomb, in the absence of American collaboration, was an 'of course' one.

The great power fixation is the factor which drives the 'special relationship'. It was quite natural, in fact unargued really except by one or two, that we should tuck ourselves in at the flank of the next superpower on the block, the United States. It is the problem, too, with Marshall Aid. Some of the most amazing minutes in the Foreign Relations series (of US documents) are when the Americans come over to set up the European Recovery Programme and want to treat us as just one of many mendicants, and we reply that we are not like France and Germany, we are a great power, do not treat us in this way. It arose, too, when Monnet approached Lord Plowden to have some kind of joint planning in 1949. It arose classically, too, at the time of the Schuman Plan, when even Kenneth Younger could say this is the black Catholic international, Schuman is a prisoner of the priests—and Morrison's famous line 'The Durham miners won't wear it'.

The problem, I think, was overload. It is far too easy to round up one or two suspects. You have got to see the thing in the round, and the really big one, if we have to single out one, is the great power fixation. It is quite wrong, however, to fall into the arms of Jean Monnet as so many English people now do both retrospectively and at the present moment. He talked about the price of victory: that we did not have to exorcise our history. Well, thank God we did not. The loss of a world war is a fairly high price to pay for economic regeneration. It is far too simple retrospectively to fall into that trap. But having said that, there was a price of victory: it was a vindication of our way of doing business, of conducting politics, which made us the smuggest nation for miles around, almost until this very moment.

Now what this period is crying for is a new generation of historians younger than me. People who are free of nostalgia, who are not susceptible to the old drumbeat, who don't still resent, as I do, Sir Anthony Eden's lying to the House of Commons in 1956 about our collusion with the French and the Israelis over Egypt, as I do at the age of 44. People who don't get a spasm of one kind or another when the word 'Suez' is mentioned. These are the people who have got to write it, not me, not the old boys. Now I am optimistic about this, I think it will be a new and a fascinating historiography and it is already under way. Many of the people who are doing it are in this room—I like to call them 'the ICBH generation'. I look forward to the day when my thoughts, my impulses, my views, have an old-fashioned, fading air, something comparable to a much-loved, cracked, 78 of the Big Band era, reprised and played periodically for reasons of nostalgia rather than enlightenment.

COMMENTARY ONE

J. Enoch Powell

Mr Chairman, I found myself in far-reaching sympathy with the cry from the heart with which Professor Hennessy ended his lecture. I think he is right to put his finger upon a factor which the historian chronically neglects: the emotional factor. One, of course, understands why the historian neglects it, it is unquantifiable, it is rather shameful, and it is difficult to handle, but without the emotional factor I do not think one can understand the turn-around which occurred in this country or some of the most surprising things which this country did in the second half of the twentieth century. When I resigned my chair in Australia in 1939 in order to come home to enlist, had I been asked 'What is the state whose uniform you wish to wear and in whose service you expect to perish?' I would have said 'The British Empire'. I would have had no doubt in giving that reply. It was a worldwide power which had at last decided to face its enemies upon the battlefield. And this gigantism, this delusion that big is great, the bullfrog mentality, has haunted Britain ever since 1945. Of course it haunted us in 1945. We defeated the Germans in 1940, but the Britain which defeated Germany in 1940 was this Britain here, it was these islands, impregnable in the face of the German armies, whom we turned around and sent eastward to their doom. But when the curtain fell, then we saw ourselves as a component in a mighty coalition, and we said to ourselves, 'It is the big boys who count now, it is the big forces'; we no longer said to ourselves 'We are great, we are impregnable, because we are small, because of the way in which in our small kingdom we behave.' Wherever I look, in the striking events of the last thirty or forty years, I see this gigantism overtaking us.

We had been great, because, Joseph Chamberlain told us, we had a great empire. So as we had manifestly lost a great empire, we must substitute for it something which we could claim to be equally extensive and equally great. In order to deceive ourselves in this way we deferred the modernisation of our law of citizenship which had left this country open to the immigration of some 800 million persons located in all parts of the world. The profound change in the population of this country which took place in the 1950s and 1960s and will progressively continue is traceable directly to the mania of gigantism: 'We are still great, we are still a world power, because we have a wonderful thing, a remarkable thing, a unit which is no unit, a political entity which is not political. We have the Commonwealth of Nations.'

Then, when we looked across the Channel, we said 'There is something big that can be made there, they are making something big there. We used to be big, we must get on to the bandwagon with it, we must join whatever is big.' And so one had the absurd British profession, absurd in the mouth of any offshore island, that we are going to 'lead Europe'. 'There is a big thing coming which will be big enough to match the Soviet Union and its allies and the United States. We must be in on the big thing. If necessary we must be amalgamated with it. We must deny the very characteristics of our polity in order to be still in the big league. It is Europe which offers us a place in the big league.'

And then there was our obsession with the United States. The United States was great because it was big; and the ideological American empire was a kind of ghost of the British Empire. Since Suez—Suez is an emotional word to me too, Professor Hennessy—it has been the axiom of the British state that you must never be separated from the policies or the perceptions of the United States. It was the way in which we could secure ourselves a place amongst the giants. We would be a great power because we would be aligned with the great power against the other great power. So our whole behaviour was coloured and characterised by this world into which we had been born, the world in which we were a 'great power'.

I know it is not so; but I also know that on my deathbed I shall still be believing with one part of my brain that somewhere on every ocean of the world there is a great grey ship with three funnels and 16-inch guns which can blow out of the water any other navy which is likely to face it. I know it is not so; indeed I realised at a relatively early stage that it is not so. But that factor, that emotional factor, that gigantism, will not die until I, the carrier of it, am actually dead. And I suppose, as a politician, I really share Professor Hennessy's death wish, as a historian, that we may be superseded. I do not really know whether he is a Nietzscheian, but the wish to be superseded is a true authentic wish for a Nietzscheian to announce; and it has been forced out of me by Professor Hennessy's paper.

COMMENTARY TWO

Keith Middlemas

I was very struck, when Peter read his paper, both by the CIA document and by the European Recovery Administration papers saying just how backward the state of much of British industry was, and just how little effort we were making to justify so much American help. That I think gave me the counter-point from which I would like to approach this central issue, which is the relationship between macro-economic policy and micro-economic. First, however, on Corelli Barnett, I think my chief issue with him is that he describes a fantasy world. He is subject to the peculiarly English disease of the optative mode, 'would that it were so'. It was not so. He ignores the context, he imagines somehow that British governments and parties and public were in a position to go through a sort of Bismarckian or possibly even Leninist (Lenin of the war communist era) process, and it was not so. And I think that vitiates his entire thesis. However, many of the points made about the micro-economic level are indeed very good, and, of course, particularly when he talks about education.

If I could just take Peter's key points fairly quickly. The first and second, about modernisation and the developmental state, are linked. I think here there is a new orthodoxy, or perhaps a long prevailing orthodoxy to which Sir Alec Cairncross also subscribes, that the thing that really matters is macro-economic policy and what is done from the centre, which ignores the fact that the Attlee government did have a micro-economic or perhaps supply-side policy which has largely been ignored. It concerned things like housing, the mobility of labour, industrial relations, research and development, and the planning of certain industries. Now some of those industries were good and some were bad. In civil aviation, many of the plans were made as early as 1943, and they led in the long run to us achieving for a brief moment a world leadership with the Comet, which as you all know collapsed under unfortu-nate circumstances. But that I would argue was a success story, building on potential going back to the early part of the war. Conversely the textile industry would be a case which was a poor one, where the management and ownership of the textile industry conspicuously failed to fulfil the plan.

So there was a supply-side part of the Attlee government, and when it comes to the developmental state one needs to advance an argument about the cooperative state. This was a government which saw the future of industry not in direct planning, not of the central European type, nor of the Jean Monnet type but what was later to be called indicative planning in which you absorb the energies of industry and organised labour and indeed the City of London. I have put that case myself at some length and I think I hardly need to put it again.

So the failure is not so much in the ideas or the initial plans but in the execution and, as Peter has pointed out, it becomes progressively more obvious by about 1949. The main deficiency that I would highlight is the failure of the Attlee government to achieve some concept of good manage-ment. They saw good management in terms of humane management and good industrial relations. They concentrated, for example, on founding the British Institute of Management. Their concept of national industries was one derived from Richard Tawney, probably, a concept which embodied the humane side of industry. It inhibited them from paying proper managerial salaries in the new nationalised industries, and as a result they got poor, if not actually derelict managers—a tradition which lasted perhaps thirty years. This is my explanation of why the nationalised industries failed as an exemplar. The Labour Party did have a link, it was called the 1944 Association which Attlee himself sometimes attended, and they met, well-minded businessmen; but though they had access to the Labour centre, I don't think that ever led to very much; it certainly didn't lead to a concentration on the supply side which might have fulfilled their initial plans.

On his final point about Europe, I think one needs to emphasise how much Attlee and his ministers admired the United States. This is partly Enoch Powell's emotional point. It is also the ideological mean in 1945. They admired the United States because it was democratic, it was a supreme power and it had the New Deal tradition. They ceased very rapidly to admire the Soviet Union the more it was discovered how it actually operated, and, of course, looking across the Channel at the states of Europe there was nothing to admire in any of them except possibly Belgium, with whom we tried bilateral trade and didn't succeed. So I think that again I would put out a plea for the Attlee government; there was not much else that they could have done at that time.

It is the third and fourth points I think that need to be analysed most. We were growing out of great power status. I do not want to say anything about the external aspects of this, but about the domestic side. It seems to me there are three areas in our approach to industry in which that habit of mind cast us in a mould for the whole of the post-war period. The first illusion is that we were a producer nation, we could produce anything. We believed we did not have to focus like Finland or Sweden on a particular group of industries, we could actually produce the whole lot. And this led I think to the depressing history of the British nuclear power industry. I remember once talking to Sir George Bolton, special adviser to the Bank of England and an author of the ROBOT scheme, and he said that there were only two efficient industries in Britain in the post-war period, agriculture and the City of London. The rest should have been allowed to go bankrupt. That is the City equivalent of Peter's Luftwaffe bombing the factories.

The second illusion is that somehow defence expenditure related to civil industry, the old spin-off argument, that our very heavy defence expenditure, which Sidney Pollard has criticised so much, would in some osmotic way benefit civil industry. I do not think this happened in the 1940s and 1950s in the way that it had done in the 1930s. This was partly for technical reasons.

The final one is our belief in secure markets, and here I would think not so much of the empire markets, not so much of the reciprocal trade agreements of the 1930s, but countries like Egypt which, of course, went down the drain—as far as the UK was concerned—when Nasser came to power; Argentina until Peron; and the Middle East, which we lorded over, in terms of the way our managers behaved towards their clients, particularly on public service contracts. We just assumed it was our patch until Suez, and we lost it very quickly, and the shock for firms like William Press when the Italians began to win the big pipeline contracts, was horrific. South East Asia was the same. One could throw in all those, and India and Pakistan, which were our economic empire of the 1930s, which by the late 1950s had largely been shut to us.

If you look at those three illusions, to which we only woke up in the late 1950s, the real people to blame are the Conservative governments of Churchill and Eden. This is part of Corelli Barnett's problem, that the real villains of the piece are people who, in terms of the politics which Peter described at the beginning, could not easily be blamed. It is so much easier to go back and blame Attlee.

I have only one other point to make, which goes back to the theme of this conference, the idea of change and continuity, and Peter's proposal that we should have history written by younger historians. I am not sure that we should not have history written by older historians, who remember the 1930s, because so much of this is to do with the 1930s. What the Attlee government did was to give the better life of the 1930s to everyone. If you look at Britain in terms of its design, arts, letters, literature, film, the type of cars that were produced, by the late 1940s we had brought to a pitch the best things of the 1930s. Forget all the Depression, forget the unemployment. For those in work the 1930s was a very good period indeed. We went on into the 1960s building a council house that was actually designed for John Wheatley in 1924. The turning point only comes in the 1950s, when it is possible to see that we cannot live that way any longer. This is the domestic and even perhaps the emotional side of what had happened. In short, the war did not produce the sort of catharsis that has been claimed. It encouraged people to extract the best from their experience, while at the same time addressing the worst problems that they had from their own experience also, such as unemployment; at the same time it inhibited the production of alternatives. The alternatives could not therefore emerge until the early 1960s.

Note

1. The Clarke Diaries are unpublished but can be read in the Churchill College Archive, Cambridge, with the permission of Lady Clarke.
2. PRO CAB 66/65.

References

Addison, Paul (1975), *The Road to 1945: British Politics and the Second World War*, London, Jonathan Cape.
Ashford, Douglas (1986), *The Emergence of the Welfare State*, Oxford, Blackwell, pp. 241–2.
Attlee, C.R. (1937), *The Labour Party in Perspective*, London, Victor Gollancz.
Barnett, Correlli (1986), *Audit of War: The Illusion and Reality of Britain as a Great Nation*, London, Macmillan.

Cairncross, Alec (ed.) (1989), *The Robert Hall Diaries 1947–53*, London, Unwin Hyman.

Central Intelligence Agency, *Review of the World Situation*, CIA, 6–49, 15 June 1949, p. 2.

Gowing, Margaret (1984), *Independence and Deterrence: Britain and Atomic Energy 1945–52*, Vol. I, London, Macmillan.

Hennessy, Peter (1992), *Never Again: Britain 1945–51*, London, Jonathan Cape.

Hennessy, Peter (1989), *Whitehall*, London, Secker & Warburg.

Howson, Susan and Muggeridge, Ronald (eds) (1990), *The Collected Papers of James Meade*, Vol. IV, *The Cabinet Office Diary*, London, Unwin Hyman.

Joseph, Keith (1987), 'Escaping the Chrysalis of Statism', *Contemporary Record*, vol. 1, no. 1.

Marquand, David (1988), *The Unprincipled Society: New Demands and Old Policies*, London, Jonathan Cape.

Morgan, Kenneth O. (1984), *Labour in Power, 1945–1951*, Oxford, Oxford University Press.

Pollard, Sydney (1982), *The Wasting of the British Economy*, London, Croom Helm.

2 Britain: a comparative view

Eric Hobsbawm

The central problem of British history since the Second World War is the continued relative decline of the British economy. It is particularly acute since apart from the United States, Canada, Australia and the neutral Switzerland and Sweden, the British economy survived the war better than the rest of Europe and Japan, recovered more quickly and at the end of the recovery period remained one of the countries with the highest per capita GDP. In 1950 only the countries just mentioned had a higher per capita GDP than we, and the difference between us and the Swedes and the Swiss was small. By 1979 we were fifteenth among the sixteen most developed OECD nations, having been passed since 1950 by Austria, Belgium, Denmark, Finland, France, the Federal Republic, Japan, the Netherlands and Norway, though not until the 1980s by Italy as well. Again in 1950 western Europe had barely passed the 1938 level of GDP, by about 2 per cent, but Britain stood 14 per cent above it.[1]

By the way, the statistics must only be taken rather like dates in history, to give relative relations but not absolute figures at all. So many of modern statistics, as it has emerged since the collapse of the eastern bloc, are pure artefacts, even when they are constructed by international organisations, so I wouldn't necessarily put too much emphasis on the actual data.

The slow subsequent growth of the economy is in contrast with its relatively good start or, conversely, the spurt of the other countries is all the more impressive because of their initial lag. Germany, for instance, did not reach its pre-war output until 1950, its pre-war export peak until 1951. Japan did not reach its pre-war output until 1954, its pre-war output per capita until 1957.[2] An anecdote may illustrate the difference. It was told to me by a Japanese friend whose school comrade had gone into the Japanese motor industry after the war with Toyota. Their ambition, he was told, was to make cars like Austin. Our motor vehicle production per capita in 1950 was still the highest of any country outside the United States as it had been before the war. By 1978 it was lower than all other European producers, including Spain, not to mention Japan and the United States.

The problem before us is why the British record was so much worse than anyone else's in the early 1960s. It is of course possible that there was nothing to be done; our decline was inevitable. Historians, especially Marxist ones, are quite reconciled to the concept of historical inevitability, though this has always outraged some philosophers, most theologians, and politicians would have to commit mass suicide if they believed in it. A lot of our decline is undoubtedly rooted in a past about which we cannot do much now, just as much as the post-war rise of Germany and Japan is not due to political wisdom but to the resumption of an upward trend which had been interrupted. Nevertheless the post-war period contains enough examples of economies whose transformation cannot be explained by simple extrapolation.

Consider the comparison with France and Britain. From 1870 to 1950 total French output consistently grew more slowly than the British, although output per capita was more favourable given the stability of the French population or rather the more rapid growth of the British. Whilst in 1950 French GDP per capita was about a quarter below the British, in the course of the next thirty years with far more rapid growth in relation to a reverse, in 1980 our GDP per capita was a quarter below the French. In this, as in other cases, we must conclude that human intention and decision had something to do with the change, even allowing for the severe and sometimes insuperable objective limits which constrain public and private policies.

All states seeking to transform or modernise their economies after 1945, breathed the same policy atmosphere: the mixed economy, in which private enterprise and the market operated in a framework of government initiative, control and planning, and often over economies with the public and nationalised sector greatly expanded since the 1930s, for various reasons, as in the case of Great Britain, France, Italy and Austria. This applied even to the economies most committed to free market allocation such as the United States and the Federal Republic, which, to quote Ludwig Erhard, 'wished to remove the last vestiges of state control'. But they did not. Indeed, as not only growth but rapid growth became the international policy objective, as it did, I think, in the 1950s and early 1960s, even governments hitherto abstentionist became more enthusiastic about planning in the 1960s. There was probably more of the so-called pro-*dirigiste*, or at any rate interventionist consensus internationally in the mid-1960s, the Wilson period, than there had been earlier on. Belgium is a very suitable example. We are not of course talking about the communist states which operated overwhelmingly by central command planning and which nobody really wanted to imitate.

Not that all governments followed a specific policy such as Keynesian demand management. Not even that there was actual agreement in any particular government on any particular way in which these things should be done—I am not claiming that. Though, of course, in the Marshall Plan period the United States was interested in encouraging some kind of cohesion of policies, not necessarily with great success. I merely argue that a common language was spoken, and there was substantial agreement about the role of the state in ensuring, to quote Alan Milward, 'high increasing output, increasing foreign trade, full employment, industrialisation and modernisation' if only because these were the only bases for political consensus in most western countries. Strong believers in the free market like Jean Monnet became champions of planning. In 1946 in the United States, Averell Harriman, not normally noted as a Bolshevik, stated, 'People in this country are no longer scared of such words as planning. People have accepted the fact that the government has got to plan as well as individuals.'

In short, in those days it was inconceivable that champions of capitalism should argue or act in the manner of the neo-liberals in the 1980s. It is difficult for people who have lived all their adult lives in the Britain of the 1980s to believe that the champions of free enterprise and capitalism in 1945 or 1950 would simply not even dream of talking in that way. I would only add that while the international consensus included a welfare state in principle, the ways in which this was achieved differed widely from one country to another, and so, at least initially, did the share of GDP devoted to social security expenditure. In 1950, it varied between 5.7 per cent in Norway to 14.8 per cent in West Germany, and Britain, with 10 per cent, was somewhere in the middle. Below were Austria, Belgium and France. It is worth noting that while the share of such expenditure rose strikingly over the next thirty years, and the difference diminished, seven countries now spend more than 20 per cent of GDP on social security, Britain notably lagging with 14.5 per cent.

As so often, the Continent was invisible to most Britons simply because they did not look across the Channel. The famous old anecdote, 'Fog in Channel, Continent isolated', represents a great deal of the old perspective of most people in Britain. It is something of course which Professor Hennessy has already stressed, that our belief that we were the only ones who had a welfare state, and we had the best welfare state, became actually increasingly unrealistic, but it is worth reminding ourselves of this.

As the name Marshall Plan suggests, planning was far from a dirty word, certainly far from the dirty word it was to become in the 1980s. It is therefore, as Peter Hennessy has already pointed out, very puzzling that Britain, which was the only non-communist country in Europe other than Norway and Sweden that was solidly governed for several years by a single labour and socialist party 'succeeded in retaining her status as Europe's most reluctant planner'. This is something of a puzzle. All the more puzzling since a very powerful *dirigiste* machinery had served Britain rather well in the war. The British equivalent, envisaged in Christopher Dow's words, was 'that unemployment would be cured by managing total demand . . . inequality by redistributive taxation and monopolistic restrictions by selective nationalisation.'

The wartime *dirigiste* machinery was dismantled and neither party thought we needed a Planning Agency. When I say neither party I will insist on the degree of consensus between both sides which was really very surprising, as Peter Hennessy has quite rightly pointed out. Even if Labour had not won we would have had a very marked advance towards a welfare state; if there had been a post-war Churchill government I think that is a fairly safe counterfactual proposition. Even though there are signs that under Stafford Cripps the necessity of planning was envisaged, and the Economic Planning Board was set up, I think most people would agree that Cripps was only engaged in short-term operations which had not very much in common with planning as otherwise understood.

Kenneth Morgan perceptively hints at one ideological reason for this. Social democrats wanted to distinguish themselves from totalitarian communism, or at least to protect themselves against accusations of being too left, and central economic planning was indeed identified with this. And the argument that we are not like the communists and therefore we must have freedom and so on was a powerful one and not only in Britain. In fact in other non-communist countries, technocrats and non-socialist ministers and non-socialist politicians were far more ready to take planning up. In France, François Bloch-Lainé, the director of the Treasury from 1947 to 1953 and a major figure in the early operations of the French planning system, bitterly complained in interviews and writings of the 1970s of the intellectual and political feebleness, not to mention the economic illiteracy of the French socialist party of this period, a party with which his own personal sympathies lay, as he makes clear in his book. He was later to write, 'Having spent so much of its knowhow, its *savoir* and its energy on countering the communists, did it have too little left for offensives on another front?' This is possible.

Still, there is no question that the anti-socialist governments in France, in Italy, even, following the French model, the Franco government in Spain in later years, and the South Korean government, planned. But the British Labour government after 1945 did not. It even had considerable difficulty with the systematic corporatist arrangement by which, as in Sweden, the Netherlands, Belgium and Austria linked themselves to longer-term or at least middle-term policies, but which essentially depended on national consultation on wage policies with employers and unions. Essentially these arguments decided the share of prosperity growth over the coming years which would accrue to workers, and without some kind of forward-looking decision it is obviously very difficult to have a long-term forward perspective.

The British TUC, in the first place, was not in a position to commit anyone, unlike in this respect some Continental trade-union centres. Moreover, the British trade unions were probably more committed to unrestricted free-market bargaining than any other economic interest group in the country. The most that could be achieved, and it served the 1945–51 governments well, was a general predisposition of the majority-controlling big unions to go along with the Labour government, partly out of common anti-communism, but perhaps even more because it was after all visibly a government largely composed of actual workers and ex-workers, which was and is rather unusual even among Labour governments and, with all these people like George Isaacs and Ernie Bevin and so on, this does make a difference and probably would not apply to more recent governments.

In the days of Cripps this actually meant the acceptance of a wage freeze, but this was a temporary concession which only lasted until the 1950s. No national economic policy could be based on such *ad hoc* emergency concessions, as the 1970s were later to confirm. Nevertheless the British lack of planning cannot just be ascribed to the characteristics of social democratic parties or even of the British Labour movement. Essentially, other non-communist countries adopted planning or its equivalent because they recognised the need for a dramatic national rescue operation—a dramatic national regeneration by means of a systematic modernisation of the economy. They needed a Great Leap Forward. In other words, countries like France, Italy, the Low Countries, not to mention Germany and Japan, had no illusions about their situation in 1945, but Britain had.

The case of France is the most obvious. The politicians, starting with General de Gaulle, agreed that the restoration of the country to the status of great power, or at least a great European power, was the overwhelming priority. Everything since 1940 combined to demonstrate to both resisters and Pétainists how far France had fallen, not least and most recently the exclusion of France from Yalta, unlike Britain. An inadequate and archaic economy had evidently contributed to the collapse of the economy in 1939–40, and this alone would have been enough to make a massive attempt at modernisation indispensable, but economic and political considerations merged and this made the impetus for it even stronger. The first strategy of the modernisation of France was to get West German coal and steel under French control, thus simultaneously preventing West German recovery and providing France with a ready-made resource basis for becoming an industrial power, and incidentally shifting the economic centre of gravity of the Continent westwards. We remember that from that day to this Germany is what French policy is fundamentally about. It was then and it is still today. As Calais was inscribed on the heart of Queen Mary, Germany is inscribed on the heart of every French president and every French prime minister.

When after the Morgenthau Plan sank from sight, and it proved to be a non-starter to demilitarise and deindustrialise Germany, the French looked to an Anglo-French partnership. And, according to at least one French historian I have read, in 1948 France offered the United Kingdom a steel cartel. Britain, or at any rate Cripps, still saw the Commonwealth as more important than Europe, which indeed it was in trading terms at that time, and the French policy shifted to Franco-German integration, the Schuman plan, which was dressed up in European costume, because the United States was keen on Europe. But essentially it was, if you can't beat them, join them, tie the Germans so closely to you that they cannot take any independent action, which is still the basic principle.

Essentially, as Frances Lynch argued so many years ago, the Monnet plan went through, unlike a number of different plans different people were suggesting, because the Quai d'Orsay at this time put its weight behind an effective economic plan for political purposes. So there was a lot of political muscle as well as economic argument saying now we have got to get a real major operation going. The impetus for massive industrialisation elsewhere was equally political or nationalist. In Italy the de Gasperi government immediately after the war called for a new Risorgimento to overcome defeat, economic ruin and overpopulation (which is a code word for communist danger) through a policy of industrialisation. Charles Kindleberger has argued that the post-war Finnish economic miracle, which without anyone taking much notice over here has brought that country virtually up to the Swedish standard, was due to political determination to gain economic elbow-room, even though politically they were completely dependent on the USSR. They exploited the fact that the USSR was a permanent captive market for the purposes of modernising the Finnish economy.

The politico-ideological element also seems to be dominant in Spain, after the original, so to speak, medievalist conception of Franco, in the 1940s and 1950s, had collapsed. The Opus Dei technocrats then borrowed the French form of indicative planning in order to create an industrially dynamic, neo-capitalist economy from the 1960s onwards. I am not concerned, you see, whether the planning is aimed at creating a large national centre or not, but that the initiative and the actual operations should be organised as they so often were by the governments, as a policy. For all such great leaps forward, planning was practical because it was an obvious way of pursuing economic objectives fixed a priori on non-economic grounds. As has been recently observed—I read it in the *Financial Times* the other day—of the far eastern NICs, 'these countries were not thriving testaments to the virtues of free market competition. Command capitalism, not free market capitalism was the system that enabled the NICs to become major players on the world economy. Export success, not efficient resource allocation, was the overriding goal of the NICs.'

I am not claiming that these various forms of command capitalism all worked the same way, or had the same objective, or that their policies were the decisive elements in ensuring a rate of growth which was in all cases superior to Britain. I am merely observing that while both capitalism and Continental social democratic regimes were ready to plan for the long and medium term, and the future of their economies, Britain showed no such willingness.

The different ways in which Britain and other countries used Marshall Aid has been mentioned as underlying this difference. I think we must agree with Sidney Pollard, 'While all other major recipients carefully used it for investment purposes, in order to build up their economic future, in Britain the Treasury used it to plug temporary holes.' Or rather, to put it more positively, in the words of a French historian, France insisted that Marshall Aid should finance a plan for capital equipment, 'whereas Britain made the opposite choice, using it to reduce the public debt, trying to re-establish its financial power.' In fact at its peak in 1949, Marshall Aid paid for over 70 per cent of investment in all major nationalised French industries, according to papers I have seen. In Austria, the point has been made by Milward again: three-quarters of Marshall funds went into new investment and modernisation. But not so far as I know in Britain.

Why the difference? I suspect it was because Britain was too slow to recognise the depths of the problem in its economy, and the impossibility of restoring its old position of political and economic power, even to maintain what had been left. There were understandable political reasons why we felt less desperate in our situation than countries which had been defeated, occupied and sometimes pulverised. We had had a good war, I am even tempted to say the best of all the belligerents' wars. Those of us old enough to remember still look back on 1939–45 with all the qualifications, with pride, even complacency. It is one of the rare times in the past hundred years when the country lived up to what the British citizens thought it was.

We had won, we were accepted, if only just, as one of the Big Three. There was also a plausible but less convincing economic reason for not feeling too dramatic about the British situation. Tight as things were, especially when the United States began to turn the screw, if we look back on the inter-war record, Britain's share of world manufacturing, though much smaller than before 1913, had remained more or less stable in the inter-war period, which was a better record than any other major industrial economy except Japan and the USSR, because we had suffered relatively less from the Great Depression. In Europe we were smaller only than Germany, we had more than twice the manufacturing industry of France, and were, per capita, still superior to all larger countries except the United States. A.J.P. Taylor was not alone to feel (Taylor, 1965, pp. 726–7) 'that the Second War, unlike the First, stimulated or created new industries which could hold their own in peacetime.' And he saw electricity, motor cars, iron and steel, machine tools, nylons and chemicals as all set for expansion. The fact that A.J.P. Taylor was notoriously not an economist only makes his views more representative of what a lot of other people, in the country and out of it, were apt to feel in the period after 1945. Moreover, remember that as late as 1952 Jean Monnet argued for continued development investment, his own premier saw the French record in industrialisation 1945 as better than the Italian, Belgian and German but he only saw it as equally good as the British. In other words, it seemed in the early 1950s that there was not really need for all that much drama.

This complacency, which a glance at the reports of the Anglo-American Council of Productivity in the late 1940s should have dispelled, continued with diminishing self-satisfaction, until well into the 1960s. Let me simply remind you of a mainstream discussion on Britain and the new Europe, the future of the Common Market, that Michael Shanks and John Lambert published in the early 1960s (Shanks and Lambert, 1962) on the occasion of the first application, the one that was vetoed by de Gaulle. It admitted that our growth in the 1950s had been relatively sluggish, but this, the authors argued, meant that our competitors' labour costs would catch up with ours as they became more prosperous and exhausted their labour reserves. We had a broad industrial base in the 1960s. The City was clearly superior. Britain had 'all the necessary ingredients if only she could organise'. Our cars were hard hit—but commercial vehicles, tractors, sports cars and accessories 'will do very well'. Engineering was mixed, with the good slightly predominating— this at least was some concession to realism—but there were really bright prospects in electronic and automation equipment, office equipment, farm machinery, some plastics, and multiple tailoring. Retailing was just mentioned; retailing only became very big in what you might call the image of the British economy when everything else had collapsed. What is very interesting, however, is that Japan was not mentioned at all.

The left was as blind to the basic predicament of the British economy, insufficient industrial capacity and insufficient investment, as anyone else. Crosland's revisionism was about distribution not production. The only exception to this is ironic. The Wilson governments of the 1960s, though congenitally unwilling to think more than a week ahead in politics, did actually gesture in the direction of modernising the economy, though they were unable to do anything about it. This was the first governmental recognition that they thought something really seriously was wrong in the British economy. Incidentally, they also gestured in the direction of planning for efficiency.

Ironically, the very success of the reconstruction effort of the 1945 Labour government reinforced complacency. I would not go as far as to speak with Peter Clarke of an incipient British *Wirtshaftswunder*, for the tremendous and successful export drive was based more on the absence of competitors and, as has been said, on using existing capacity, because the qualities of British technology, especially in engineering and of British management, were not really good. Still, it was the only time when, especially under Cripps, something like a coherent systematic national productive effort was made. And yet our very success seemed to suggest that we were stronger than we actually were. And the rhetoric which you found in America in 1945 and 1946 that somehow or other Britain might turn into the European competitor, in retrospect only rings falsely.

As always the extraordinary provincialism of the British vision also played its part. Just as, in the Thatcher era, the illusion of some enormous British renaissance in the 1980s was based simply on not looking at what had actually happened outside the City and a few other areas in the 1980s, so the surge of the Continental economies in the 1940s was not taken much notice of until some time after it had already visibly got going.

Does this explain the persistent political megalomania of Britain to which allusion has already been made? The willingness to undertake commitments which our economy could not really sustain? I do not really know. But this was an old tradition. After all, on paper, neither the First nor the Second World War was an economically cost-effective proposition. We couldn't afford either. Britain almost certainly spent a higher proportion of its GNP on defence than anyone in the West, even before NATO and the Korean War drove it to the point where it directly clashed with civilian economic growth. And I do not think it was merely the point mentioned by Middlemas that we thought there would be an automatic spin-off of defence expenditure into the civilian economy. Conversely, of course, the absence of serious military expenditure and more importantly military R & D in Germany and Japan were major assets to their economies, as we all know.

Some things as always seem to be all too clear. In spite of obvious signs to the contrary, neither the armed forces nor the Foreign Office nor the Labour government believed that Britain's international position and interests had basically changed. The only exception, which has been plausibly argued recently by John Saville (Saville, 1983), was Clement Attlee himself, who initiated the only major piece of decolonisation in the 1940s, the Indian subcontinent, against opposition within the Labour Party, and who was sensible enough to observe that an imperial policy predicated upon the position of India made no sense once India had gone. He was criticising our position and expenditures in the eastern Mediterranean partly with this in mind. But even Attlee fell silent from 1947, partly because in that year the world was frozen into two blocks, partly no doubt also because he depended on the support of Bevin, whose identification with the Etonians in the Foreign Office appears to have been total.

It could have been different. It was clear from the start that Britain depended on dollars for its domestic programme as well as for the restoration of its international position. Economically the cost of this dependence was actually not high, since as Keynes realised the dollars would become available one way or another without effective strings, for instance through convertibility, in much the same way that the yens flowed into the United States in the 1980s without the Americans having to make any very notable concessions to Japan. However, politically, the strings bound Britain firmly to the United States and, with all the western governments' genuine fear of the Soviets and welcome to American commitment, this did create problems. While dependence on US policy cramped the policy objectives of the French, which is why their country tried to maintain some freedom of action and, incidentally, later on some sense of reality about the alleged Soviet threat, the Cold War gave Britain a justification for maintaining a world position as a junior partner or, as the British would no doubt have put it, the world adviser to the United States.

Britain, I suggest therefore, plunged into the Cold War not just willingly but enthusiastically. It helped to prolong the illusion that was so long in dying. But it also diverted resources which would have been better devoted to other purposes. And yet the puzzle remains. There was no argument about the dramatic nature of our post-war economic problem, because Keynes himself had talked about a financial Dunkirk. Outsiders could see what needed to be done even then. Here is an assessment made by a fairly left-wing social democratic American from the Berkeley Economics Department in 1950. He had been around and interviewed everybody in the Labour government (Brady, 1950):

> Virtually all the causes of the low level of British production show that they cannot be eliminated by piecemeal measures. They are rooted in the whole British industrial system. In its need for vast new investment before it can begin to catch up, in the prevalence of small scale plant unequipped for modern mass production, in relatively low levels of installed mechanical horsepower, in the well-nigh universal resort on the part of management and worker, to practices of a restrictive character in virtually all lines of industry.

He concluded gloomily:

> What makes future prospects seem very dim indeed is the government's failure to see that nothing less than a revolutionary replanning of all the factors bearing on the problem of improving British production methods is required of them, and that a drastic reorientation of both colonial and foreign policy is needed abroad. Should it continue to remain complacent about domestic problems, and to follow traditional patterns overseas, then on the available evidence to date Britain only needs a Gibbon to write their chronicle.

This was published in 1950. It was written not after the relapse into complacency of a Tory Britain in the 1950s, to which Middlemas attributed the failure to carry on from the Labour government, but at the end of a period when, especially in the Cripps years, the government's commitment to a major economic effort was undeniable and its success in no way negligible (Middlemas, 1986).

Again in the first ten post-war years I don't think it is even possible to claim what the late Mounia Postan claimed in the middle 1960s, that what was lacking was the conviction that a country victorious in war and basking in the heat of post-war prosperity was in fact face to face with a national emergency. We were face to face with a national emergency, and in fact 'basking in the heat of post-war prosperity' is probably not true of any period before the middle and late 1950s, at least as far as most of the British citizens were concerned. However, until 1953–4, neither had British manufacturing export declined relative to the rest of the industrial world compared to pre-war. A major reason for our complacency was the typical concentration of Britain on trading in the financial rather than the manufacturing side of our economy, which goes back a long way in our history and is dramatically exemplified by the Thatcherite 1980s.

It is fair to say that for any one man-hour spent between 1947 and 1979 discussing the problem of Britain's low investment and low productivity in manufacturing and how to solve it, at least 200 were spent on the strength of sterling and the balance of payments. As Pollard has put it, the exchanges were saved at the expense of productive investment. In the last analysis, the visible economy was sacrificed to the invisible.

Could things have happened other than they did? As always this is a pointless question to ask. What actually happened in the past was the only thing that happened, and because it was the only thing that happened it was the only thing that could happen. To that extent it was inevitable. But it is not a pointless question for the future. Counterfactual history has some sense where the options are still open, not where the decision has already been made and the consequences have followed. What light does the period that we are dealing with today throw on our present difficulties? I want to conclude with three observations.

Firstly, do we recognise today that Britain is in an emergency and something must be done? Yes, I think so. However, secondly, the forty years since 1950 have destroyed that British confidence which Peter Hennessy noted so correctly in the 1945 government. A recent poll in *The Guardian* of fifty historians reports that over half of them think British industry is in terminal decline. This is a discouraging but perhaps not totally surprising finding, but it indicates something about the spirit in which a lot of people in Britain in the 1990s look at the future prospects. But there is a third and even more discouraging side to the situation. If there is one thing about which I think a lot of people are agreed, it is that the great economic miracles of the period from 1945 to the 1970s were not achieved by letting the free market rip. As the OECD put it, articulating the then consensus in the early 1960s, 'Economic progress is not an autonomous historical process which happens accidentally, but an evolution that can be promoted by deliberate action and planning.' It may be wrong but that is what everybody believed and that is what they acted on.

Now on paper a Labour government in Britain today should be in a better position to undertake such action and planning than the market theologians who have been in office. Yet the left has been in retreat for so long before an economic liberalism, which in less extreme form was probably necessary, that it has been frightened away from its traditional and even more necessary insistence that the modernisation of Britain, mixed economy as it is and will remain, requires above all action and planning by the state and where necessary economic controls and interference in the free market. Without it, we shall continue to decline. With it, we may not get out, but nevertheless we must try. A Labour government must undertake some necessary and almost certainly unpopular steps, to lay the foundations for the regeneration of the British productive economy. It will probably be defeated at the end of its five years. But, like the Labour government of 1945–50, it will have set the country's agenda for the next forty years. A Labour government which fails to take these steps will be another edition of the Wilson years. It will not have been worth having.

COMMENTARY

John Barnes

I wanted to start with a couple of detailed points, but they make a more general point about the trickiness of international comparisons. We heard a certain amount from Professor Hobsbawm about the way in which the welfare state in Europe had ranged ahead of us by the end of the 1970s. The measure there was the amount of spending of GDP. Now that may be a reasonable measure, but if at the same time you are contending that the Health Service is actually a more effective user of resources than the Continental systems of welfare, then it is not actually going to give you the proper comparison.

I make that point as a tight point in itself, but I suspect the more I have actually looked at the international comparisons, and it is a literature which has been growing because it seems to have lent us much greater enlightenment, the more difficult it is to find successful models which are anything other than *sui generis*. I am sceptical, for example, about the amount of planning that actually went on in Europe, although there does seem to be a different state model in operation. It is not so much a planning one but a state partnership with industry, though to whose real benefit that was I am not sure. It sometimes seems to me that the industries are taking the state for a ride rather than the state taking industry along.

Indeed, the most fashionable comparison of all, which I suppose is that of Japan, again seems to me a slightly bogus one, because as far as I can see the big industries in Japan tend to get their second-rate scientists and their second-rate people, actually to work along with the state, and they cheerfully and busily go on with their own research, their own development and their own investment programmes. I am not so sure that the state plays quite the part in Japan that we have come to think.

I am sceptical therefore about the alternative models. What seems to me quite clear is that British industry does not develop either an interest in research or an interest in skilled manpower, or in higher education; that it doesn't in fact develop a policy of training, it doesn't actually concentrate very much on industrial investment in the way that some of our Continental counterparts do. That seems to me to start at the micro-level, but perhaps we ought to start at the micro-level, because I suspect that economic performance is not actually best measured in terms of nations and states but in terms of international competitiveness between firms, particularly if, like us, you actually have an economy that is relatively open to the world, and actually has a very high trading component.

I make a second point and that is the extraordinary dominance of a City interest which is not fundamentally locked into industry in a way that one might look for in other countries. I just make that point very briefly—it is too familiar to do anything other than that.

As somebody again who lived through this period, rather younger, I suspect, than Professor Hobsawm but rather older than Peter Hennessy, I don't remember this degree of complacency around that they seem to remember. I think that Brady's rhetoric of 1950 spells out much more, what was a really driving element of that Labour government, which was to recover in some sense our international solvency. I remember again the imperatives that were driving the cutbacks in the defence programme in the early 1950s, and indeed the whole rhetoric that underlay the defence White Paper of 1957 was essentially to get our resources out of defence research and development and into things which were much more industrially useful. Indeed, the nuclear weapon itself was actually seen as a cheap way of retaining Great Power status because you couldn't afford to do it with your present manpower levels in the services, with your present levels of R & D and scientific technology. It wasn't exactly a recipe for complacency, it was an attempt to square a circle people knew was an impossible circle.

Nor indeed was Attlee's realism about the Empire unmirrored by Macmillan's. Macmillan actually drew up a balance sheet of Empire in 1957, and was as keen on getting shot of the unproductive colonies as anybody I think before or since. That complacency, as an answer, does seem to me a rather bogus one. There does seem to me, though, something about our feeling that we are only happy living on a world stage, which does seem to come from that imperial past. You find it on the left as well as on the right, it is very interesting, it seems to me, to read the rhetoric of CND, that somehow if we give a lead, the world will follow. It is a kind of moral imperialism of the left which is mirrored, I think by this sense that we have got to be part of some larger network, some larger entity on the right. And that clearly does come out of our long-term political culture and is very difficult to do away with.

But I don't think anyone was complacent about that in the 1940s and the 1950s, and indeed that there was very little consensus in the 1940s and 1950s. There was a real experiment with economic liberalism, to some extent in the early 1950s, which seems to have been misplayed by people like Anthony Seldon; they tend to conflate things. It is very easy to jump from the 1940s to the early 1960s when there was a real degree of consensus. Funnily enough, the consensus was around planning, it was around intervening in industry. We got it wrong, I suspect, for two reasons. The first is that political consensus broke down in the 1964 election campaign, in a quite massive way. If you are actually going to run through that experiment which we were trying from 1962 onwards, it had to be done on a consensual basis, but for electoral reasons, well understood, Wilson talked up the balance of payments crisis and tied an albatross around the incoming government's neck. And that undoubtedly handicapped all the early years of the Wilson government. Secondly, they also did it very badly. They did not actually spot winners. What they tended to do was to merge for short-term efficiency reasons not longer-term growth reasons. So our micro-policy also went wrong in the 1960s pretty badly.

I suspect that the state can only do certain things well, I am not sure that it can actually plan well, but that is obviously a point at issue between Professor Hobsbawm and myself. One of the things which we quite clearly did not do was to invest in our training, in management, in trying to get rid of restrictive practices, in developing the kind of higher education sector which suits the modern state instead of our present high-cost, low-productive higher education sector. All those things the Continentals were doing. All those things were clearly things which the state alone can do. And again in terms of infrastructure it is probable that the state was not doing enough. When I look at the successful Continental examples it seems to me that it is not the state trying to pick the winners but to try and create a climate in which the winners will emerge, that is going on. Now whether I am right or wrong, I none the less have a feeling that we exaggerate the degree of complacency, we exaggerate the degree of consensus, we exaggerate the sense of what went wrong in the 1960s when we did actually try to move towards Continental models.

Clearly we have had a political culture that is centred on imperialism in a way in which we haven't begun to analyse in sufficient depth but, over and beyond that, the sense that things had gone right too long. We would not face up to the fact that the war had bankrupted us. It is very nice to sit back and bask in reflected glory as the one country which did the right thing in 1940. The truth is that but for the Americans we should have been out of the war by midway through 1941, we had lost the war that mattered, we were then bailed out by the Americans. We then found that building up the sterling bloc which had got us out of the Depression was very congruent with the ways that the whole world moved out of depression. What we failed to notice was that the sterling bloc had actually peaked in 1948 and no longer offered us a viable future. But we did not actually flirt—well, some did—with trying to link the remnants of Empire – remember all Continental countries had colonial interests at that stage. The notion of welding those together in some kind of European preferential bloc with Empire, which was an imaginative idea in the 1940s, took no grip at all on the Labour Party and very little on the Conservative Party.

Notes

1. For increase in GDP in OECD Europe and the UK, 1938–9, see Alec Cairncross (1992), *The British Economy Since 1945*, Oxford, Blackwell, p. 278.
2. For the growth of the Japanese and other economies in the post-war period, see Andrew Graham and Anthony Seldon (eds) (1990), *Government and Economies in the Postwar World: Economic Policy and Comparative Performance 1949–85*, Routledge, London.

References

Brady, Robert (1950), *Crisis in Britain: Plans and Achievements of the Labour Government*, Cambridge, Cambridge University Press.

Dow, Christopher (1970), *The Management of the British Economy 1945–1970*, Cambridge, Cambridge University Press.

Middlemas, Keith (1986), *Power, Competition and the State*, Vol. 1, *Britain in Search of Balance 1940–1961*, London, Macmillan.

Milward, Alan (1970), *The Economic Effects of the Second World War in Britain*, London, Macmillan.

Milward, Alan (1984), *Reconstruction of Western Europe 1945–1951*, London, Metheun.

Pollard, Sidney (1983), *The Development of the British Economy 1914–1980*, London, Edward Arnold.

Saville, John (1983), 'Clement Attlee: an assessment', *Socialist Register*, Vol. 20, pp. 144–67.

Shanks, Michael and Lambert, John (1962), *Britain and the New Europe: The Future of the Common Market*, London, Chatto & Windus.

Taylor, A.J.P. (1965), *English History 1914–1945*, Harmondsworth, Penguin.

II

What difference did the war make to society and the citizen?

3 The changing nature of the British state, 1929–59: the historiography of consensus*

Malcolm Smith

I think I need to begin by defining what I mean by the state. I may not have to: historians have been writing about the state for most of this century without even trying to define the term, and it has not seemed to matter. Defining the state is, in fact, a difficult thing to do, although political scientists might find such a statement typical of the worst kind of historian's abstention from theoretical reading. Looked at historically, however, a difficulty of definition does in fact arise in this country because we have no written constitution in Britain, no contract between people and state which defines for us exactly who is supposed to be responsible for what and why. This has meant that governments can change in just three sittings in Parliament what it might take months of working through the Supreme Court in the United States to do. For most people in Britain 'the state' means, basically, 'the government'. In a sense, trying to define the state in Britain is a bit like trying to define social class. Virtually no one in Britain can define social class because virtually no one has read Karl Marx, but we all know what it is when we see it. It is the same with the state: we all know what it is when we get a tax bill, queue up to sign on, pay a prescription charge, or land up in an ambulance after a traffic accident. Yet in popular political discourse the concept of 'the state' is not very well defined at all. Recent debates on Declarations of Rights and Citizens' Charters seem to me, at least, to be belated attempts to deal with the confusions and misunderstandings which understandably and inevitably arise when a government has the right to move the goalposts virtually at will, spuriously legitimised by reference to some incomprehensible sentence half-way through a sixty-page election manifesto. If there is a popular concept of 'the state', and this appears to have been true even at the height of the popularity of the welfare state, then it is probably seen as something rather sinister, shades of secret police and 1984, certainly a concept of 'them' as opposed to 'us'.

* I am especially grateful to my colleague, Anne Borsay, for her comments on an earlier draft of this essay.

This is ironic, even a little sad, in a period when governments at least tried hard to make the state look benevolent. In itself, it almost certainly says something either about the failure of welfare politics to deliver the New Jerusalem or, at least, the failure of politicians to explain fully what was intended or, perhaps, simply the failure of electors to believe them. But that is to move into an area which will be discussed a little later. For our purposes, it is enough to define the national state in its domestic role—and I am going to be talking very little about the local state—as the formal organisation of the relationship between the social classes, the genders, professional and other interest groups, as that relationship is recognised by government, manifested in the ideology of the institutions of government. In other words, the term 'the state' is being used here to describe the ideology of the institutions of government, the network of laws and assumptions which construct the individual as citizen in relation to other citizens, with duties as well as rights.

In what follows, no attempt is made to go through all the many areas in which the role of the state has changed in these dramatic thirty years. I do not have the expertise, and many of the areas will be discussed in other essays in this publication anyway. It did seem important, however, to see that there was a role at this stage in the debate for a discussion of the changing nature of the state. This is not all that easy, either. I came to suspect, looking through the library cards, that there was a remarkable dearth of serious theorising on the nature of the state in post-war Britain. It is an extraordinary thing: Britain gives away an empire and develops a welfare state. These are momentous changes, but without their subliminal theorist. Where is the Hobbes? Where is the Locke or even the John Stuart Mill? We have plenty of explanations of what can be done—from the Keyneses and the Beveridges, the Croslands and Crossmans and the T.H. Marshalls—but very little on *why* it should be done and what it all *means*—until the late 1960s that is, by which time it was all coming unstuck. The state as a concept emerged from the Second World War still tainted by fascism and by Stalinism, even though the 'welfare state' was intended as a direct juxtaposition to the 'warfare state'. Perhaps it is this which explains the very muted fanfare for welfarism, certainly nothing to compare with the dire warnings of *1984*, published in the climactic year of Labour's post-war legislation. The welfare state developed largely pragmatically, in a theoretical vacuum, sustained almost wholly by its apparent popularity, by the supposedly widely held view that it was the right and practical thing to do. It was simply assumed to be the democratic collectivist nirvana for which liberal political theorists of the past had campaigned for so long and which no longer even needed explanation or legitimisation. In fact, what theory of the state there was in this period appeared more pragmatic than visionary. Keynes's notion of citizenship, for instance, seemed to imply that if there *were* constraints that people would not like (even though they might be necessary for the future) then people should not be made to endure them. 'In the long run we are all dead' was a humane but hardly responsible or even sustainable theory of state intervention in a sustained economic crisis. Beveridge's principles of universality and comprehensiveness were designed only to produce a floor to social provision, not a ceiling, leaving continued space for voluntary agencies and private insurance schemes. This in turn left room for major confusions about the rights of citizenship, how far entitlement to universality and equity conflicted with individuality and choice. Neither were these confusions wholly ironed out by writers such as T.H. Marshall in the concept of citizenship developed in the 1950s and 1960s. Marshall proposed that, while the rights of citizenship should inhibit such tendencies, inequality was in some measure necessary for the production of wealth, and that the purpose of the welfare state was actually to iron out poverty rather than inequality.[1]

Into this gap in theory, however, the historians have moved. If it be allowed that historians are themselves evidence—if only in the obvious sense that in explaining the past to the present they must take up a position, if only semi-consciously—then the developing historiography of mid-century Britain may provide us with the nearest to a description we have got of changing perceptions of what it was that the state both ought to be doing and was in fact doing. The contention is that it is potentially significant for the historian to consider the development of the historiography of mid-twentieth-century British politics, to examine the ways in which key terms such as 'the 1930s', 'the people's war', 'the welfare state' and 'the Butskellite consensus' have come to change their load of meaning over the past thirty years, and to consider what this suggests about the development of the notion of the state. The historiographical debate has centred on the role of conflict, on the one hand, and of consensus, on the other hand, in changing notions of how society should formally be organised, the changing ideology of government. In this debate, it soon becomes clear, historians have actually been talking about the historical construction of the citizen and about how the state changes.

In developing overviews on the period from 1929 to 1959, we are crossing a great historiographical divide which, until comparatively recently, constructed the Second World War as the great turning point in twentieth-century British history. The war in general, and 1940 in particular, acted through the 1950s , 1960s and into the 1970s as the fulcrum of contemporary British politics. The prevailing view, to put it at its simplest, was that 1940 marked the end of the 'bad times' and the beginning of the 'good times'. In what is perhaps its classic formulation, this periodisation of British history was most succinctly put in Charles Mowat's *Britain Between the Wars*, first published in 1955 and still featuring on most twentieth-century history undergraduate reading lists. Mowat wrote at the end of a study which still repays detailed reading for its balanced survey of that complex and paradoxical period:

> In the summer of 1940, as they awaited the Battle of Britain, [the people of Britain] found themselves again, after twenty years of indecision. They turned away from past regrets and faced the future unafraid. (Mowat, 1955, p. 657)

Mowat's book was written in the context of the mature welfarism of the mid-1950s, when the reforms of the wartime coalition and the Labour governments of 1945 to 1951 had been confirmed (and apparently made irreversible) by the ascendancy of the Tory reformers in the government of 1951 to 1955. In many ways, that book is itself a monument to welfare culture, the sort of book which ought to have been given free to everyone on the National Health. It stands as a useful touchstone to mark the way in which the savaging of Neville Chamberlain and his interwar colleagues in *Guilty Men*, written in 1940 itself (Cato, 1940), was transformed into respectable academic underpinning of the notion that in the Second World War the nation had fused with the state. *Guilty Men* suggested the need for a new beginning. *Britain Between the Wars* suggested that, historically, that new beginning had indeed occurred. The age of conflict was over. Consensus was now and forever.

In Mowat's formulation, the war marked a fundamental shift in the nature of the state, with 1940 as the sharp point of focus. The dole queues, poor housing and appeasement were replaced by welfarism and the Cold War. But Mowat's picture of the inter-war years was not entirely black, of course. It was also he, after all, who first picked up on the evidence of major social and economic benefits enjoyed by large sections of the population in the 1920s and 1930s. This was to be taken up and made central to the treatment of the interwar years in the work of the so-called revisionists in the 1970s, notably Aldcroft and Richardson, Glynn and Oxborrow, Stevenson and Cook.[2] Emphasis shifted from the monochrome image of the inter-war years, centred on the depressed areas, which had largely predominated since the war, to the rise in the standard of living that affected the majority (i.e. those who were not unemployed) and which may have fed the consumer boom of the 1930s. The notion that the interwar years had been primarily years of conflict and division was challenged by the view that evidence of such conflict and division had to be set against the huge electoral support for the Conservative Party and for its very moderate opponents on the Labour benches.

While the revisionists argued that most of the improvements that took place in the inter-war period occurred in spite of, rather than because of, state policy, the implication was that the notion of the war years as a new beginning had to be recast. The consumer economy that was to be such a major factor in post-war Britain was already making a major impact in the inter-war period. Intervention in the workings of industry was becoming common practice, if not actually the mainstay of state policy, by 1939 (the revisionists pointed to the rationalisation schemes in steel, textiles and agriculture, as well as the nationalisation of commercial aviation and mining royalties). Meanwhile the development of social policy, in the view of one admittedly controversial analysis from the late 1960s at least (Gilbert, 1969), had produced—in effect if not yet in theory—a welfare state. By implication, then, the effects of the war were simply to apply a gloss, a more positive policy statement, to the pragmatic reaction of government in the inter-war years to the problems of living with a prolonged depression. This gloss was provided by Keynes and Beveridge, most of whose ideas stemmed not from the experience of wartime as such but from pre-war experience. It was that same pre-war experience, moreover, which raised practical 'blueprints' for change, such as the Hadow Commission in the case of education, the minority report of the Royal Commission of 1926 in the case of health, or the Barlow Commission in the case of inner-city deprivation.

It was not just changing views of the interwar period that were gnawing away at the idea that the war marked a new beginning, because studies of the impact of the war itself were also challenging the post-war historical and political orthodoxy. As early as 1961, Anthony Howard had suggested that 1945 marked 'the biggest restoration of traditional values since 1660' (Sissons and French, 1964), but such views were more surprising than acceptable until the publication of Calder's *The People's War* in 1969—which argued that a radical groundswell in the war had been sat upon by a reformist state in 1945 and thereafter—after which time such arguments became pretty much mainstream in New Left history (Calder, 1969). But a major synthesis and rebalancing of the debate on the inter-war and the war years was left until Paul Addison's *The Road to 1945*, which accepted implicitly the revisionists' case on the 1930s but still argued for a major shift occurring in the war years. This may not have been as great a shift as writers such as Calder would have wished or thought possible, perhaps, but nevertheless Addison saw it as a decisive shift in emphasis, particularly in terms of the commitment of the state both in economic management and social engineering. This marked a move, in Addison's view, not from conflict to consensus (as the orthodoxy of the 1950s would have had it) but from one consensus to another, from Baldwin's consensus to Attlee's (Addison, 1975). At this stage of the debate, then, conflict had been effectively ironed out of the process of change. What we have instead is a supremely sensitive hegemonic machine in the state which is able to deal consecutively with crises as momentous as the Great Depression and the Second World War. Consensus becomes the theory of the state: it is what the state is there to engineer. Addison's views in fact reflected those of Beveridge himself, who had declared in his Report that 'a revolutionary moment should be a time for revolutions and not for patching', but who had gone on to suggest that the form that this revolution would take would be incremental and consensual: a 'British revolution.'[3] A variant and more detailed example of this kind of argument has been advanced by Keith Middlemas in his monumental analysis of the development of economic corporatism as a product of wartime, an alliance between government, employers and TUC (Middlemas, 1986). This is best considered as a 'variant' on Addison because Middlemas gives more prominence to the term 'balance' rather than 'consensus', and argues that it was already under serious threat as early as 1961.

More recently, Addison's synthesis has itself come under attack. Charles Webster, in his work on the National Health Service, has suggested that it was not consensus which produced the NHS but conflict: and the result was not consensus, either, but uneasy compromise (Webster, 1988, 1991). Kevin Jeffreys has suggested that pressure for change in the wartime coalition came from some intellectuals, from the press and from specialist pressure groups, not from consensus at the top. Politicians mostly agreed to disagree, so that the White Paper chase produced ambiguous and vague documents, no blueprints for action (Jeffreys, 1987, 1990). José Harris (Harris, 1986) and Ben Pimlott (Pimlott, 1989) have suggested that the idea of there being a post-war consensus is virtually a conspiracy of historians once you get down to details, while Rodney Lowe, though suggesting that consensus is not so easily dismissed, argues that consensus was constantly shifting and that it was passive rather than active, dictating what could *not* rather than what *could* be done by the state in the new dispensation (Lowe, 1989).

The point that should be made here is that the historiographical debate has centred on the role that consensus and conflict in the political establishment —or conflict with consensus (see Ashford, 1981)—has played in the development of the state and is therefore, in itself, a discussion of the nature of the modern British state. To a large extent, of course, this debate has itself been a product of, or at least a reaction to, changes in the dominant political discourse. It is difficult to believe, for example, that the revisionists' case on the 1930s could have gained credibility had it not been for the fact that Britain was getting used to large-scale unemployment once again. In the 1950s, the fact that there were never less than one million unemployed from 1920 to 1940 appeared appalling; in the 1990s, if unemployment went down to one million it would be seen as incontrovertible evidence of economic recovery. Calder's work similarly reflected the frustrations with the apparently limited achievement of Labour after 1945 and after 1964. The problem both with using and with opposing the consensus argument is that a consensus is only a consensus as long as there is a consensus that consensus exists. That having been said, it does appear that there may be something of a vacuum in analysis at the heart of the explanation of change in the state in terms of consensus. It does not in itself explain how consensus (if it happens) is arrived at, the mechanisms by which general agreement is reached, or how general agreement changes over time, how resistant or alternative stances are incorporated into a new, replacement general agreement. It is not just that consensus as analysis tends to be static rather than dynamic; there is also a danger, here, of reversion to basically self-congratulatory arguments; one suspects sometimes that the subtext of the consensualist argument is a discourse on the British national character. Certainly, there may be involved here a throwback to the Victorian notion of the organic community, reborn after the trials and tribulations of two world wars and the Depression. It would not be going too far to say that the notion of post-war consensus plays a similar role in the study of twentieth-century British history to that played by *Coronation Street* in popular culture: it produces a warm glow. It may well be that the problem may be intrinsic to the term itself. 'Consensus' has complicated, innately hegemonic semantic implications, suggesting only the predominance of agreement over dissent and actually implying that dissent is itself an important element in the make-up of consensus. Dissent and consensus make up a binary opposition because of the implication that dissent is not simply ignored in consensus but constantly engaged with in an active attempt to appease or, if appeasement is impossible, to brand as deviant. But consensus certainly does not preclude dissent, as some of the more head-on attacks on the consensualist argument seem to suggest. Perhaps it would be better for historians to abandon such a complicated and loaded term altogether and seek something rather more neutral. We might feel happier with the phrase 'compromise equilibrium', for example. It may well be that that phrase conveys more accurately than the term 'consensus' the conflict between interests that is only temporarily frozen, rather than wholly undermined, in periods of broad political agreement. The melting of this agreement in political reactions to periods of crisis finds these interests still at odds until a new but, again, temporary coalition can be engineered (Smith, 1990).

Naturally, the evidence for continuity, for cumulative and incremental rather than sudden surges in state intervention, is great, but this should not be misconstrued as evidence for consensus as such. The constraints on change are inbuilt in the structure of the state. Central government expenditure rose from about 12 per cent of GDP before 1914 to an average of 25 per cent in the inter-war years, to 36 per cent in 1963 and 49 per cent in 1975. Even a decade of Thatcherism only reduced it to just under 40 per cent, such is the ratchet effect of state intervention. An ever-growing civil service is difficult to shift in its ideas, is naturally 'consensualist' in that it may have to deal with the opposition in government within a few years. It also takes a great many years to reach a position in the civil service where advice has any effect on politicians. It is not therefore all that surprising that chancellors in the 1950s had to fight for their Keynesian principles against Gladstonian Treasury officials or, conversely, that chancellors had to battle against a now Keynesian Treasury in the 1980s. Professional groups, such as the British Medical Association or the teachers—in two key areas of state involvement in this period—are not easily ridden over, with the result that they may well retain their privileged status within the social services, arguably at the expense of the public good and government intentions. Centralisation, at the expense of the local authorities, may well have benefited professional groups rather than the consumer. But such failures may be the unavoidable side-effects of a welfare state. It is difficult to conceive how it might be possible to side-step the need to work through a policy community which involves professionals as well as state and consumer, but which necessarily gives extraordinary power both of obstruction and direction to the group which will have to work the system. At this point, we may switch attention to the political mechanisms through which conflict produces compromise equilibria in this period, though without underrating these institutional difficulties in the everyday practice of the state. The interests that we should be really considering in examining the notion of compromise equilibria are social and economic rather than institutional.

The mechanisms by which compromise equilibria were engineered in this period were twofold. There was, first, the simple fact of political coalition in reaction to crisis: the coalition of 1931 in reaction to the financial crisis and the coalition of 1940 in reaction to the international crisis, accounting for fourteen of the thirty years under discussion. Secondly, it has been suggested that Baldwin was a natural coalitionist and it is probably important to emphasise more generally, since it has been in power for such large periods of this century, that the tradition of one-nation Conservatism has itself contributed to the significance of the consensus argument in relation to the state. Baldwinism at least used the rhetoric of consensus and concession in worried reaction to the possible social and political consequences of the depression and renewed war. It is also true that, though the coalition governments of the 1930s may have isolated the leadership of the left, they did produce a number of opportunities for cross-party contacts which may have gone some way to fray the edges of political conflict. Specifically, there were groups like Political and Economic Planning, of course, as well as the Next Five Years Group and the League of Nations Union. In reaction to appeasement, the Popular Front produced the strongest evidence in the 1930s of the development of a new political centre, prepared to sacrifice party loyalties and traditions for the sake of defending democracy against fascism. Even though Labour could broadly agree with the Churchillian right over Munich, it was highly unlikely in the circumstances of the late 1930s that they could mount a combined challenge to Chamberlain at the top—there was too much which separated them—but these signs of developing links at the edges of the political parties suggested that if such a challenge to Chamberlain could ever be mounted, it might carry real political weight.

Hence the significance of 1940 is perhaps not so much a case of the right and left coming together simply to fight the war, but rather of the opportunity it brought for the nascent centre groupings of the 1930s to come into prominence as back-bench pressure groups, and in a situation which demanded fairly radical alternatives if the war were to be won. This was accompanied by the drafting into the Ministry of Information of many of the alternative cultural mandarins of the 1930s, who brought their politics with them and who attempted to turn the series of patchwork, pragmatic responses of government to the problems of reconstruction into a crusade. This is not to say that there existed a consensus in the state; the Tory reformers and the Gaitskellite revisionists—the political heirs of the centre groupings of the 1930s—did not gain control of their respective parties until the end of the decade, and one must not overstate the importance of the propagandising zeal of the MoI. The debate over the Beveridge Report and the hedging in the White Paper chase which followed showed the many 'ifs' and 'buts' which stood in the way of full agreement.

Nevertheless, coalition had forced the major parties to fill the ideological vacuum produced by the fall of Chamberlain, and the wartime acceptance of the Keynes–Beveridge axis—in principle, if not in practice—depended upon an implicit acceptance of the kind of assumptions that had dominated PEP and Next Five Years in the 1930s, as well as the 'people's war' rhetoric of MoI public presentations of the issues involved in wartime. Whatever the shortcomings of the argument for wartime 'consensus', it is important not to lose sight of the wood for the trees: no serious politician with an eye on the future could have stood up publicly in 1945 and said that Keynes and Beveridge were wholly unacceptable. On the other hand, it is equally important to note that war produced two antipathetic self-images for Britain. The democratic collectivist self-image associated with Keynes and Beveridge, Labour and Tory reformer, was to coexist unhappily with the Churchillian legacy. If the people's war had been a fight for freedom through collectivism, Churchill's war had been a fight for freedom through individualism, and that difference of emphasis remained as a grumbling appendix even in the most obvious moments of post-war consensus. The central features of the post-war settlement only disguised what was, finally, an irreconcilable difference of opinion. The Churchill legacy also left the unfortunate impression that Britain still counted in the world, a delusion which affected Labour as much as Conservatives. The cost of the defence commitment which resulted gnawed away at the nation's ability to develop the social services. This much was clear as early as five years after the end of the war, when Nye Bevan resigned from Attlee's Cabinet.

Compromise equilibria were not produced simply by the mechanics of coalition in reaction to crisis, however. Coalitions can only come into existence if there is already enough of a fit between the outlooks of the political parties concerned, even in a major crisis. To explain the mechanism which made coalition possible in time of crisis it is necessary to look at the socio-economic conditions which shaped electoral geography in this period. Ramsay MacDonald's strategy of the 'respectable alternative' in the interwar years, whatever else it might have been, was a simple rational reaction to the fact that Labour could not hope to win a general election simply on the votes of the unemployed. In the interwar period Labour began to pile up the huge majorities in what became known as the 'Labour heartland', but were stymied by the fact that the Conservatives could sweep the board in the South and South East where the large majority were not unemployed, not badly housed and, in fact, relatively prosperous. Unless Labour could appeal to these areas then the Conservatives would be in for ever, unless they made some disastrous mistakes. The real political battle in the 1930s and beyond was for the votes of the lower-middle class; already 40 per cent of all families in Britain according to the census of 1931. Election victory in a first-past-the-post system depended on attaching a large portion of their support to the bedrock support of the working class for Labour or the middle class for Conservatives. Between 1950 and 1959 the parties were within 5 per cent of each other in the share of the popular vote in every general election; the size of their parliamentary majorities depended on the geographical distribution of those votes. Back in the 1930s, Labour was certainly further behind in the popular vote anyway, but it was their failure to appeal to seats in suburban areas, particularly in the South and South East, which severely skewed the results against them. Simply fighting for the same support is likely to bring the political parties within sighting distance of each other on the major political issues. The conclusion that may be drawn is that the appearance of consensus in the state is the product of the electoral consequences of economic and social geography. On the other hand, the bedrock support for the two major parties continues to make their fundamental interests quite different. Party leaders charged with the direction of electoral strategy over the past twenty years have been quite blatant in their appeal to the hundred or so key marginals which have largely controlled general election results; the agenda of modern politics have probably been controlled by not much more than 15 per cent of the entire electorate. Backbenchers with 20,000-plus majorities feel no such compunction in putting forward their particular electors' doorstep point of view. It is always likely, therefore, that those fundamental interests will reassert themselves if they see themselves threatened by the consensual consequences of courting the electoral middle ground. While the gap between the political parties was lessened by these pressures, gaps within the parties might well appear. Consensus may therefore be simply an optical illusion caused by focusing simply on electoral strategy rather than on these bedrock sympathies.

After 1945, as the war crisis receded and the rhetoric of the 'people's war' died away, those fundamental interests soon began to reassert themselves, while the political leaders strained hard to maintain a centre position as the only means of attaining power. In the period of Conservative ascendancy between 1951 and 1964 the emphasis therefore shifted from the application of the principles of comprehensiveness and universality as such to the use of welfarism and corporatism to create the basis for a rejuvenated popular capitalism. Welfarism and corporatism, in their 'consensual' application, washed away many of the assumptions on which welfarism and corporatism had originally been based, though without actually destroying the fundamental political frictions. It is an ironic if obvious fact that privatisation in the 1980s would have been impossible without nationalisation in the 1940s: Morrison's idea of the state corporation, seen at the time by opponents either as a sell-out to the interests of private capital or as creeping socialism, led finally in fact to the share-owning democracy. In the same way, the fight against the slums destroyed the solidarity of the working-class communities on which Labour had depended for much of its traditional support and in its place, in its Tory application, produced the property-owning democracy. In similar fashion, the National Health Service finally undermined the idea that capitalism led only to rickets and TB. The democratisation of education, by the 1980s, apparently gave every young person the wherewithal to make £1,000 a day in the City. Already by the late 1970s, the clear failure of welfarism to produce 'socialism by consensus' had produced near civil war within the Labour Party. At the other end of the political spectrum, these same unexpected results of welfarism had given the New Right the critical mass finally to overthrow 'Butskellism'.

Welfarism depended upon a new relationship between nation and state, but there was never any consensual or consistent argument deployed by politicians to explain what this new relationship was supposed to be. 'You've never had it so good' was a long way in sympathy from the programme for democratic collectivism central to the ideology of the people's war and set out in Labour's 1945 manifesto. This was something that Richard Titmuss had been clear about in the late 1950s, admitting 'that we put too much faith in the 1940s in the concept of universality . . . Mistakenly, it was linked with economic egalitarianism' (Titmuss, 1960). Yet Macmillan had been talking about exactly the same social benefits as Labour. The success of the notion of the social wage—the idea that wage demands should take into account the benefits provided by welfarism—was crucial to welfarism's success, but after the stop-go budgeting of 1951 to 1964 it was clear from increasing industrial militancy over wages that the argument simply had not stuck. And resistance to the social wage can only be interpreted as a lack of consent, or a lack of belief in the welfare state. The rapidly expanding role of the state between 1929 and 1959, predicated on a new relationship between the social classes, a newly integrated national family, disguised the fact that the consensus taken to be the manifestation of that new integration was only a mechanism for containing the clash of interests. At this distance in time, we can see that the road to 1945 was only the first stage of the roller-coaster ride to 1979.

Notes

1. See T.H. Marshall (1950), *Citizenship and Social Development*, Cambridge, Cambridge University Press; (1963), *Sociology at the Crossroads and Other Essays*, London, Heinemann.
2. D.H. Aldcroft and H.W. Richardson (1969), *The British Economy, 1870–1939*, London, Macmillan; S. Glynn and J. Oxborrow (1976), *Interwar Britain: A Social and Economic History*, London, Allen & Unwin; J. Stevenson and C. Cook (1978), *The Slump: Society and Politics During the Depression*, London, Cape.
3. Cmd. 6404 (1942), *Social Insurance and Allied Services*, HMSO, London.
4. See the distinction between corporate and competitive pressure groups, formalising this tension, in A. Cawson (1982), *Corporatism and Welfare: Social Policy and State Intervention in Britain*, London, Macmillan.

References

Addison, P. (1975), *The Road to 1945*, London, Cape.

Ashford, D.E. (1981), *Policy and Politics in Britain: The Limits of Consensus*, London, Macmillan.

Calder, A. (1969), *The People's War*, London, Cape.

Cato, (1940), *Guilty Men*, London, Gollancz.

Gilbert, B.B. (1969), *English Social Policy*, London, Batsford.

Harris, J. (1986), 'Political values and the Debate on the Welfare State', in Harold L. Smith, ed., *War and Social Change*, Manchester, Manchester University Press.

Jeffreys, K. (1987), 'British politics and social policy during the Second World War', *Historical Journal*, vol. 30, pp. 123–44.

Jeffreys, K. (1990), *The Churchill Coalition and Wartime Politics*, Manchester, Manchester University Press.

Lowe, R. (1989), 'The Second World War: Consensus and the foundation of the welfare state', *Twentieth Century British History*, vol. 1, pp. 152–82.

Middlemas, K. (1986), *Power, Competition and the State*, Vol. 1, *Britain in Search of a Balance, 1940–1961*, London and Basingstoke, Macmillan.

Mowat, C.L., (1955), *Britain Between the Wars*, Methuen, London.

Pimlott, B. (1989), 'Is the Postwar Consensus a Myth', *Contemporary Record*, vol. 2, no. 6, pp. 12–14.

Sissons, M. and French, P. (eds) (1964), *The Age of Austerity*, Harmondsworth, Penguin.

Smith, M. (1990), *British Politics, Society and the State Since the Late Nineteenth Century*, London, Macmillan.

Titmuss, R. (1960), *The Irresponsible Society*, London, Fabian Society, reprinted 1963, *Essays on the Welfare State*, London, Unwin.

Webster, C. (1988), *The health service since the war, Volume 1: problems of health care*, HMSO, London; 1990.

Webster, C. (1991), Conflict and consensus: explaining the British health service, *Twentieth Century British History*, Vol. 1, No. 1, pp. 115–51.

4 The road to *Nineteen Eighty-Four*: Orwell and the post-war reconstruction of citizenship

David Morgan and Mary Evans

This essay suggests some preliminary thoughts on George Orwell and the social reconstruction of citizenship during and immediately after the Second World War. By comparison with the heated controversies surrounding the direction of the post-war economy, or over specific issues such as the nationalisation of iron and steel, citizenship was not a contested or prominent issue. However, major reforms and legislative changes in health, education and welfare significantly altered the status of citizenship by shifting the boundaries between public and private interests towards the public domain. Henceforth, responsibility lay with the state to ensure the conditions of a healthy and productive life. These reforms offered unprecedented protection to those most vulnerable to what Ernest Bevin called 'the economic whip', but, together with the commitment to 'full and stable employment', they raised complex questions—and equally confused expectations—about the limits of this 'new society' and, *inter alia*, the changing relationship of citizens to the state.

The main beneficiaries of these changes were the sick, the elderly, children and the poor. However, the rationalisation of welfare expressed the belief that society has an obligation towards *all* its members to provide what Orwell commonly referred to as a 'decent standard of life'. It was a sentiment of which he wholly approved. As a socialist, Orwell passionately believed that in relation to education, health and domestic security, ability to pay should be replaced by universal criteria of need. But equally, as a liberal with an idiosyncratic strain towards conservative and anarchist sympathies, he had a deep distrust of authority and especially the collectivist tendencies of the modern state. However benign its purpose, the centralisation of power threatened to undermine the autonomy of civil society and hence the individual and political freedoms upon which, he believed, democratic socialism should rest. Orwell did not claim to be a political theorist, yet amongst contemporary writers he offers a characteristically distinctive view of the tensions between liberty and equality, socialism and democracy which marked the changing relationship of citizenship to an emerging corporate state.

In *The Lion and the Unicorn*, Orwell noted that 'War is the greatest of all agents of change. It speeds up all processes, wipes out minor distinctions, brings reality to the surface. Above all it brings home to the individual that he is *not* altogether an individual' (Orwell, 1941, p. 117). Feelings of mutual obligation and the expectation of impending change permeated the prospect of a New Jerusalem and influenced thinking about citizenship for some years after the war. T.H. Marshall's classic essay, *Citizenship and Social Class*, published shortly before Orwell's *Nineteen Eighty-Four*, catches the optimistic mood of the time. Marshall claims that the post-war expansion of social and economic rights—what he calls 'social citizenship'—is the basis of a new form of social solidarity (Marshall, 1963). Citizenship binds together different interest groups, parties and—most of all—social classes into a single community whose boundaries form the nation state. Clearly, Marshall attributes to citizenship a moral and symbolic significance that goes well beyond the formal recognition of civil, political and social rights. Post-war Britain is seen rather like a 'friendly society' which confers upon all members a fundamental human equality in relation to each other and the state. Indeed, he ventures to suggest that citizenship goes some way towards legitimising class inequalities by establishing a common basis of individual entitlements and social rights (Marshall, 1963, p. 73).

This idea of citizenship as a kind of 'social cement' might easily be dismissed nowadays as romantic conjecture, but Marshall's essay has to be read in historical context. The shared experience of war had created a strong sense of national cohesion. Food rationing, mass evacuation, conscription and the strategic use of labour and scarce resources had demanded massive civilian cooperation and—in a contemporary phrase—'equality of sacrifice' irrespective of class. For the first time since the Great War, the efforts of ordinary wage earners were identified not just with the labour process, but with the values and aspirations of society as a whole. Bitter memories of the Depression, means tests, unemployment, and the General Strike, as much as the war effort, contributed to a groundswell of radical sentiment in favour of improving the life chances of ordinary citizens after the war. Indeed, the aims of the war were inseparable from expectations of future prosperity, equal opportunity and a decent standard of material life.

Against this background, thinking about citizenship was both utopian and pragmatic. It was moved by a concern for social injustice, and by the conspicuous deprivations of large sections of the population who had long endured disease, ignorance, squalor, idleness and want. These were marks of an unfair society—the five 'giant evils', as Beveridge called them, on the road to a safer and better world. With the publication of Beveridge's Report, demands that private suffering should be treated as a public issue were hard to resist. Almost immediately, popular aspirations for a more compassionate, egalitarian society found practical expression in early plans for what later became known as the 'welfare state'. Citizenship was conceived as a *social* status that in the New Jerusalem would confer an unconditional right to participate fully in the life of the nation, irrespective of market situation or accidents of birth.

But it wasn't just idealism—there were more strategic issues at stake, not least the immediate task of mobilising a subordinate and largely disaffected working class to cooperate in what many within the labour movement saw as yet another capitalists' war. As A.J.P. Taylor observed

> Men talked of reconstruction as they had done during the First World War. This time they were determined not to be cheated, and therefore demanded the formulation of practical schemes while the war was on. This demand was hard to resist. The governing classes were on their best behaviour, from conviction as well as calculation. (Taylor, 1965, p. 567)

War gave reality and legitimate purpose to the collective interests of the nation and the corporate role of the state. Between the government and the labour movement, it was tacitly agreed that it was unacceptable for gross material and social deprivations to exist when an unconditional commitment was being demanded to defend the nation at war. It was an agreement that transformed the outward face of the state from a force of aggression and repressive control to an agency of restitution and conciliation. The declared aims of a war in defence of freedom, democracy and justice made this development virtually unavoidable. In any case, after the First World War, the idea of a modern nation waging an imperial war had become ideologically indefensible. Nationalism, in a crude nineteenth-century sense, was no longer sufficient justification for either civil authority or war; both had to be presented ideologically in terms of moral ideals and abstract rights.

This shift in the legitimacy and the role of the state was part of the broader context in which proposals for social reconstruction and reform took shape. Much has been made of legislative achievements, and the so-called political 'consensus' which facilitated the relatively smooth transition towards a social democracy after the war. But whilst these changes went some way towards modernising the infrastructure of British society, bringing measured improvements in material and public life, much less has been said about the cultural and ideological tensions which accompanied corresponding expectations of citizenship and the corporate aims of the state. Orwell's pessimistic warnings suggest one of the few contemporary counterpoints to the buoyant assumptions of planners, reformers and the enlightened Establishment of his day.

The very idea of *social* democracy entailed the radical and none too welcome prospect of the mass participation of an army of servicemen and ordinary citizens in a society traditionally governed by patronage and networks of almost caste-like exclusivity. Although Churchill had declared in the midst of war that the aim of victory was '. . . the forward march of the common people towards their just and true inheritance', he was less forthcoming on what this inheritance should be. Nor was he particularly well placed to judge: as his wife remarked, 'He knows nothing of the life of ordinary people. He's never been on a bus and only once on the Underground' (Soames, 1981). Churchill's experience was not atypical of his class. As Andrew Sinfield wryly observes,

> the British governing elite had no conception of how most of the population lived, and could therefore neither understand nor anticipate their experience of the war. They installed a network of 'Home Intelligence' to find out. Prime Minister

Chamberlain, learning of the malnutrition revealed in the evacuation of children, observed, 'I never knew such conditions existed, and I feel ashamed of having been so ignorant of my neighbours'. (Sinfield, 1989, p. 9)

The image of a common people, to which Churchill returned time and again, was drawn from mythology and historical fantasy, rather than a shared social past. Yet, ironically, this man whose life had been cushioned by wealth and privilege invoked a sense of common identity quite unlike any prime minister before or since. When Churchill spoke of Britain's lonely fight against tyranny and injustice, he gave the language of British politics an altogether new resonance. To speak in one sentence of the march of the common people and their fight for freedom extended the meaning of democracy in new directions. The possibilities were quickly seized upon in the early years of the war by others who recognised the shifting discourse of political debate. A much quoted *Times* leader, published during the Battle of Britain, develops the point:

> If we speak of democracy, we do not mean a democracy which maintains the right to vote but forgets the right to work and the right to live. If we speak of freedom, we do not mean a rugged individualism which excludes social organisation and economic planning. If we speak of equality we do not mean a political equality nullified by social and economic privilege. If we speak of economic reconstruction, we think less of maximum production (though this too will be required) than of equitable distribution. (*The Times*, 1 July 1940)

Here is explicit recognition by a leading newspaper of the British establishment that notions of 'democracy' and 'freedom' were open to radical reinterpretation. Renegotiating the meaning of these terms and their implications for the direction of change produced a diversity of competing and frequently conflicting opinions on the nature of citizenship and the proper functions of the state. In what was already a highly pluralistic society, these views commonly cut across such familiar configurations as labour versus capital, individualism versus collectivism, left versus right (Harris, 1986). There were many on the left, for instance, who supported the proposed expansion of social benefits and rights yet were fearful this would bring the inevitable encroachment of materialist values and the corporate power of the state. Others saw the centrally planned redistribution of material resources as a substantive condition of individual freedom and a more democratic way of life.

Many of these tensions and misgivings are reflected in the writings of George Orwell. His essays offer rich insights into the condition of the English working class both before and during the Second World War; however, they reflect a self-conscious ambivalence towards the direction of change that was shared by many liberals and others during the war. Orwell's agnosticism had little in common with the blustering resistance of Tory backbenchers who believed a 'welfare state' would bring socialism or worse. His sympathies, as always, were with the working class, yet he feared that the collectivism implicit in these reforms would undermine the integrity and cohesion of working-class life. Even worse, he feared that without a democratic revolution 'to transform the nation from top to bottom', the centralisation of state powers could destroy the inherent 'gentleness of English civilisation', imposing a tyranny of impersonal officialdom on a world that would become unremittingly utilitarian, drab and grey. Orwell's nightmare vision of *Nineteen Eighty-Four*—conceived as wartime plans for social reconstruction were taking shape—echoes Max Weber's earlier pessimism that modern forms of mass administration will eventually negate intellectual and democratic freedoms and envelop society in an invisible 'iron cage' from which there is little hope of escape (Orwell, 1949; Weber, 1968, p. 987ff.).

In common with many on the left, Orwell was deeply suspicious of all forms of state intervention and bureaucratic planning. Although the idea of 'fair shares for all' was morally attractive, socialism was politically more problematic. For instance, whilst he endorses Hayek's critique of economic planning in *The Road to Serfdom* (Hayek, 1944), he rejects Hayek's conclusion that the only sure defence against totalitarianism is a competitive free-market economy which asserts individual liberty over collective security. Of the two systems, Orwell recognises that 'collectivism' is inherently undemocratic; on the other hand, 'capitalism leads to dole queues, the scramble for markets, and war' (Orwell, 1944, p. 144). It was a commonly recognised dilemma: the problem was how to improve the living standards of ordinary people without imposing the measured conformity of the state. Characteristically, it was seen by Orwell as a moral rather than a narrowly political problem which threatened the vitality of the culture and the integrity of working-class life.

In his essays before the war, Orwell presents an uncompromising yet comfortable image of the ordinary citizen. Above all else, ordinary people are 'decent', and it is the 'fundamental decency' of their lives to which he repeatedly turns. In *The Road to Wigan Pier*, Orwell elaborates the idea both in relation to working-class families and the conditions in which they live, suggesting an intimate connection between material circumstances and the conditions of a 'decent' way of life:

> Give people a decent home and they will soon learn to keep it decent. Moreover, with a smart looking house to live up to they improve in self-respect and cleanliness, and their children start life with better chances. (Orwell, 1966, p. 62)

Well-housed people will make good citizens and produce future generations of well-socialised children. The working class whom Orwell came to know in Wigan and the north fell mainly into two categories: tolerably housed families that 'were as decent as one could possibly expect in the circumstances', and those families living in conditions so squalid that, as Orwell said, he had no hope of 'describing them adequately' (Orwell, 1966, p. 52ff.). In documenting the plight of the working class, Orwell was struck not just by the grim conditions in which people lived their lives, but their enduring efforts to make the best of what little they had. At its best, the working-class home offered a secure and comfortable haven from the relentless wear and tear of a hostile world:

> In a working-class home—I am not thinking at the moment of the unemployed, but of comparatively prosperous homes—you breathe a warm, decent, deeply human atmosphere which it is not so easy to find elsewhere. I should say that a

manual worker, if he is in steady work and drawing good wages—an 'if' which gets bigger and bigger—has a better chance of being happy than an 'educated' man. His home life seems to fall more naturally into a sane and comely shape. I have often been struck by the peculiarly easy completeness, the perfect symmetry as it were, of a working-class interior at its best. Especially on winter evenings after tea, when the fire glows in the open range and dances mirrored in the steel fender, when Father, in shirt-sleeves, sits in the rocking chair at one side of the fire reading the racing finals, and Mother sits on the other with her sewing, and the children are happy with a pennorth of mint humbugs, and the dog lolls roasting himself on the rag mat—it is a good place to be in, provided that you can be not only in it but sufficiently *of* it to be taken for granted. (Orwell, 1966, p. 104)

Again, the word 'decent' sets the tone of this private world of hearth and home. Here is a place where people could treat each other with proper concern and respect, where a working man could escape from dirt and strife and find contentment. However, the variation Orwell found between working-class homes couldn't always be accounted for in terms of material deprivations alone: in some cases, he admits, 'the squalor of these people's homes is sometimes their own fault' (Orwell, 1966, p. 53). But that was wholly beside the point: whether by design or by default, the freedom to be different and, even in the most oppressive circumstances, to choose one's own fate, Orwell considered a fundamental human right. Moreover, it was a right worth fighting for—the only moral justification for what he later saw as an otherwise indefensible imperialist war.

In common with progressive thinking at the time, Orwell supported the need for public programmes to relieve unemployment and poverty; the problem was how to achieve this without a concomitant tendency towards bureaucratic domination and oligarchical forms of power. As in the case of the war, it was again a question of defending 'the bad against the worse' (Crick, 1982, p. 377). He despised the exploitation and gross inefficiency of *laissez-faire* capitalism, yet he thought it offered a better chance of individual freedom than a command economy and tawdry officialdom of the state. This position was common enough amongst liberals both before and during the war. Ideologically, the differences between moderate opinion and those further to the left turned upon whether state intervention was seen as a positive step towards a more efficient and responsible society, or a temporary expedient to shore up an ailing system in terminal decline. Keynes had favoured the former view when he wrote:

For my part, I think that Capitalism wisely managed, can probably be made more efficient for attaining economic ends than any alternative system yet in sight, but that in itself it is in many ways extremely objectionable. Our problem is to work out a social organisation which shall be as efficient as possible without offending our notions of a satisfactory way of life. (Keynes, 1931, p. 321)

For Orwell, that 'way of life' had to be uncompromisingly egalitarian and democratic. It was a view that readily appealed to the spirit of wartime radicalism with its rough justice and popular demands for a fairer world. But it was the radicalism of rebellion rather than revolution. In the *The Lion and the Unicorn*, Orwell comes close to capturing the vitality yet deeply parochial sentiment of wartime dissent:

It is only by revolution that the native genius of the English people can be set free. Revolution does not mean red flags and street fighting, it means a fundamental *shift* in power . . . Nor does it mean the dictatorship of a single class. The people in England who grasp what changes are needed and are capable of carrying them through are not confined to one class. What is wanted is a conscious open revolt by ordinary people against inefficiency, class privilege and the rule of the old. It is not primarily a question of change of government. British governments, broadly speaking, do represent the will of the people, and if we alter our structure from below we shall get the government we need. (Orwell, 1941, p. 108)

There is no question here of challenging the existing *system* of power: the Westminster model of parliamentary democracy is still firmly intact; the economy is still predominantly capitalist, and inequalities of income still exist. As he went on to say, 'In a country like England we cannot rip down the whole structure and build again from the bottom, least of all in time of war' (Orwell, 1941, p. 119). But what has been eliminated is 'inefficiency, class privilege and', most of all, 'the rule of the old'. It is a modernising, egalitarian revolt, led in Orwell's imagination by craftsmen, technical experts and NCOs. Above all, patriotism that will carry the day: 'the English sense of national unity has never disintegrated, because patriotism is finally stronger than class hatred, the chances are that the will of the majority will prevail. (Orwell, 1941, p. 118).

Orwell's idea that all that is needed is a patriotic shift in power appealed to ordinary people fighting for continuity yet hoping for change. Furthermore, the wartime resurgence of national unity created an opportunity, and an immediate need, to redefine the nature of patriotism and the reciprocal obligations of the state. If the ideal citizen of the nineteenth century had personified rugged and fearless individualism, then the new John Bull of the mid-twentieth century was someone for whom the struggle for freedom and liberty was inseparable from common opposition to social deprivation and material want. The John Bull who had 'stood up to tyrants' (largely Britain's commercial foes) became in the 1940s a patriot who identified tyranny not just with freedom from arbitrary rule but the inescapable drudgery of poverty, hunger and industrial decline. The old Tory idea of patriotism, marked by a readiness to do one's duty on the field of battle, gave way to a form of 'social patriotism' which corresponded more closely to the efforts and aspirations of the people as a whole (Addison, 1975). This was 'the people's war', fought by a largely conscript army against forces that demolished homes, factories, railways and docks, and killed civilians and soldiers on leave. Patriotism was no longer limited to the front line; it became a generalised quality of all citizens who endured the deprivations and dangers of total war.

In line with these sentiments, the aspirations of ordinary people were fed with plans and images of a modern, more open society which would share the fruits of victory when the war was won. As early as 1941, *Picture Post* published a special issue which contrasted in pictures and features the slums and dole queues of the past with a vision of an appealing 'new Britain'. Yet not all in this visionary society was new: in common with Orwell's comfortable domestic interior, illustrations of family life typically showed men reading or gardening and women knitting or sewing. Such images were unthinkingly patriarchal and, in relation to the rest of the British Empire, covertly racist in their assumptions. Clearly, the 'new' British citizen was not someone whose race or gender or middle-class life style were seriously questioned or open to doubt. The family is always headed by a white male, and the comfortable interiors, which indicate participation in the good life, take for granted a conventional sexual division of domestic labour. As many feminist critiques of the Beveridge Report and related policy papers have pointed out, it was assumed that the new citizen was invariably male, and the contract under negotiation was between men and the state (Land, 1976; Summerfield, 1989).

Orwell, in common with his wartime contemporaries in Whitehall, was equally biased in his thinking about citizenship. The rights to adequately paid employment and decent housing for which he pressed were aimed at making working-class life more tolerable and secure. As such they were clearly of immediate concern to women, but at no time is there any suggestion that women should be seen as other than passive (and presumably grateful) recipients of the extension of male citizenship. And yet the war effort, by comprehensively extending the influence of the state from munitions production to family diet, profoundly affected women and their participation on the home front. Women were expected to 'do their bit'—in factories and on the land, in the Auxiliary Services and Civil Defence, and not least, in the home. From child care to what women should wear, the state exhorted the 'citizen housewife' on the resourceful management of domestic life. While citizenship was defined exclusively in terms of political and civil rights, the interest of the state in its citizens stopped at their own front door. The state had formerly shown little concern, and had even less influence, upon nutritional standards, household amenities, the care of children and the elderly, contraception or personal hygiene. All these matters and many more became subject to intervention or advice during the Second World War. In effect, the war effort 'domesticated' the concept of citizenship by massively extending the sphere of the state into the private domain. Citizenship became a social, as well as a civil and political status, and the ideal citizen the embodiment of domestic virtues as well as patriotic concerns.

This domestication of citizenship permeated the privacy and 'easy completeness' of Orwell's interior. Instead of being a safe haven from the world, the household was now subject to official scrutiny, prescription and a barrage of detailed advice. Orwell had already rebuked the condescending attitudes of middle-class matrons who offered homely nostrums to the poor. Now that advice had an official stamp and the sanction of a community at war: waste was unpatriotic, extravagance offended 'equality of sacrifice', and 'under the counter' trading was against the law. The Ministry of Food and the Board of Trade employed secret inspectorates to detect abuses in the distribution and consumption of household supplies, while all manner of cumbersome systems of registration, regulation and report controlled and recorded the administration of persons and things (Calder, 1971, p. 469ff.). It was but a short step in Orwell's imagination from snooping inspectors to the thought police of *Nineteen Eighty-Four*. As he had remarked in *The Road to Wigan*

Pier, 'I sometimes think the price of liberty is not eternal vigilance but eternal dirt' (Orwell, 1966, p. 73).

Although the expansion of officialdom was accelerated by the peculiar needs of the war effort, it was also, and more profoundly, a substantive consequence of the egalitarian belief that all persons in the same circumstances should be treated in similar ways. Wartime equality presupposed uniformity and hence required an extensive apparatus of administrative control. The 'new' citizen of the Second World War became more precisely individuated (in the sense of being enumerated and classified within an administrative grid) but their individuality, that is, their subjective characteristics as persons, also became a matter of public concern. Whilst citizenship was limited to formal political and juridical rights, the distinction between private individuals and public citizens could be legally and absolutely defined: individuals as such existed only as abstractions—as voters, conscripts, taxpayers—the bearers of civil obligations and rights. However, as households became more dependent upon the services provided by the state, the boundaries between citizens and persons who embodied these rights became morally opaque and open to ideological construction and debate. As Marshall observed:

> societies in which citizenship is a developing institution create an image of an ideal citizenship against which achievement can be measured and towards which aspiration can be directed. (Marshall, 1977, p. 92).

Once citizenship became an issue about social rights—about rights to economic security, health, education and domestic welfare—the state assumed a much closer interest in the well-being of its citizens as persons, and consequently the moral no less than the material conditions in which they lived. The authors of the Beveridge Report and other wartime position papers on health and welfare tacitly assumed that the removal of private squalor—so plainly documented in *Down and Out in Paris and London* and *The Road to Wigan Pier*—would raise standards of both public and personal conduct. Like the nineteenth-century philanthropists who campaigned for improvements in working-class housing on the grounds (amongst others) that overcrowding encouraged incest, liberal social reformers of the 1940s believed that domestic squalor bred moral and social squalor. It was a view shared by Orwell who observed that under miserably impoverished conditions, it is well nigh impossible to live a 'decent' life.

Orwell was by no means a materialist but he understood from direct experience that the key to a 'decent' life was, in Beveridge's phrase, 'a reasonable chance of productive work'. Amongst ordinary people, he wrote in 1943, 'unemployment is an even greater nightmare than the war'. Neither socialism nor capitalism, he claimed, had 'much emotional appeal', yet the contentment that would follow from having a relatively secure job with enough money to support a wife and a suitably small family was self-evident to any working man. Continuity of employment underpinned all prospect of change. If that could be achieved, private and civic virtues, Orwell believed, would coincide. The ordinary man had no need of ideologies or exhorting leaders and patronising advice: in common with Churchill, Orwell assumed that a sense of fairness, good humour and community (with a proper regard for the privacy of others), together with moderation, tolerance, self-discipline and a tendency to support the 'under-dog', were universal English traits. Civil, political and social rights were needed only to ensure equal representation and to hold market forces in check; all else would naturally flow from that 'moral quality which must be vaguely described as decency' (Orwell, 1947, p. 28).

This sense of what is positive about the British fitted comfortably into the reconstruction of citizenship. Orwell, a stalwart defender of Britain and British culture, represents both the strengths and the limitations of a way of life. From cooking to the countryside to the arts, Orwell's defence of all things British, his disapproval of Bloomsbury intellectuals, ideologies or anything foreign—in either a cultural or an international sense—came close to expressing a shared ideal. The country at war did not wish to have its culture held up to critical examination; it was entirely acceptable for the left (no less than the right) to be unassumingly patriotic. In common with other popular wartime authors, notably, J.B. Priestley, Orwell elaborated the qualities of the British which Churchill rhetorically invoked throughout the war. These speeches about 'this island people' with their seemingly innate sense of 'justice' and 'democracy' touched common sentiments, but equally they brought an urgency to debates about the future of British society which was quite uncharacteristic of peacetime.

From 1940 onwards it was apparent that the legitimacy of the existing political order was at stake, just as much as national sovereignty. Identifying what was characteristic and intrinsically valuable about the nation and its people, became a central theme in reconstruction debates. There was a widespread feeling that 'things couldn't go back to the way they were', yet Orwell's faith in the 'common decency' of ordinary people was not matched by his confidence in their ability to effect a radical change. They lacked a politicised sense of the future, and were ignorant of the vested interests that would subvert a shift in power. In his essay *The English People* he outlines how attitudes and old habits must change:

> They must breed faster, work harder, and probably live more simply, think more deeply, get rid of their snobbishness and their anachronistic class distinctions, and pay more attention to the world and less to their own backyards . . . They must have a clear notion of their own destiny and not listen either to those who tell them that England is finished or to those who tell them that the England of the past can return . . . They must take their destiny into their own hands. England can only fulfil its special mission if the ordinary English in the street can somehow get their hands on power. (Orwell, 1947, p. 54ff.)

The alternative possibilities envisaged by Orwell if people failed to respond to this somewhat simplistic appeal were sketched out in *Nineteen Eighty-Four*. It portrays the tyranny of a totalitarian society in which ordinary people are manipulated and controlled by an exploitative web of commercial and authoritarian pressures and crudely fabricated lies. Truth, privacy and common decency have disappeared, along with coal fires, racing papers, dogs and the comfortable interior of working-class homes. The proletariat of *Nineteen*

Eighty-Four is defenceless against the hegemony of centralised power. Uncritically accepting everything they are given or told, they are easily manipulated by what Hoggart later described as 'a candy floss world'. As Ben Pimlot points out in his introduction to a recent edition:

> In *Oceania* the relative freedom of working class people is merely a symptom of the contempt in which they are held. 'From the proletarians', declares Goldstein, 'nothing is to be feared.' They can be granted intellectual liberty, he adds (with a kick in the groin for liberal, as well as socialist, assumptions), 'because they have no intellect'. (Pimlott, 1989, p. xv)

Not only do they have no intellect, they have no community. The private and communal world Orwell documented in *The Road to Wigan Pier* has been transformed into a landscape of atomised, conforming individuals.

The tyranny of *Oceania* is not specific to fascist or communist regimes; Orwell believed it could happen anywhere, including Britain where the novel is set. Just as the war was fought, in Orwell's opinion, to protect freedom of thought, so ordinary people should be on their guard against the centralisation of economic forces and the authoritarian tendencies of a peacetime state. Though related, these tendencies were not necessarily the same: Orwell believed that centralised planning and some form of command economy was bound to come; indeed, it was already being welcomed as a solution to unemployment and poverty, even though it was likely to restrict freedom of movement and freedom of choice. However, the real danger Orwell thought lay in accepting an ideology of any persuasion which set standards of conduct and dictated what people should think. It is this authoritarian strain towards conformity and order with its suppression of critical thinking and dissent, that has to be resisted at all costs. The point of *Nineteen Eighty-Four* is that a totalitarian states tries to control the thoughts and emotions of its subjects at least as completely as it controls their actions. This had already happened in fascist Europe; it was ostensibly the issue on which the Second World War was fought; yet Orwell feared the incipient threat it posed to liberty and democracy had not been fully grasped.

The problem with terms such as 'freedom' and 'democracy' is that they are vacuous and equivocal unless precisely defined in relation to substantive benefits and social rights. Yet the departure from formal, juridical interpretations of citizenship towards a more open-ended contract with the state, did not lead in directions Orwell most feared; nor did it encourage the 'revolution' he sought. *Nineteen Eighty-Four* was read as a prophetic fantasy, rather than a serious qualification of his earlier warning that unless people have control over their government, 'oligarchy and privilege can return based upon power rather than money' and 'the State may come to mean no more than a self-elected political party' (Orwell, 1941, p. 101). However, while Orwell was writing *Nineteen Eighty-Four* and the post-war world was being constructed, the possibilities of a commercially generated illiteracy had hardly been imagined. Fears about the potential dangers of science were commonplace after Hiroshima and Nagasaki; much less obvious were the culturally and politically distorting pressures of the media and mass market. Production for personal consumption had all but ceased to meet the needs of the war and the post-war reconstruction. Although still predominantly capitalist, debates about the new British citizen took place in a society in which there was little attempt to commodify and mass-produce cultural forms. The ordinary citizen was represented in this transitional vacuum without those needs and consumer habits which the liberal middle class would later deplore. While no one was attempting to seduce consumers with false commercial gods, the post-war citizen could emerge as someone to whom much, indeed everything, had yet to be given.

Indeed, the British citizen at the end of the war was morally above criticism. The Ministry of Information had elevated the working man to the status of wartime hero, whilst the people as a whole could be seen as deserving and grateful recipients of social reforms. The Conservative Party continued to express suspicions about the fecklessness of the working class, and the unsupportable burden upon the Exchequer of providing benefits and bathrooms, but their sentiments were far removed from the reformist consensus and the mood of the electorate in 1945. Yet despite the legislative and economic achievements of the post-war Labour government, Orwell remained less than optimistic about the long-term direction of these changes for ordinary citizens. Nationalisation and the extension of rationing and wartime controls had concentrated unprecedented powers in the hands of a peacetime state. Small incidents, such as the arrest of five people selling left-wing literature in Hyde Park, he regarded as 'importantly symptomatic' of a general decline in freedom of expression and political dissent. He was especially concerned that such incidents warranted scant mention in the press (Orwell, 1945a). Less obvious, though more insidious, was the gradual erosion of communities and family life. Orwell believed that for ordinary people the family had become 'their sole refuge from the state', yet all the while its stability and autonomy were being undermined. (Orwell, 1945b, pp. 116–17). Against these mounting pressures, Orwell doubted whether working-class communities had sufficient resilience to resist the influence of the market, the media and the centralised powers of the state. In much the same idiom as the present-day right, he anticipated that working-class families would be sucked into a dependency or 'welfare' culture created by a cross-hatch of market forces, social planning and officialdom. Collectivism, not want, would become the moral rot of the working class, undermining the values of individualism and patriarchy which had traditionally defended the integrity of the working-class home. On this view, it is not specifically capitalism or socialism which directly threatens social and cultural decay, but a corrosive combination of bureaucratic and commercial interests which gradually define the political agenda over which ordinary citizens have no control.

With hindsight, Orwell, in common with many wartime social reformers, not least Beveridge and the Tory Reform Group, whilst pressing for change, judged the past and future against the same ideals. Though recognising that poverty created the kind of squalor that had no place in a civilised society, they took for granted the universal validity and derivation of their own moral standards. Yet when Orwell used the word 'decent', he drew upon a code of behaviour which had specific connotations for his class. Historically its derivation assumed a largely inactive consumer economy, a rigid sexual division of labour and a common national culture. Those conditions existed as perhaps never before in Britain during the Second World War. On this apparently firm ground, the social reconstruction of citizenship readily assumed that the virtues of the private citizen and the virtues of the state were one and the same.

In the halting and largely passive evolution of the British citizen, it was this assumption, rather than the reforms and technocratic adjustments which followed, that underpinned the post-war expansion of social rights and legitimated the framework of social democratic government for the next thirty-odd years. The war effort accelerated this transition in an uncharacteristically radical moment of change and reform. Yet when the war ended British society was still ideologically innocent compared with most modern states. Unlike France or the United States, there was virtually no tradition of revolutionary dissent. Social and political integration continued to rest upon traditional hierarchies of deference and local ties that had for centuries assimilated changing class formations with a resilience more akin to a caste system than a secular bourgeois state. The post-war social reconstruction, though reformist and tinged with radical ideals, was mediated by the legacy of that same assumptive world with its culture of aristocratic amateurism, robust pragmatism and profound distrust of ideologies and abstract ideas. The model citizen of 1945 reflected many of these assumptions: *he* was a useful 'decent-living' individual—the long-suffering British Tommy who had loyally served his country in the expectation of a fairer world. Though women had featured prominently in wartime propaganda, the image of the post-war British citizen was unquestionably male, and unmistakably white— Beveridge's head of the household, a man with family responsibilities in need of reasonably well-paid work. The idea that women, and particularly unmarried women with children, could form a household without a male head was alien to legal expectations and common sense. In employment and the law relating to domestic property, paternalistic assumptions created an anomalous status for the 'citizen housewife' whose relations to the rest of society it was taken for granted would be mediated by men.

Sexual inequalities, racial discrimination and the position of ethnic and other minorities tended to be unthinkingly accepted as part of the hierarchical order of British society, even though there had been universal condemnation of the racial and ethnic intolerance of the Nazi regime. Perceptions of social inequality seldom extended beyond inequalities of income and wealth. Similarly, Marshall's optimism about the 'drive towards social equality' took no account of the resilience of traditional patterns of status and the enduring insularity of their legitimating beliefs. At the extremes, 'gas and water socialism' and the welfare state coexisted with feudal titles and inherited privileges, including hereditary peers in the House of Lords. Although post-war Budgets effected marginal redistributions of income and wealth, there was no attempt to challenge entrenched systems of deference and preferment, or the privileged institutions they maintained. Over the next generation, the social backgrounds from which senior civil servants, Anglican bishops, High Court judges and senior army personnel were recruited remained largely unchanged (Kelsall, 1955; Urry and Wakeford, 1973; Stanworth and Giddens, 1974).

Yet something had changed with the war. The idea of 'citizenship' promoted within the armed forces and on the home front expressed a qualitative change in relations between individuals and the state. Official pamphlets, broadcasts and the activities of the wartime Army Bureau of Current Affairs emphasised reciprocity and fairness, decency and trust which caught and endorsed the current mood. The state at war was a moral as well as a legal entity; its legitimacy was based upon a consensus of patriotic sentiments and common aims. The same sense of solidarity carried the social policies of the Labour government in 1945. Although its perceptions of inequality were relatively narrow, it was understood, albeit in confused and sometimes inconsistent ways, that civic morality had to be based upon distributive justice and a more caring relationship between citizens and the state. Labour's ideals, if not their policies, were touched by the same spirit that inspired Orwell to write 'the war and the revolution are inseparable'. Yet, in the event, the lasting tensions which Orwell reflects were not between individual freedom and authoritarian tendencies within the state, but more specifically between the boundaries of the private and public realm. As we have suggested, the post-war social reconstruction in effect 'domesticated' citizenship bringing all conditions of family and personal life within the public domain. When some decades later it became apparent that the welfare state had not produced universal decency, it was not the individual but the state that was held to blame.

References

Addison, P. (1975), *The Road to 1945: British Politics and the Second World War*, London, Jonathan Cape.

Calder, A. (1971), *The People's War*, London, Panther Books.

Crick, B. (1982), *George Orwell: A Life*, Harmondsworth, Penguin Books.

Harris, J. (1986), 'Political ideas and the debate on state welfare', in H.L. Smith (ed.), *War and Social Change*, Manchester, Manchester University Press.

Hayek, F.A. (1944), *The Road to Serfdom*, London, G. Routledge & Sons.

Kelsall, R.K. (1955), *Higher Civil Servants in Britain*, London, Routledge & Kegan Paul.

Keynes, J.M. (1931), *Essays in Persuasion*, London, Macmillan.

Land, H. (1976), 'Women; supporters or supported?', in D. Barker and S. Allen (eds), *Sexual Divisions in Society: Process and Change*, London, Tavistock.

Marshall, T.H. (1963), 'Social class and citizenship', in *Sociology at the Crossroads and Other Essays*, London, Heinemann.

Marshall, T.H. (1977), *Class, Citizenship and Social Development*, London, Heinemann.

Orwell, G. (1937), *The Road to Wigan Pier*, Harmondsworth, Penguin Books (1966).

Orwell, G. (1941), 'The lion and the unicorn', *The Collected Essays, Journalism and Letters*, Vol. 2, Harmondsworth, Penguin Books (1970).

Orwell, G. (1944), Review of *The Road to Serfdom* by F.A. Hayek, *The Collected Essays, Journalism, and Letters*, Vol. 3, Harmondsworth, Penguin Books (1970).

Orwell, G. (1945a), 'Freedom of the park', *The Collected Essays, Journalism, and Letters*, Vol. 4, Harmondsworth, Penguin Books (1970).

Orwell, G. (1945b), Review of *The Reilly Plan* by L. Wolfe, *The Collected Essays, Journalism, and Letters*, Vol. 4, Harmondsworth, Penguin Books (1970).

Orwell, G. (1947), 'The English people', *The Collected Essays, Journalism, and Letters*, Vol. 3, Harmondsworth, Penguin Books (1970).

Orwell, G. (1949), *Nineteen Eighty-Four*, London, Secker & Warburg.

Pimlott, B. (1989), Introduction to George Orwell's *Nineteen Eighty-Four*, Harmondsworth, Penguin Books.

Sinfield, A. (1989), *Literature, Politics and Culture in Post-war Britain*, Oxford, Basil Blackwell.

Soames, M. (1981), *Clementine Churchill*, Harmondsworth, Penguin Books.

Stanworth, P. and Giddens, A. (eds), (1974), *Elites and Power in British Society*, Cambridge, Cambridge University Press.

Summerfield, P. (1989), *Women Workers in the Second World War: Production and Patriarchy in Conflict*, London, Routledge.

Taylor, A.J.P. (1965), *English History, 1914–1945*, Oxford, Clarendon Press.

Urry, J. and Wakeford, J. (eds) (1973), *Power in Britain*, London, Heinemann.

Weber, M. (1968), *Economy and Society*, trans. G. Roth and G. Wittich, New York, Bedminster Press.

5 Approaches to women and social change in the Second World War

Penny Summerfield

Historians and sociologists have been interested in the idea that the Second World War significantly changed women's social position since the 1950s, when Stanislaus Andrzejewski developed the theory of the military participation ratio and Richard Titmuss wrote his essays 'War and Social Policy' and 'The Position of Women'. Andrzejewski argued that mass war involving a high proportion of the total population had a levelling effect on social differences (Andrzejewski, 1954). Titmuss followed this by suggesting that women's role as dependants in wartime stimulated the development of social policies which reduced inequalities and raised women's status. He also drew attention to contemporary demographic changes that were fundamentally altering women's position in the family and labour market. The increased incidence of marriage at a younger age after the war, and the birth of a small number of children close together early in marriage, meant that married women over 30 now became a major source of recruitment to the labour force (Titmuss, 1958).

In 1956 Alva Myrdal and Viola Klein investigated the trends that Titmuss had identified and defended the married woman's dual role in domestic and paid work. They considered the impact of the war on women to have been significant in three ways. Firstly, they believed that 'sex discrimination in matters of employment almost disappeared'. Secondly, they argued that the 'reorganization of working conditions to meet the needs of women workers assumed such dimensions that it may well be called a social revolution.' Thirdly, they claimed that there was a sizeable reduction in the number of married women in paid work post-war, in spite of evidence that women wished to stay in work after the war (Myrdal and Klein, 1956, 2nd edn, 1968, pp. 52–4). The thrust of their argument was that what the war had proved possible could be repeated in the 1950s and 1960s: married women could be persuaded to join the labour force, and they could combine responsibilities to their homes and to the work-place without having detrimental effects on either.

In the 1960s and 1970s Arthur Marwick popularised the view that the Second World War contributed significantly to the growth of equality between the sexes. Like Myrdal and Klein he argued that women did men's jobs in wartime and received equal pay, and that these were lasting gains.

Unlike them he believed that government conscription 'played a very minor role in the changes in women's employment'. He also argued that married women became more acceptable as employees. (Marwick, 1968, pp. 291–4) More generally, Marwick's approach was to see the war as crucial for the 'modernisation' of women's position, that is giving women greater self-confidence and a more public and visible role in paid work, politics and social life. For example, Marwick concluded a discussion of the effects of the war on British, American, Russian and German women, published in 1974, thus: participation as workers in the war effort 'can be seen at work everywhere in further developments in the status of women' (Marwick, 1974, pp. 137–61).

Titmuss, Myrdal and Klein, and Marwick all subscribed to the idea that the war and post-war years constituted 'a period of increasing emancipation for women' (Titmuss, 1958, p. 101). But feminist scholars of the 1970s could not accept such a reading. There was abundant post-war evidence that women, especially working-class women, were not free from the home, that they were typically dependants and that they were in subordinate positions at work. If women had achieved higher status during the war it appeared that they had not retained it afterwards. The dispute hinged on the understanding of 'emancipation' and 'status'. Myrdal and Klein were not thinking in terms of absolute equality between the sexes but of the recognition of what they saw as women's special abilities, which included both practical competence and motherliness. The war had required women to put these qualities at the disposal of the nation, and 'women had met the demands made on them' (Myrdal and Klein, 1968, p. 3). Likewise, Marwick was arguing about a shift stimulated by both wars, from subordinate forms of femininity to what one might call transcendant ones: from a situation in which women's actions were constrained by Victorian dictates of modesty and propriety to one in which women could go to pubs, travel, have sex outside marriage, wear lipstick and shorter skirts, and smoke in public (Marwick, 1968, p. 127; 1976, p. 138).

However, in the 1970s and 1980s feminists took the view that changes in manners and morals were misleading guides to the real determinants of women's position, their economic role in paid work and housework. In response to Myrdal and Klein, feminists suspected that the idea that women had special aptitudes served to reinforce discrimination against them. Rather than applauding the practice of women taking on paid work on top of domestic work, and seeing this as raising women's status, feminists asked why domestic work should be identified solely with women, and why women's paid work was typically less valued than men's work. Emancipation was now equated not with women making their special contribution as women to society, nor with women apparently becoming more independent, but with the complete removal of sexual divisions in the home and at work.

The question of what had happened in the war remained an important one for understanding the opportunities historically open to women, and what women had done with them. Work published by Juliet Mitchell, Denise Riley and myself in the 1970s and early 1980s concerned the extent of wartime change and its degree of permanence. In this writing the three issues highlighted by Myrdal and Klein were pursued: the role of social policy in freeing women from domesticity, the impact of the war on women's position in the labour force, and the problem of women's subjective responses to work during and after the war.

Women and wartime social policy

In terms of social policy the question concerned the extent of substitution for women's domestic functions such as child care, and the development of appropriate legitimising ideologies. Mitchell in *Psychoanalysis and Feminism* (1974) argued for extensive substitution accompanied by a temporary ideological transformation *vis-à-vis* women's role, both of which were abruptly withdrawn at the end of the war to force women back home. In this the family, 'a primary ideological institution', was successively deconstructed by wartime pressures, and then reconstructed after the war particularly within the discipline and practice of social psychotherapy. Women's centrality to the family was reasserted.

> After the war political stabilization and economic reconstruction brought about a restoration of conservative social forms. Nurseries and communal restaurants were closed down. Where women had been recruited to industry they were now encouraged to marry and, if married, barred from most professions and many jobs: instead of national workers they were to be private wives [and above all mothers, whose place was at home with the children] . . . From the psychoanalyst John Bowlby, whose work was popularized on radio and in women's magazines, we learnt that a person sucked his emotional stability literally with his mother's milk. (Mitchell 1974, pp. 227–8)

Denise Riley in *War in the Nursery* (1983) investigated the connections between wartime social policies and ideologies more thoroughly than Mitchell, and argued for a less clear-cut picture. There were contradictions in wartime social policy, which was neither so extensive nor so abruptly withdrawn as Mitchell had thought. On the one hand, the full-time mother was expected to be an active citizen. On the other, she was required to do paid work. There were gaps between psychological theory, social policy and social practices. The idea that 'the postwar government used Bowlby's theory of "maternal deprivation" to get British women out of their jobs and back into their kitchens' was wrong (Riley, 1983, p. 189). All the same, wartime ideology conflated 'woman worker' with 'wife and mother', and in post-war pronatalist discourses a woman's destiny was that of full-time mother bearing major responsibility for the physical and psychological development of her children.

> Women's war work, even in presentations of their collective heroic capacities, was work done by *women*, marked through and through by the gender of its performers, and consequently by the especial temporariness of the work of women who were mothers . . . Everything about the employment of married women in industry militated against their being taken seriously as real workers: by 1945 the dominant rhetoric held out an opposition between the mother and the woman worker. The postwar collapse of the war nurseries only underlined the 'special nature' of temporary concessions to working mothers. (Riley 1983, p. 195, emphasis in original)

In *Women Workers in the Second World War* I analysed the formulation and application of wartime social policies towards women in greater depth than either Mitchell or Riley. I argued that there were competing discourses concerning women's role during and after the war in areas such as child care, shopping and feeding. Conventional patriarchal expectations about women were in tension with the pressures of wartime production which demanded solutions to the problem of mobilising the female labour force. Thus within government ministries such as Labour and Supply during the war there were those who advocated collectivist methods of dealing with domestic work, and justified them in terms of national needs and progress for women. And there were also those in these ministries and in Health and Food who based policy on the idea of the sanctity of the home and the mother's place with her child within it, in spite of wartime pressures (Summerfield, 1984, 2nd edn, 1989). The state was driven neither entirely by the interests of capital nor by those of patriarchy. The outcome of the conflict of interests was unprecedented discussion at government level of the work involved in running a home, partial and temporary provision of collective child care, and official insistence that paid work should be organised on a part-time basis to mobilise women who were also running homes. But 'the great bulk of wartime domestic work was thrown back to the private sphere of a woman's own resources and those of her family, friends and neighbourhood' (Summerfield, 1989, p. 185). In the area of social policy there was, then, little to undo at the end of the war. Wartime nurseries were handed over to hard-pressed local authorities which returned to the pre-war policy of providing day nurseries for special cases of poverty or hardship rather than as a service for any working woman. And employers were left to decide whether it was worth their while to continue part-time working arrangements. There was no 'social revolution' arising from wartime social policy of the sort Myrdal and Klein had imagined.

Women in the labour force

As far as women's place within the labour force was concerned, Mitchell's argument implied an understanding of women as a reserve army of labour which was pulled in during the wartime crisis of production, and pushed out afterwards. I also subscribed to this view in an early publication (Summerfield, 1977) and it remains popular among sociologists. Global figures appear to support the theory. Following an increase of 1,500,000 women in the work-force between 1939 and 1943 (from approximately 6,250,000 to 7,750,000), there was a decrease of 1,750,000 women in employment between 1943 and 1947. The shrinking size of the younger-age cohorts in the population as a whole partly explains this big decrease. But the proportion of all adult women in paid employment also dropped, from 51 per cent in 1943 to 40 per cent in 1947, and 35 per cent in 1951, similar to the 1931 proportion of 34 per cent (Summerfield, 1988, pp. 97–8).

The reserve army theory, as developed by Marx, concerned the creation of a reserve of labour by capital, which served two functions: to depress the wages of those in employment because there were always substitutes waiting in the wings, and to provide a source of cheap and easily dispensable labour should it be required by developments in production. Marx did not place women specifically in any of the three layers he identified: the floating (temporarily unemployed), the latent (chronically unemployed) and the stagnant (the virtually unemployable, on the very edge of the labour market). Later writers such as Veronica Beechey thought that married women's position in the family placed them in the latent category. They were an unemployed group which could be drawn into the labour force at low rates because they were being supported by a husband's breadwinner wage, and pushed back into that dependency when no longer needed, without becoming a state responsibility (Beechey, 1977).

Two conditions need to be fulfilled for this theory to be helpful in explaining the position of women in the work-force in the Second World War. One concerns where those women came from. If they were members of the latent layer of the reserve army, they should have been unemployed before the war or even (given the economic depression of the inter-war years) totally inexperienced 'green' labour. The second concerns where women went to afterwards. The crisis of production over, they should have subsided into dependency on their husbands in the home.

An immediate problem with the theory concerns the size of the pre-war female work-force. Over six million women were in paid employment in 1939, 80 per cent of the number employed in 1943. Thus it looks as though the majority of the women in paid work in the war cannot be considered part of a reserve mobilised for war work. The aggregate figures are snapshots, however. The six million in work in 1939 might not have been the same women as those counted in 1943.

The Wartime Social Survey, which interviewed a representative sample of 2,609 women in civilian industry in 1943 tells us more about the flows of women in and out of the labour market. Women who were not in paid employment immediately before the war constituted 28 per cent of the sample. A minority (6 per cent of the whole sample) had entered war work straight from school, and so were new entrants to the work-force rather than members of a reserve. Most of the remaining 22 per cent had done paid work at some time before the war, so they were not completely 'green'. The last paid occupation of some was on munitions in the First World War (Central Office of Information, 1944, pp. 7, 10). This group, mainly women who had ceased work on marriage, bears the closest resemblance to the reserve, but formed only part of the total female labour force.

It is clearly not helpful to think of wartime women workers in general as a reserve army of labour. However, there might still be a case for regarding *married* women war workers as members of a reserve, as Beechey's interpretation of the reserve army theory would suggest. However, the Wartime Social Survey shows that not *all* married women war workers had been pulled in from home. Over half of those in its sample who were married in 1943 (59 per cent) were in paid work in 1939 (though the Survey does not tell us whether they were married then). Only the 41 per cent of married women war workers who were 'at home' before the war look as though their experience might fit the description of the reserve army. If this was to be the case, one would expect them to have dropped out of the labour force at the end of the war, so that the post-war marital composition returned to its pre-war shape. In fact, although the proportion of married women in the work-force dipped slightly from its wartime peak, it remained well above the 1930s level in the 1940s and climbed steadily in the 1950s (as Titmuss and Myrdal and Klein observed). In 1931 only 16 per cent of working women were married. In 1943 this had risen to 43 per cent, it fell to 40 per cent in 1947, then climbed again to 43 per cent in 1951 and 52 per cent in 1959 (Summerfield, 1988, p. 100, n. 20). The proportion was 64 per cent in 1985. Titmuss pointed out the demographic changes behind this in the 1950s. There was a rising proportion of married women in the population (because the imbalance between the sexes righted itself, the age of marriage fell and life expectancy rose) (Titmuss, 1958) and at the same time the size of the adult age cohorts was falling. But the fact remains that married women did not drop out of the labour force after the war as the pull–push mechanism of the reserve army theory would suggest.

The reserve army theory is, then, of limited use in understanding women's labour force participation in the Second World War. In particular it does not say anything about the majority of women war workers, married as well as single, who were in paid work at the outbreak of war. The Wartime Social Survey of 1944 revealed a high degree of transference between different types of work and industries among these women. For instance, only 47 per cent of women machine and assembly workers in 1943 were in this category before the war. The rest came from a range of occupations. Twenty-eight per cent were 'distributive workers, waitresses etc', 19 per cent were 'labourers and domestic servants' and 6 per cent were in the 'professional, administrative and clerical' group (Central Office of Information, 1944, p. 9). Taking industries as opposed to occupations, the recruitment pattern in engineering showed the greatest changes. Only 22 per cent of the women in engineering in 1943 had worked there pre-war; 51 per cent came from another job, 24 per cent from home and 4 per cent from school (Central Office of Information, 1944, p. 7). In terms of industrial distribution, numbers of women dropped in many of the industries which had employed large proportions of women before the war, such as textiles, where the number of insured women fell from 656,000 to 456,000 between 1939 and 1943. There was a similar contraction of numbers in clothing, pottery, leather goods, food, drink and tobacco, distribution and consumer services (Central Statistical Office, 1951, p. 9). On the other hand, numbers of women rose in industries in which the proportion of women was relatively small before the war. For example, the number of women in engineering rose from 97,000 to 602,000 and from 10 to 34 per cent of workers in the industry between 1939 and 1943. Large increases also occurred in the metal and chemical industries, vehicle building, transport, gas, water and electricity, and shipbuilding (Beck, 1951, Table 40).

Though much more dramatic, the wartime redistribution of women across industries was not inconsistent with what had gone before. In the 1920s and 1930s the textile industry contracted, and the numbers and proportions of women employed in transport, chemicals, vehicles, engineering and metals rose, even though the extent of the increases was small. In engineering, for example, the proportion of women rose from 6.5 per cent to 10.3 per cent between 1923 and 1939. This is not what the reserve army theory suggests should have happened in a period of economic depression when women should have been the first to lose their jobs. With reference to the same phenomenon in the United States, Milkman argued that women were protected by occupational segregation from unemployment between the wars (Milkman, 1976). Women were being employed in new types of work, for instance on production lines in electrical engineering factories and behind typewriters and adding machines in offices. They were regarded as belonging in separate sections of work commanding lower rates than men (Parliamentary Papers, 1930; Holtby, 1934).

The war hastened this process. At its end there were readjustments involving considerable job loss for women and a big drop in the proportions of women employed in many industries and white-collar jobs as men returned. However, the gender restructuring of the labour force that had begun slowly before the war carried on, stimulated by wartime acceleration of changes in labour processes and in the deployment of women. After the war the numbers and proportions of women in engineering, vehicles, metals, gas, water and electricity, transport and government fell compared with 1943 but were higher than they had been in 1939. In 1950 the industrial distribution of women was markedly different from that of 1939, as Table 5.1 shows.

Table 5.1 The proportion of women in a number of industries, 1939–50 (%)

	1939	1943	1950
Engineering	10	34	34
Metal manufacturing	6	22	12
Transport	5	20	13
Government	17	46	38

Source: C.E.V. Leser, 1952.

These long-term trends meant, according to the economist C.E.V. Leser, 'not so much that women took men's jobs as that women-employing sections of the industries concerned gained at the expense of men-employing sections' (Leser, 1952, p. 330). In other words, the war did not win women permanent access to 'men's jobs', but enlarged the number of segregated and subordinate positions open to them in these industries. Simultaneously job opportunities shrank in many of the traditional major employers of women such as textiles and domestic service. All the same, when the fall in the size of the adult-age cohorts is taken into account, there was an overall expansion of the female work-force compared with pre-war. By 1948, if there had been a return to the *status quo* in 1939, 'the number of insured women would have fallen by more than 400,000. But in fact the number increased by about 350,000' (Leser, 1952, p. 335).

The reserve army theory was too simplistic a model to elucidate this complex process. In its place historians like myself and sociologists such as Sylvia Walby developed an alternative understanding of women's place in the labour force, seeing it as determined by the interaction of capitalist and patriarchal interests (Walby, 1986). To summarise, the capitalist interest in forming a cheap, semi-skilled work-force which also engaged in the reproduction of male labour power and children was seen as intersecting with the patriarchal interest in women as an unpaid work-force in the home that would not challenge the power of the male breadwinner and would provide him with domestic and other services. This intersection produced a powerful set of forces (including the state, employers, male trade unionists, and husbands) which contributed to labour force segregation.

Thus in the Second World War, trade unionists did not see it as in the interests of the working class as a whole for men and women to be treated as an undifferentiated work-force with identical interests *vis-à-vis* capital. Rather they sought to defend men's jobs against the encroachment of lower-paid women by two methods. On the one hand, they engaged in 'gate-keeping' through agreements under which women in men's work received equal pay (to protect men's rates from being undercut) on the understanding that they would be removed at the end of the war (to protect men's jobs). On the other hand, male trade unionists tried to resist the classification of work (in particular the numerous new jobs thrown up by labour process changes in the war) as women's work, which would be paid at women's rates and lost to men thereafter. Both strategies were prompted by patriarchy, and were opposed by capital. Employers looked for ways round the equal pay agreements, to avoid paying women the same as men and to keep them on as cheap labour. And employers took the offensive in the gender classification of work on the basis of their perceptions of the national employment picture and beliefs about women's innate capacities, such that many types of work, from sweeping the floor to coremaking, were redefined as women's work (Summerfield, 1989, chapter 7). The evidence does not support Myrdal and Klein's assertion quoted earlier, that 'sex discrimination in matters of employment almost disappeared'.

Women's subjective responses

Harold Smith in 1986 produced what was intended to be the final crushing of the Marwickian approach, arguing that the war contributed very little to the increased size of the female work-force, and that it did not undermine the sex segregation of jobs. Thus far he was following previous writers. He also raised the issue of women's subjective responses to wartime changes.

He argued that women did not welcome wartime opportunities to do paid work and that wartime work did not make them dissatisfied with traditional sex roles. According to Smith, women were anxious to return to their pre-war way of life, and the war's 'most important legacy for women' was 'a strengthening of traditional sex roles rather than the emergence of new roles' (Smith, 1986, pp. 56, 57).

Smith regarded the evidence as sufficiently clear-cut to offer this categorical interpretation. Other writers, including Myrdal and Klein, Denise Riley and myself, saw the data concerning what women wanted from the war as more problematic. Myrdal and Klein cited wartime investigations which showed that 'the proportion of those who wished to stay at work, particularly among the older women, was astonishingly high' but all the same 'with the end of the war most of the married women returned home' (Myrdal and Klein, 1968, p. 53). They looked for explanations of this seemingly contradictory situation in external factors, such as the decline of shifts for part-time workers and the closure of nurseries, and they also speculated that a cause was 'the feeling that the jobs ought to be "kept for the boys" and that women should make way' (Myrdal and Klein, 1968, pp. 53–4).

Denise Riley's response to the problem of such apparently discordant evidence was to discuss it as a major example of the difficulties of historical reconstruction. It was part of the deeper problem of discovering 'why and how people produce particular formulations about what they want' (Riley, 1983, p. 190). Coming from a socialist feminist perspective which associated paid work with liberation from domestic dependency and progress for women, she confessed that she had found herself oscillating between two explanatory models, the one saying:

Women really did want to work, they did want nurseries; if we read the responses to these flat questionnaires correctly, we can surely decipher these wishes; or we can uncover the buried evidence of meetings, demonstrations and petitions to reveal their wants.

And the second saying:

Well, no wonder women were, on the whole, indifferent: what else, given these political conditions and these circumstances of work, could these women have done in 1945? (Riley, 1983, pp. 190–1)

She rejected both these models because they presupposed that women had a set of clearly defined needs and wants which could be revealed 'by stripping away a patina of historical postscripts and rewritings' (Riley, 1983, p. 191). Yet though she did not believe this to be possible she had no alternative approach to offer, in spite of continuing to see the problem of identifying what women wanted historically as important.

Like Riley I scrutinised investigations conducted by the Wartime Social Survey and Mass-Observation for evidence of women's post-war intentions. Both organisations asserted that the majority of women wanted marriage and domesticity, rather than paid work, after the war. For example, Mass-Observation stated: 'The most general opinion seems to be that women will want to go back home, or take up the jobs which were usually considered suitable for women before the war, while awaiting marriage' (Mass-Observation, 1944, p. 66). In contrast to Smith's acceptance of such interpretations, I have drawn attention to the inconsistencies between the surveys' own data and the conclusions drawn (Summerfield, 1989, p. 190; 1992). Both organisations in fact collected data showing that the majority of women surveyed either definitely wanted to carry on in full- or part-time paid work or felt that their decisions about the matter would depend on a number of factors, including the availability of work, how much their husbands earned, and economic circumstances generally (Central Office of Information, 1944, pp. 12–13; Mass-Observation, 1944, pp. 54–63). Contrary to Riley's uncertainty about the capacity of women's responses to reveal what they really wanted, I have regarded their answers as indicative of women's perennial uncertainty about how to balance the demands of domestic work and the pressure of economic constraints. I have also seen the gloss put on them by the surveys' authors as part of the domestic facet of progressive as well as reactionary approaches to post-war reconstruction. Whatever women actually wanted they should not compete with men in the labour market but should devote themselves to home-making and childbirth (Summerfield, 1992).

The questions with which Riley approached women's post-war intentions were, as she herself admitted, somewhat loaded. Instead of asking why women did not want paid work or to fight to keep nurseries it is perhaps appropriate to relax the pressure of inquiry so as to allow those things which were important to women themselves to surface. Autobiographical sources, including oral history, offered such a possibility, for all that they would inevitably bear the marks of retrospection. In collecting such material for the book I wrote jointly with Gail Braybon, *Out of the Cage: Women's Experiences in Two World Wars*, it became clear that decisions about whether to work or not were by no means the only things that women remembered about their wartime experiences. It is possible to list others, many of which had both positive and negative sides to them. Such a list would include going into different work settings away from home, mixing with new people and coping with separation; learning different types of work and finding satisfaction or boredom in it; enjoying new opportunities for sociability and courtship as well as experiencing sexual harassment; dealing with fatigue and work-related health problems; coping with wartime shortages of food and clothing and with readjustments at the end of the war; feeling the exhilaration of contributing to the war effort as well as doubt about producing instruments of death (Braybon and Summerfield, 1987). It was impossible to ignore the fact that many women found that war necessitated changes in their lives, and that many also regarded it as a key phase in terms of personal change and development. As Mona Marshall, a Lincolnshire nursemaid who became a steelworker, said of the war when interviewed in her 70s, 'It made a great deal of difference to me. It made me stand on my own feet, gave me more self-confidence' (Thames Television/Channel 4, 1985). And Marjorie Wardle, the middle-class daughter of an industrialist, said that her wartime experiences in the Women's Royal Naval Service became 'the foundation of my life' (Oral History Interviews, 1986). They were both young, unmarried women at the outbreak of the war. For an older woman with young children like Muriel Windle, whose husband was posted to the Far East in 1941 and did not return until 1945, the war was more of a test of endurance. 'At the time one just did not have time to think, life had to go on, each day brought its routine and problems and often it was a case of pushing yourself to the next job . . . Still it ended, and we survived!' (Windle, 1975).

Autobiographical evidence emphasises the diversity of wartime experience as well as its importance for women.

The challenge now is to combine an approach to women, war and social change which dismisses exaggerated claims that the Second World War emancipated women with one which acknowledges that the war was an experience of major personal significance for many women. At the same time it is necessary to unpack the category 'woman' and to ask in what ways the effects of war were different for women whose life circumstances were different. Thus one wants to know about the wartime experiences of, for example, young and old, married and single, working class and middle class, black and white women, and how wartime changes in their lives fitted into longer-term trends. Ethnic differences have barely begun to be explored (Bousquet and Douglas, 1991). However, it is possible to outline differences in the impact of the Second World War according to age and marital status as I have previously begun to do (Summerfield, 1988) and to say something about class differences, as Margaret Allen has done (Allen, 1983).

Diverse experiences

Statistics, as well as personal testimony, reveal the extent and permanence of the effect of the war on the position of married and older women in the labour force. We have already noted that the war contributed to a permanent expansion in the number of women workers who were married from 16 per cent in 1931 to 43 per cent in 1943 and 1951. The proportion of all married women who did paid work also rose between 1931 and 1951, from 10 to 22 per cent. Unfortunately there are no reliable figures of the proportion of wives in employment immediately before and during the war. However, estimates for the post-war period do suggest that the war contributed to a permanent upward trend. Geoffrey Thomas stated that in 1947 22 per cent of all married women were in paid work, the same proportion as in 1951 (Central Office of Information, 1948, p. 8).

A similar permanent shift occurred as far as the age of women workers was concerned. Before the war the age profile was heavily weighted towards the youngest age groups. In 1931 41 per cent of women workers were under 25. In the context of heavy wartime recruitment from older age groups, the proportion in this youngest age group fell to 27 per cent in 1943. But after the war it did not return to its former size. In 1947 only 24 per cent of women workers were under 25. The age groups over 35 showed the greatest increase during and after the war: 32 per cent were aged 35–59 in 1931, 42 per cent in 1943, and 49 per cent in 1947. The result was that the average age of women in employment was much higher in 1947 than even in 1943 (Census 1934, Table 3; Central Office of Information 1944, p. 1; 1948, pp. 6–7).

The two sets of changes went together. Geoffrey Thomas, author of wartime and post-war social surveys on women workers, comments that the war saw a 'very great modification of customary patterns of employment' especially in respect of married women over 35 (Central Office of Information, 1944, p. 7). After the war younger women, single and married, moved out of industry. They were the group most inclined to see domesticity as a full-time option. Their reasons for leaving work included getting married, expecting a baby, and home duties and responsibilities. Thomas applied the X^2 test of statistical significance to these reasons, and found that 'marriage is by far the most important factor which dissuades women from work', outstripping children some five times (Central Office of Information, 1948, p. 10). It seems that the convention of devoting oneself to a husband and a marital home was a stronger deterrent to work than the presence of children in spite of the post-war ideology of motherhood. Children under school age were a barrier, but 'married women with children aged five and over work as frequently as married women with no children' (Central Office of Information, 1948, p. 8). Indeed, the group which the government thought most likely to want to leave work at the end of the war, older married women with children, continued to come into paid work. As I have argued before, the war played a major part in the transition from the pre-war situation in which the majority of women workers were young and single to the 1950s when the typical woman worker was the older married woman with children (Summerfield, 1988).

Statistics alone tell us nothing about how women experienced these changes. Is it true that, as Harold Smith insists, the majority of married women 'fervently wished themselves back into their prewar way of life' in 1943 (Smith, 1986, p. 225)? Did the phenomenon of older wives, including mothers of children under 14, going out to work make any difference to marital styles and the domestic role?

The wartime government's recruitment policy contributes to the impression that married women were reluctant war workers. It was based on the assumption that older married women should not be taken away from their conventional roles in domestic work and childrearing, and that young, single women (the conventional female labour force) should be the prime target of mobilisation policy. It was only severe labour shortage which persuaded the government to begin to direct any women into work, in March 1941, and to conscript them in December 1941. The process was riddled with exemptions determined by official perceptions of women's domestic duties. For example, a childless serviceman's wife could not be sent away into war work since it was considered vital that she was available for him, in 'his' home, when he returned on leave. Above all, while being a husband and father exempted a man from nothing, no wife could be called up into the Armed Forces and no mother of a child under 14 living with her could be directed even into local war work. The problem with this was that it did not produce a large enough labour force. In 1943 the government took two steps towards encouraging older women to enter war work. Firstly it extended the upper age limit for direction from 40 to 50, and secondly it began to direct previously exempt housewives into part-time work.

It is perhaps hardly surprising that older married women expressed doubts during the war about taking up paid work, especially in the context of the conservatism of employers' recruitment practices which favoured young, single, white, British women, and demonstrated prejudice against older married women and those recruited abroad, from, for example, Ireland and the British colonies in the Caribbean. A survey in 1941 revealed that one-third of women apparently available would not take up war work because of domestic responsibilities and dislike of the prospect of leaving home, and these reasons applied particularly to older women (Central Office of Information, 1941, pp. iii, 6). Younger women, especially members of the middle class, were more inclined to welcome war work for the opportunities to travel, mix and learn new skills. The two smaller and more select women's armed services, the WRNS and the WAAF, and the Women's Land Army were particularly popular with this group. On balance, young middle-class women considered mobility in relatively high status, if temporary, jobs preferable to (and more patriotic than) the continuation through the war of a restricted role as 'daughter of the house' (Central Office of Information, 1941).

In contrast, older women's doubts about entering war work focused on practical considerations about how a balance could be struck between domestic responsibilities and the demands of paid work (a problem which, as we have seen, was to confront increasing numbers of women in the 1950s and after). Many were critical of the government's lack of clarity on hours, wage rates and facilities for child care and shopping. For example, in 1941 a middle-class Coventry wife and mother told the public opinion research organisation Mass-Observation that she had unsuccessfully requested part-time work at the Labour Exchange. 'They could give us full-time work but we would get war in our homes if we took it' (MO-A, TC 66/4/C-H, 18 November 1941). Official encouragement of employers to organise part-time work in 1942-3 and direction of older women into it in 1943 appears to have lessened women's anxiety about managing the work–home balancing act. Part-time certainly recruited well: from 20,000 in 1942 to 900,000 in 1944. Employers learned quickly that part-time was to their advantage since they could give the most monotonous, unpleasant and low-paid work to part-timers without productivity suffering (PRO Lab 8/634, 1942-3). Even so there is abundant evidence that it was popular among women and that, as Myrdal and Klein believed, if part-time work was available they would carry on with it post-war. Mass-Observation collected a number of comments like the following from a 45-year-old woman:

> You see, to me it's freedom. It's such a change after your own house . . . the old house you know too well. It makes you feel younger and it makes you *look* younger, going out to a job each day. I can do my housework and shopping in the morning—and I do let me house go a bit now. My husband comes home at night and I give him a proper dinner. And that's how we live. And now I don't have to scrape every penny together. I wish part-time had come to stay (Mass-Observation, 1944, p. 58).

Not all older married women worked part-time. On the one hand, Mass-Observation found that some felt they needed full-time work in view of absent husbands and rising prices (Mass-Observation, 1944, p. 57). On the other, there were social class differences. It was not hard for a middle-class woman to evade even part-time war work. Margaret Allen cited Ministry of Labour sources for examples of middle-class married women resisting its efforts to draft them into work dissimilar from that which they had done before marriage, usually teaching and clerical work (Allen, 1983, pp. 410–11). The Wartime Social Survey confirms that in practice there was a high degree of continuity as between pre-war and wartime employment for women in the 'professional, administrative and clerical' group (Central Office of Information, 1944, Table 14, p. 9). Allen also used autobiographical evidence to illustrate the disinclination of this group to undertake war work at all. For example, she quotes an ex-shorthand typist from Bristol whose account of her war experiences was a tale of escaping the Ministry of Labour's clutches. This woman took up part-time clerical work which she found for herself in preference to going 'to any place the Labour Exchange may send me', then left but later found similar work 'to appease the Labour Exchange'. She left that job to care for her 18-year-old daughter and refused further offers of part-time secretarial work: 'since I had been home nursing Joyce the Labour Exchange had not worried me and I had therefore been "lying low" for some time' (Allen, 1983, p. 410).

Nevertheless the organisation of 'non-casual' factory, clerical and service work for women on a part-time basis was, like the work participation of older and married women, a permanent wartime legacy, and a major means by which those women were drawn into the labour force during the war and subsequently. In 1947 approximately one-quarter of women workers were in part-time work, and by 1973 the proportion was one-third (Central Office of Information, 1948, p. 3; Routh, 1980, p. 46).

The evidence concerning older married women does not appear to support Smith's generalisation that women did war work on sufferance and longed to give it up. Young single women, on the other hand, appear to have been more worried about their futures after the war, expressing anxieties about their marital as well as employment prospects (M-O, 1944, p. 61). As Geoffrey Thomas's statistics reviewed above indicate, single and married women under 35 were the groups readiest to give up work and devote themselves to marriage at the end of the war. There is, nevertheless, evidence that some at least had qualms about full-time domesticity once they had experienced it (Braybon and Summerfield, 1987, p. 280) and it is presumably from this group that the older married women part-time workers of later decades were recruited.

Let us now look at the question of whether the wartime shift towards older married women working made any difference to marital styles and the domestic role. Harold Smith argues that it did not, that there was no transformation of the sexual division of labour within marriage during the war. Certainly part-time working arrangements made it possible to keep homes going in much the normal way, as the woman quoted above made clear. Myrdal and Klein and others advocated part-time largely because it did not disturb sexual divisions (Myrdal and Klein, 1968, chapter 10; Political and Economic Planning, 1948). Housework and shopping could be fitted in around working hours, husbands and children could be given their main meals at home, and child care for young children was easier to arrange for a few hours than a full day. The government was thus under less pressure to provide substitutes for the housewife, employers did not experience so much absenteeism, and women workers did not get 'war in their homes' as a result of the challenge to conventional domestic arrangements represented by full-time work.

There is evidence, nevertheless, that the war contributed to changes in marital styles, though it is impossible to measure the extent to which it did so. Various reports referred to a restlessness among women about marriage during and after the war. For example, Mass-Observation claimed that women particularly resented 'the wife being tied to the house, loss of freedom of movement and an inability to take part in the outside pleasures and amusements of single life' (M-OA, File Report 2495, June 1947, p. 17). And autobiographical evidence that I have quoted elsewhere suggests that even some women who did not intend to continue in paid work after the war felt that wartime experiences meant they would not return to being quite the same sort of housewives as they had been before. Zelma Katin's experiences on the Sheffield trams and buses made her determined that her husband would share the washing up with her; Nella Last's role in her local Women's Voluntary Service made her perceive her husband differently and gave her the confidence to insist on a room of her own (see Summerfield, 1988, p. 109).

When Zelma and Nella wrote of their beliefs that post-war wives would not want to be 'caged up separately in their separate spheres' and that 'in the world of tomorrow, marriage will be—will *have* to be—more of a partner-ship', they were echoing a new orthodoxy (Katin, 1944, pp. 49, 123; Broad and Fleming, 1981, p. 255). Public discourses were increasingly emphasising new styles of marriage based on partnership, teamwork and companionship (see Finch and Summerfield, 1991). There was nevertheless considerable uncertainty about the wisdom of encouraging marital styles that would make women less confined to domesticity. Both the falling birth-rate during the war and the rising rate of divorce during and after the war were blamed by some on the greater freedom of women in marriage, while others advocated companionate styles as the solution to both issues. In practice, policy did little to encourage it. For example, though William Beveridge emphasised that marriage was an equal partnership, in his proposals for post-war social insurance a wife was dependent on her husband's contributions and on the benefits he received on her behalf. Surveys in the 1950s showed that the ideal of companionate marriage was more popular with women than with men, and was rarely realised in practice (Finch and Summerfield, 1991, pp. 29–30). All the same, it became a new marital objective to which the war does appear to have made a significant contribution.

To conclude, I have urged here an approach to women and social change in the Second World War which avoids exaggerated claims about emancipation or an inaccurate picture of sweeping changes and sudden reversals or an equally unrealistic depiction of nothing changing at all. I have suggested an approach which avoids regarding 'women' as a homogeneous category, mak-ing it possible to identify the effects of wartime change on distinct groups. Further research is needed here, especially more thorough investigation of ethnic and class differences. Breaking up 'woman' into subcategories makes it possible to observe the restructuring and redistribution of the female work-force, even if it was not greatly enlarged, nor given better opportunities. It also brings into focus the creation of new expectations and new social norms even if they were not necessarily realised. In short, I am arguing for an approach which dismisses the idea that the war transformed women's position, without throwing the baby out with the bathwater.

References

Allen, M.V. (1983), 'The domestic ideal and the mobilization of womanpower in World War II', *Women's Studies International Forum*, vol. 6, no. 4, pp. 401–12.

Andrzejewski, S. (1954), *Military Organisation and Society*, London, Routledge.

Beck, G.M. (1951), *Survey of British Employment and Unemployment 1927–1945*, Oxford, Oxford University Institute of Statistics.

Beechey, V. (1977), 'Some notes on female wage labour in capitalist production', *Capital and Class*, vol. 3, Autumn, pp. 45–66.

Bousquet, B. and Douglas, C. (1991), *West Indian Women at War. British Racism in World War Two*, London, Lawrence and Wishart.

Braybon, G. and Summerfield, P. (1987), *Out of the Cage: Women's Experiences in Two World Wars*, London, Pandora.

Broad, R. and Fleming, S. (eds) (1981), *Nella Last's War: A Mother's Diary 1939–1945*, Bristol, Falling Wall Press.

Census of England and Wales (1934), *Occupation Tables 1931*, London, HMSO.

Central Office of Information (1941), *Wartime Social Survey*, 'An investigation of the attitudes of women, the general public and ATS personnel to the Auxiliary Territorial Service'.

Central Office of Information (1944), *Wartime Social Survey*, 'Women at work: the attitudes of working women towards post-war employment and some related problems' by Geoffrey Thomas.

Central Office of Information (1948), *Social Survey*, 'Women and industry: an inquiry into the problem of recruiting women to industry carried out for the Ministry of Labour and National Service' by Geoffrey Thomas.

Central Statistical Office (1951), *Statistical Digest of the War*, London, HMSO.

Finch, J. and Summerfield, P. (1991), 'Social reconstruction and the emergence of companionate marriage 1945–1959', in D. Clark (ed.), *Marriage, Domestic Life and Social Change: Writings for Jacqueline Burgoyne (1944–88)*, London, Routledge.

Holtby, W. (1934), *Women in a Changing Civilisation*, London, Lane.

Katin, Z. (1944), *'Clippie': the autobiography of a wartime conductress*, John Gyifford, London.

Leser, C.E.V. (1952), 'Men and women in industry', *Economic Journal*, vol, 62, no. 246, pp. 326–44.

Marwick, A. (1968), *Britain in the Century of Total War: War, Peace and Social Change 1900–1967*, London, The Bodley Head.

Marwick, A. (1974), *War and Social Change in the Twentieth Century*, London, Macmillan.

Marwick, A. (1976), *The Home Front: The British and the Second World War*, London, Thames & Hudson.

Mass-Observation (1944), *The Journey Home*, London, John Murray.

Mass-Observation Archive (MO-A) (1941), TC 66/4/C-H, War Work Coventry.

Mass-Observation Archive (MO-A) (1947), File Report 2495, 'The state of matrimony'.

Milkman, R. (1976), 'Women's work and the economic crisis: some lessons of the Great Depression', *Review of Radical Political Economy*, vol. 8, no. 1, pp. 73–97.

Mitchell, J. (1974), *Psychoanalysis and Feminism*, Harmondsworth, Penguin.

Myrdal, A. and Klein, V. (1956), *Women's Two Roles, Home and Work* (2nd edn, 1968), London, Routledge & Kegan Paul.

Oral History Interviews (1986), (in author's possession).

Parliamentary Papers (1930), 'A study of the factors which have operated in the past and those which are operating now to determine the distribution of women in industry', Cmd. 3508 (December 1929), London, HMSO.

Political and Economic Planning (1948), *Planning*, vol. xv, no. 285, July.

PRO Lab 8/634 (October 1942–January 1943), 'Part-time women . . . in the engineering industry'.

Riley, D. (1983), *War in the Nursery: Theories of the Child and Mother*, London, Virago.

Routh, G. (1980), *Occupation and Pay in Great Britain 1906–79*, London, Macmillan.

Smith, H.L. (1986), 'The effect of the war on the status of women', in Harold L. Smith (ed.), *War and Social Change: British Society in the Second World War*, Manchester, Manchester University Press.

Summerfield, P. (1977), 'Women workers in the Second World War', *Capital and Class*, vol. 1, Spring, pp. 27–42.

Summerfield, P. (1984), *Women Workers in the Second World War: Production and Patriarchy in Conflict* (2nd edn., 1989), London, Croom Helm/Routledge.

Summerfield, P. (1988), 'Women, war and social change: women in Britain in World War II', in A. Marwick (ed.), *Total War and Social Change*, London, Macmillan.

Summerfield, P. (1992), 'Mass-Observation on women at work in the Second World War', *Feminist Praxis* (forthcoming).

Thames Television/Channel 4 (1985), 'A people's war', documentary series: interview transcripts.

Titmuss, R.M. (1958), *Essays on 'The Welfare State'*, London, Allen & Unwin.

Walby, S. (1986), *Patriarchy at Work*, Cambridge, Polity.

Windle, M. (1975), 'War and social change', unpublished paper, Durham University Extra Mural Department.

6 From the Roaring Twenties to the Swinging Sixties: continuity and change in British youth culture, 1929–59

Bill Osgerby

Within the writing of British history the Second World War invariably appears as a decisive turning point, a watershed in the nation's social, economic, political and cultural development. Nowhere is this more apparent than in the study of British youth, where 1945 often assumes the aspect of a yawning gulf dividing two entirely different cultural worlds. However, while elements of truth exist in such a perspective, a faithful overview of British youth culture demands an appreciation not only of the discontinuities but also of the continuities to be found in the cultural frameworks of young people during the pre- and post-war periods. Furthermore, while national trends and developments must inevitably figure prominently within any examination of modern youth culture, approaches can be valuably enhanced by the addition of a more localised dimension to provide concrete illustration of complex issues and relationships, thereby avoiding the tendency towards abstraction and over-theorisation common to many more sociologically orientated accounts. The present study, therefore, draws not only on nationally based sources but also on materials relating to a specific locality—the coastal town of Brighton in South East England.

'The Young Ones'

From reading many sociological and historical accounts it is easy to get the impression that British 'youth' suddenly materialised in the 1950s amid an astonishing welter of rock 'n' roll records, D.A. haircuts and brothel-creeper shoes. Peter Lewis, for example, writes of the mid-1950s as representing a 'youthquake' encompassing the 'explosive discovery of teenage identity' (Lewis, 1978, p. 118), while Ernest Cashmore contends that before the 1950s 'there was no such thing as youth' and young people 'had no distinct music, nor styles of dress or leisure patterns . . . they were not different but simply younger versions of their parents' (Cashmore, 1984, pp. 9, 23). Nor are these feelings confined to retrospective analysis. Notions of post-war youth as uniquely separate from wider, 'adult' society also stood at the forefront of efforts to comprehend social and cultural developments during the 1950s and early 1960s themselves. Indeed, the enduring myth that youth culture was 'born' in post-war Britain is largely indebted to the strength with which convictions to this effect were held during the period itself.

From the mid-1950s a wealth of official research responded to and reinforced perceptions of youth as an increasingly distinct and significant social category. In the sphere of education the Crowther Report of 1959 and the Newsom and Robbins Reports of 1963 institutionalised adolescence as a discrete age span with particular needs and problems, while in 1960 the Albermarle Report did the same in relation to the youth service. The theme was further emphasised by the work of innumerable agencies and organisations throughout the period. For example, 1959 saw both the publication of the Report of the Labour Party Youth Commission and the British Medical Association's choice of *The Adolescent* as its 'Subject of the Year' (British Medical Association, 1961). National research, moreover, was mirrored by a profusion of locally based studies, reflected in Brighton in 1959 by the local Education Committee's investigation into the 'needs' of the town's youth, its aim being to 'get to the minds of young people and see what they want to do and what Brighton is providing for them' (Brighton Education Committee, 1959, p. 1).

The Brighton study is revealing. It was prompted not only by generalised concern regarding local youth provision, but also by specific anxieties engendered by a series of violent confrontations between Brightonian youth and the police which had come to characterise the town's annual Bonfire Night celebrations. This local disquiet was indicative of general preoccupations with a perceived upsurge of youth crime and delinquency in the aftermath of the Second World War. The belief was widespread that the destruction of the war, the absence of fathers and the long working hours of mothers had contributed to a general breakdown in processes of socialisation, 'war babies' growing into post-war problem adolescents. The most notable exposition of this theme appeared in 1963 with the publication of T.R. Fyvel's *The Insecure Offenders*, Fyvel contending that post-war increases in juvenile crime were, at least partly, 'the expression of a particularly disturbed generation, a delayed effect of the war' (Fyvel, 1963, p. 51). Juvenile delinquency was regarded as endemic to the post-war milieu, Fyvel going so far as to talk of a 'Teddy boy international', the war having disrupted the lives of young people around the globe (Fyvel, 1961). Further support for these arguments came from research conducted for the Home Office by Leslie Wilkins and published as *Delinquent Generations* in 1960. Juggling with reams of statistics, Wilkins claimed that children born between 1935 and 1942 were especially prone to delinquency, though he judged that wartime conditions alone could not fully account for subsequent rises in levels of juvenile crime. As an important contributory factor Wilkins cited the stylistic adaptations of post-war youth, proffering that the 'crime-wave' among young males had been 'associated with certain forms of dress and other social phenomena' (Wilkins, 1960, p. 9).

Throughout the post-war period the new fashions of the young were a recurring theme in attempts to understand the apparent wave of juvenile crime. In Brighton in 1959, for example, a local rabbi told two hundred youth workers attending a mayoral reception that 'Britain today is suffering from a new disease—that of the maladjusted young men who don special clothes and rebel against any form of discipline' (*Brighton and Hove Herald*, 28 February 1959), while the previous year the Brighton press had conjured with images of a new style of young, vicious assailant—the perpetrator of a violent robbery being described as wearing 'a zip fronted, black, shiny, windcheater and dark coloured jeans, the uniform of the "Wild Ones", youths who ape the dress worn by Marlon Brando in the film of the same name' (*Brighton and Hove Herald*, 11 January 1958). In 1960, meanwhile, reporting on the conviction of seven Brighton youngsters after a street fracas, the local press drew readers' attention to the attire of one of the accused, who had appeared in court sporting the racy ensemble of 'black shirt, pink tie and pink-trimmed jacket' (*Evening Argus*, 23 November 1960).

It was the Teddy boy, however, who stood out as the pre-eminent example of links being drawn between post-war delinquency and young people's sartorial preferences. First identified by the media in the working-class neighbourhoods of south London, the Ted was soon presented as a shockingly new apparition haunting street corners and dance halls across the country. In 1954 the *Brighton and Hove Herald*, for example, conjectured that its older readers must have been puzzled by recent references to 'Edwardian hooligans' and saw fit to explain that the new 'Teddy' boys were, in fact:

> groups of teen-age youths who affect what they fondly imagine to be the costume of King Edward's golden days—black knee-length jackets, with fobbed pockets and velvet collars, 'bootlace' ties, drainpipe trousers, fancy waistcoats and curling hair which bubbles all over their ears and necks . . . [and] hooligans amongst [them] are not above walking five or six abreast and pushing elderly people off the pavement. (*Brighton and Hove Herald*, 8 May 1954)

Closely associated with these perceptions of post-war youth as a generation uniquely disposed to delinquency were beliefs that after 1945 young people had come to possess economic muscle as never before. As early as 1947 the Clarke Report had drawn attention to the financial power accruing to the young worker, observing that:

> when juvenile workers are scarce, as they are now, and are likely to continue to be, he quickly realises that he may not be so unimportant as he seemed at first; and after two or three years his income may be larger compared with his needs and with his contribution to his maintenance than at any other period of his life. (Ministry of Education, 1947, p. 47)

The equation of 'youth' with 'affluence' became a prevalent theme throughout the post-war era, owing a considerable debt to Mark Abrams' research on young people's spending patterns at the end of the 1950s. According to Abrams, youth, more than any other social group, had materially prospered after 1945. Compared to pre-war levels Abrams calculated that young people's real earnings had risen by 50 per cent (roughly double that of adults) with male teenagers earning, on average, £8 per week and their female peers about £6 (Abrams, 1959, p. 9). Moreover, Abrams estimated that youth's 'discretionary' spending had risen by as much as 100 per cent, collectively representing an annual expenditure of around £830 million (Abrams, 1961, p. 3). Furthermore, Abrams contended, this spending was concentrated in particular consumer markets (representing, for instance, 44 per cent of spending on records and record players and 39 per cent of spending on bicycles, motorcycles, etc.), a concentration which, he claimed, represented 'distinctive teenage spending for distinctive teenage ends in a distinctive teenage world' (Abrams, 1959, p. 10).

Recited almost verbatim in a multitude of contemporaneous books, newspapers and articles, Abrams' figures went a long way towards sedimenting notions of a newly affluent body of young people patronising a commercial youth market of unprecedented scale. In Brighton dominant opinion shared Abrams' observations. In 1959, for example, a local headmaster was reportedly convinced that 'the "barrage" of advertisements, diversion and passive entertainment aimed at teenagers today [is] far greater than in any past generation and'; he concluded, 'adolescents have the purchasing power in our present economy as never before' (*Brighton and Hove Herald*, 14 March 1959). And his convictions appeared to be borne out by the local Education Committee's findings that:

> commercial interest has developed apace. 'Youth' is a new found market with its increased spending power and its less ordered ways. In the last three years, particularly, the regular attraction of the picture houses and the ice rink have been augmented by the mushroom growth of Coffee Bars, and the opening of a special 'Record' evening at the Regent Dance Hall. (Brighton Education Committee, 1959, p. 2)

The growing association of youth with consumer spending was exemplified, above all, by the addition of the term 'teenager' to everyday vocabulary. First coined in the mid-1940s by American market researchers and imported into Britain at the end of the decade, the term 'teenager' was incorporated within popular discourse as a cornerstone in explanations of post-war social change. Taken as the quintessence of transformations in British cultural life, 'teenagers' were conceived as the sharp end of the new consumer culture, distinguished not simply by their youth but by their particular style of conspicuous, hedonistic and 'classless' consumption. As Peter Laurie contended in his 1965 anatomy of the 'Teenage Revolution':

> The distinctive fact about teenagers' behaviour is economic: they spend a lot of money on clothes, records, concerts, make-up, magazines: all things that give immediate pleasure and little lasting use. (Laurie, 1965, p. 9)

However, while notions of post-war youth as socially, economically and culturally distinct from previous generations held (and continue to hold) considerable currency, such assumptions demand much deeper scrutiny than has hitherto been the case.

'Mad, bad and dangerous to know'?

Throughout the 1950s and early 1960s official opinion consistently caricatured, overstated and generally misrepresented the behaviour and cultural orientations of British youth. There was, for example, nothing especially novel about patterns of juvenile delinquency after the Second World War. During the 1930s Brighton's *Evening Argus* had complained of 'gangsterism' among youngsters, 'too many of whom have nothing to do and no interest in life except gambling and getting easy money' (*Evening Argus*, 4 September 1936), while a leading magistrate had been appalled by 'boy gangsters . . . [who] committed offences largely for self-glorification' (*Evening Argus*, 17 September 1936). Indeed, Geoffrey Pearson (1983; 1984; 1987) has uncovered a long and connected history of moral panics around youth and crime stretching back at least until the Victorian era and he attributes the rise in recorded levels of delinquency after 1945 largely to changes in the scope and organisation of law enforcement and to the 'formalisation' of police procedures following the war. These 'hidden' influences on the 'manufacture' of post-war crime, moreover, were not lost on contemporaries. In 1954 Brighton's Senior Probation Officer, speaking at a community 'Any Questions' session, refuted notions of a quantum leap in the scale of delinquency, assuring his audience that current juvenile crime figures could not be directly contrasted with those produced before the war when 'public opinion was not directed against the subject as it is today' (*Brighton and Hove Herald*, 20 November 1954). In fact, immediately after the Second World War the local Chief Constable's Annual Reports actually showed a decrease in offences committed by Brighton juveniles, while in nearby Hove during the mid-1950s numbers of young offenders were so low that juvenile crime officers were reported as 'enjoying an off-season' (*Evening Argus*, 23 June 1954).

Nor did the Teddy boy represent a Copernican break in the cultural traditions of British youth. Historians such as Pearson (1983), Gillis (1975) and Springhall (1986) have produced a wealth of evidence to show that the streets of Victorian and Edwardian Britain were no strangers to subcultural groups of working-class youths distinguished by particular styles of dress and who were subject to official opprobrium akin to that attracted by the 1950s' Teddy boy. Stephen Humphries' (1981) research and Robert Roberts' (1973) autobiographical account, meanwhile, testify to the continuation of these patterns during the first half of the twentieth century. Moreover, contrary to popular opinion, the Teddy boy 'look' did not represent a seismic shift in subcultural style.

Conventional wisdom holds that 'Edwardian' designs were created in 1950 by Savile Row tailors catering for respectable young gentlemen, the fashion subsequently appropriated by working-class youngsters. The Ted's style, however, can be more reasonably understood as a variant of the American-based fashions which had been popular among sections of working youth since at least the 1940s, inspired by the iconography of the Chicago gangster and the zoot-suit styles imported with the arrival of GIs during the war. These styles were originally associated with the 'spivs', the cockney wideboys who wheeled and dealed in the black market of the 1940s. Though used to denote any kind of 'flashy' petty villain, the term 'spiv' often bore specifically youthful connotations. For example, in 1946 the *News Chronicle* associated 'the spiv' with a particular section of working-class youth. 'Spivs', the paper contended, 'begin being spivs when other boys are joining in activities at their clubs; and they stop being spivs, rather suddenly, when they reach Borstal' (*News Chronicle*, 15 December 1946). In the mid-1940s the same equation between 'spivs' and sections of working-class youth was made by a Mass Observer at a London dance hall who described a group of youngsters of what he termed 'the "Dago" or "Spiv" type':

> They are dressed in their own, or rather the American singular style—i.e. cut back collar with large knotted tie; 'Boston Slash Back' hair cut; and a 'house coat' style of jacket usually in a light fawn with brown flannels to match' (Willcock, 1949, pp. 49–50)

The same styles were also in evidence on the south coast. In 1948, for example, a young Brightonian, signing himself simply 'Teen-Ager', wrote to the local press, complaining:

> Why is it that boys who wear brightly-coloured clothes are considered to be 'spivs'? . . . Why can't I wear ankle-length trousers or a drape jacket without being called 'flash boy'? This doesn't happen in America, where people are less Victorian and conservative. (*Evening Argus*, 16 September 1948)

Important elements of continuity also existed within the post-war growth of a commercial youth market. Between the wars young people's spending power was constricted by the effects of the Depression, social researchers voicing concern at levels of youth unemployment which remained high throughout the 1930s, and in hard-hit urban areas unemployment was cited not only as a factor contributing to juvenile crime but also as a cause of youngsters' general demoralisation (Bagot, 1941). Nevertheless, traditional views of this period as being typified by mass unemployment and industrial decay have now been modified (Stevenson and Cook, 1977). Although heartlands of heavy industry such as South Wales and the North East certainly suffered, areas of the South and Midlands fared much better, sustained by the growth of 'new' industries like vehicle manufacture and electrical engineering. For workers in full employment standards of living actually rose between the wars and for many people access to leisure and amusement was considerably enhanced. For working-class youth, for example, the demand for labour generated by the Great War and the cost-cutting of the Depression meant that throughout the inter-war period there was always a significant group of working youngsters with a margin of income available for personal consumption. Recent research by historians such as David Fowler (forthcoming) shows that during the 1930s there certainly existed a notable youth market for particular consumer goods and commercial entertainments. For instance, although it is difficult to prove that the American-style dance music and the new dance halls of the 1930s were specifically targeted at young people, it is undoubtedly the case that this section of the population took up the new crazes with greatest enthusiasm, as Bert Healey's autobiographical account of a working class youth in inter-war Brighton recalls:

> There was a bit of the Roaring Twenties and early Thirties as they called it . . . It was jazz, jazz, jazz all the way. Young giggling youths and girls going to work would suddenly twist their feet around doing the Charleston on the pavement. Errand boys on bikes would be whistling 'Ain't She Sweet' all day long. Music

shops would have gramophones, and trumpet speaker radios blaring out hot jazz. The dance halls opened about one p.m. and carried on to one or two in the morning, filled to capacity. (Healey, 1980, p. 113.)

The growth of a youth market for mass entertainment was constituent in a general expansion of commercial leisure and consumer consumption between the wars. Moreover, just as these broader trends traced their origins to the emergence of prototype leisure industries in the late nineteenth century, it is also possible to identify elements of a nascent youth market in this much earlier period. In 1905 in Manchester, for example, C.E.B. Russell observed that a 19-year-old semi-skilled youth working in an iron foundry might earn a pound a week and after giving his parents twelve shillings for board might spend the remainder on clothes, gambling and the music halls (cited in Springhall, 1986, p. 89). Indeed, from the late 1880s policy-makers became preoccupied with the issue of 'boy labour'. Public concern focused on working youngsters' propensity for 'blind alley' jobs that offered high immediate rewards but few long-term career prospects, the problem being cited as a cause of adult unemployment, declining 'national efficiency' and rising juvenile delinquency through the independence afforded by a high earning capacity.

As well as casting doubt on the 'unique' qualities of the post-1945 youth market we should also be wary of exaggerating the status of 1950s' youth as a fully formed consumer group. After visiting Britain in 1954, and again in 1956, Eugene Gilbert—who had made his name as 'the George Gallup of teenagers' through his market research on American youth—concluded that no potential existed for his company to have a permanent office in London. Even in the early 1960s the Managing Director of Thomson Newspapers could assure Peter Laurie (1965, p. 62) that 'As far as advertising goes the teenage market does not exist. As far as we are concerned, as magazine publishers, there *are* no teenagers.' In this light, therefore, Abrams' proclamation of 'a distinctive teenage world' looks suspect at the very least. It is, perhaps, unfair to subject Abrams' data to rigorous criticism. Produced for the London Press Exchange, it was never intended as a thoroughgoing piece of academic investigation. However, many otherwise excellent studies (Chambers, 1985, pp. 26–7; Dunning, Murphy and Williams, 1988, p. 160; Weeks, 1989, p. 252) have uncritically accepted the validity of Abrams' figures and, given the regularity with which they have been cited, it is essential that their accuracy be scrutinised.

Room exists to qualify Abrams' findings in several important respects. To begin with, his definition of teenagers as 'those young people who have reached the age of fifteen but are not yet twenty-five years of age and are unmarried' (Abrams, 1961, p. 3) would undoubtedly have disguised considerable differences of earning and expenditure within this group, while his discussion of *total* expenditure and *average* earnings would also have concealed major differences and disparities. Abrams, furthermore, took no account of regional variations which were undoubtedly present. Indeed, the picture he painted was at variance with less well-known, locally based research produced during the period. According to Brighton Education Committee's 1959 study, for instance, most boys in the town spent under £2 a week while most girls spent between £1 and £1.10s—approximately half the levels calculated by Abrams (Brighton Education Committee, 1959, pp. 8–9). The methodology of the Brighton study was less than rigorous, but more thorough research produced during the 1960s cast similar doubt on notions of 'teenage affluence'. Pearl Jephcott's (1967) study of Scottish youth found that 59 per cent of 15–17½-year-olds had less than £1 a week spending money while 81 per cent of 17½–19-year-olds had less than £3. Cyril Smith's (1966) study of youth in Bury, meanwhile, found that only 5.5 per cent of 15–18-year-olds spent over £2 per week with 61.5 per cent spending less than 15 shillings. 'The popular picture of affluent teenagers', Smith concluded, 'grossly simplifies the very real differences in income among them' (Smith, 1966, p. 17). Nor should we overlook the fact that Abrams' figures themselves showed that the greatest proportion of young people's consumer spending went on goods that were essentially 'non age-specific'—for example, meals out and cigarettes.

In these terms claims about the 'novelty' of the post-war British youth experience appear distorted and exaggerated. Rather than representing a dramatic break with the past, subcultural styles of the 1950s were an extension of cultural responses long evident among sections of working-class youth, while such 'teenage affluence' as existed (together with those markets which sought to exploit it) had been prefigured by social and economic trends originating as far back as the late nineteenth century.

'I was a teenage consumer'

Questions therefore arise as to *why* post-war British society should have perceived its young people as so different from previous generations and *why* youth should have become the focus for such a surfeit of investigation and comment after the Second World War. After all, one of the main difficulties in examining youth consumption before 1945 lies in the sheer scarcity of data. It is only after the war that youth consumption begins to attract, in its own right, the avid interest of media and social researchers. The crucial question is why this should have been so.

The answer comes in two, closely related parts. Firstly, a number of real developments *did* take place in the lives and culture of young people after the Second World War which, while not unprecedented, nevertheless represented a marked contrast with the past. Secondly, these changes were inextricably bound up with broader transformations taking place in Britain during the period, transformations which the 'youth question' came to epitomise—the 'teenager' emerging as an ideological axis around which cohered debates about more fundamental shifts in social and cultural relations.

The post-war 'profile' of youth was heightened by processes of social and economic change. Michael Blanch (1979, p. 103) has argued that the past two hundred years have been punctuated by 'troughs' and 'peaks' in the identifiability of youth as a distinct generational category, citing the turn of the century as one such 'peak' in young people's social 'visibility'. The mid-twentieth century represents a comparable 'peak', the outcome of a combination of social, economic and cultural variables.

The post-1945 period saw a profound apprehension that demographic shifts were affecting societal make-up. The aftermath of the war saw a significant, if temporary, 'baby boom' with the British youth population during the 1950s and 1960s growing both in absolute numbers and as a percentage of the national total, prompting the Albermarle Report of 1960 to remark that 'for every five 15–20-year-olds today there will be six in 1964' (Ministry of Education, 1960, p. 1). Consciousness of demographic change prompted a scramble of initiatives, at both national and local levels, aimed at expanding provision for youth. The implementation of the 1944 Education Act saw public expenditure on education double within ten years, while the raising of the school leaving age to 15 saw adolescents segregated for a greater period of time within age-specific institutions. Under the 1944 Education Act it also became the statutory responsibility of Local Education Authorities to provide adequate recreational facilities for the young people of their area, LEAs being encouraged to set up committees to discharge these responsibilities in cooperation with local voluntary groups. The 1950s, however, saw mounting concern that these agencies were failing in their task and there followed an avalanche of initiatives attempting to extend and professionalize the youth service. These developments were not unprecedented and in many instances marked the implementation of plans made either during or before the war. Nevertheless, an expanded education system and an augmented youth service served to magnify and reinforce conceptualisations of 'youth' as a discrete social entity with its own demands and interests.

Even more crucial in accentuating the visibility of post-war youth was the intensification of long-term economic trends. After 1945 Britain's traditional staple industries—the so-called 'smoke-stack' industries—increasingly declined, capital moving into lighter forms of production—especially the manufacture of consumer durables—involving the expansion of production-line technologies and 'de-skilling'. The trend originated in the previous century but after the Second World War accelerated, registering a much greater impact on the composition of labour. This transformation of traditional labour markets had implications for the structure of the working class as a whole but it was young workers who felt the greatest consequences, their unskilled and semi-skilled labour being sought by employers as never before or since. Indeed, during the 1950s and early 1960s many working youngsters successfully exploited the exceptionally buoyant job market, their peripatetic orientation to employment often provoking official concern. For example, the authors of the Brighton Youth Study of 1959 were unnerved by the attitudes to work they uncovered among local youngsters, reporting that:

> a disappointing number of those with whom we talked seem to have no ambition in other than financial terms. It seems as if they do not expect to be excited or deeply satisfied in their work. This makes them prone to change their jobs easily and often appear to get no joyful satisfaction out of working hard. (Brighton Education Committee, 1959, p. 10)

After 1945, then, demand for youth labour began to outstrip supply, with the result that young people's earning power was significantly augmented. Though exaggerated by many contemporary commentators, the 'affluence' of post-war youth was not entirely mythological. Figures such as those collated in the *British Labour Statistics Historical Abstract* (1971, Table 49, pp. 116–17) indicate that young manual workers made particular material gains in the 1950s and 1960s and, while not bulging, their wage packets were more replete than those of previous generations.

In this context it is hardly surprising that the post-war drive to find new markets and products spawned a youth market far surpassing its antecedents. The post-war period witnessed growing levels of consumer spending within the working class generally, but it was young workers—unfettered by family responsibilities—who were most able to enjoy the fruits of the consumer society. Moreover, the consumption patterns of young people were especially conspicuous. Unlike their parents' home-centred spending, youth's consumption of goods and entertainments took place primarily in public arenas, this exposure contributing toward impressions of a new, affluent 'young generation'.

The range of products geared to the post-war youth market was innumerable, consumer industries interacting with and re-enforcing one another in their efforts to cash in on youth spending. The prime example, of course, came in 1956 with the arrival of rock 'n' roll, a genre of popular music tied much more closely than any of its predecessors to processes of mass marketing and youth demand. The film industry also began to orientate itself to the youth market. John Doherty (1988) has documented the post-war rise of the American 'teenpic', exemplified in the films of Roger Corman and Sam Katzman, but the British film industry also began explicitly to seek out youth audiences, the 1950s and 1960s seeing the release of a host of films featuring pop idols such as Cliff Richard, Tommy Steele and later, of course, the Beatles.

British radio, however, was much less associated with post-war changes in popular music and youth culture. Restricted by limits on 'needle time' and official antipathy towards the 'Americanizing' influences of rock 'n' roll, it was only with the appearance of pirate stations in the early 1960s that British radio began broadcasting programmes specifically geared to a youth audience. Television, on the other hand, responded swiftly to the post-war 'youth scene', BBC and ITV both making numerous forays into the field. However, while the cinema was able, indeed was economically forced, to seek out age-specific audiences, John Hill (1991) has shown that early television programmes always had to allow for the domestic environment of their viewers, shows like 'Six-Five Special' and 'Juke Box Jury' having to embrace a heterogeneous, 'family' audience. Nevertheless, by the early 1960s concessions to adult viewers had vanished, programmes like 'Ready, Steady, Go!' revelling in their teen exclusivity. As Ken and Sylvia Ferguson observed in their 1965 television guide:

> 'Ready, Steady Go!' is not . . . so much a programme—more a way of life. It is a mirror of teenage tastes, the stars they worship, the way they dress, all reflected in one huge television series that unfolds to a vast viewing audience every Friday night. (Ferguson and Ferguson, 1965, p. 24)

Indeed, television became crucial in promoting and propagating all aspects of post-war British youth culture, George Melly describing how 'Ready, Steady, Go!' 'plugged in direct to the centre of the scene and only a week later transmitted information as to clothes, dances, gestures, even slang to the whole British teenage Isles . . . *RSG* made pop work on a truly national scale' (Melly, 1972, p. 72). In fact, without the definition and dissemination that the media and other commercial institutions afforded, it is probable that the Teddy boy, mod and skinhead would all have remained regional subcultural variants—much as 'scuttlers' and 'peaky boys' had been in the nineteenth century.

In short, then, after the Second World War market penetration of British youth culture went far deeper than anything that had gone before. As Derek Hawes observed in his report published in consultation with the Standing Conference of National Youth Organisations during the mid-1960s:

> The quality of life lived by the average young person in Britain today is much affected by the realisation by commercial interests that the age group fourteen to twenty-five represents, in economic terms, a vast multi-million pound market; a well-defined consumer group, affluent and innocent, to be attracted and exploited and pandered to; second only to the housewife in potential spending power. (Hawes, 1966, p. 25)

It is also worth noting that the role of young women within youth culture and the youth market was significantly extended after 1945, to the extent that in the early 1960s Laurie could confidently assert that 'the real dynamo behind the teenage revolution is the anonymous teenage girl . . . Although girls spend less than boys, the dominant sales efforts for clothes, records, and cosmetics is aimed at girls' (Laurie, 1965, p. 151). Pearl Jephcott's studies (1942; 1948) show that before 1945 young women already possessed a degree of disposable income, but labour-market shifts after the war offered them particular benefits. As late as 1931 nearly a quarter of working girls were subject to the rituals and regulations of domestic service, but after 1945 this area of employment contracted into insignificance. In place of the constraints of domestic service and 'living in', girls took advantage of the opportunities opened up by the expansion of consumer industries, retailing and especially the clerical sector. Whether they were secretaries or production-line workers, therefore, girls were (albeit partially) liberated by changes in employment structures, better paid in relative terms and increasingly able to leave behind the disciplines of the work-place in the evenings and at weekends.

Post-war Britain, therefore, witnessed developments in social provision, labour markets, earning power and market exploitation which served to accentuate the appearance of 'youth' as a distinct social category. None of these trends was entirely new, but after 1945 they intensified to a degree that warrants seeing the period as a crucial turning-point in the development of British youth culture. Moreover, the post-war era was also distinguished by the way in which 'youth', or more accurately 'the teenager', was mobilised as an ideological mainstay within dominant accounts of shifts in patterns of class relations.

'Be there or be square'

Many authors (Clarke *et al.*, 1976; Davis, 1990) have commented on the capacity of youth, since at least the turn of the century, to play a metaphorical role in the ways sense is made of more general social developments. Although chronological age seems to have always figured in notions of change and renewal, this 'ideological' dimension to the 'youth debate' becomes powerfully extended at moments of dramatic social transformation. As John Clarke and his associates have argued (1976, p. 71), the 1950s and 1960s represented just such a moment—the tensions and conflicts of the period being embodied within themes and images of 'youth' which impinged on the public consciousness as never before.

Discussion of social change during the 1950s and early 1960s was dominated by the vocabulary of consensus, affluence and classlessness. From this discourse emerged a number of constructed social types that seemed to epitomise the new cultural order—most notably the 'bourgeois worker'. Home-centred, instrumentally orientated and materially prosperous, the 'bourgeois worker' was prominent in popular debate, was courted by Conservative Party electioneering and was given academic recognition in the research of such authors as Ferdynand Zweig (1961). 'Teenagers' represented a similar ideological construct. They were the young nephews and nieces of the 'bourgeois worker', the image of the 'affluent teenager' coming to embody dominant notions of social change in which the generation gap was displacing the class war as Britain's most crucial division.

Throughout the 1950s and 1960s 'youth' was deployed as a shorthand signifier for unbridled pleasure in a new age of forward-looking prosperity. 'Youth' seemed to embody all that the new age of hedonistic consumerism stood for, representing a dynamic and uplifting contrast to the tired, worn-out traditional order of the pre-war years. The general mood was caught in 1960 by the *Brighton and Hove Herald* under the headline 'It's Great to be Young These Days!', the paper declaring that 'In a world of bewildering—often alarming—uncertainties one thing is unassailable: That it is a great age in which to be excitingly young, vibrantly energetic, confidently optimistic' (*Brighton and Hove Herald*, 23 July 1960).

'Teenagers', however, always possessed a Janus-like quality. Almost in the same breath, they were both lauded as a refreshing foretaste of good times waiting around the corner for everyone, and vilified as the deplorable evidence of a growing moral and cultural bankruptcy. In post-war Britain youth was taken as symbolic of not only the best but also the worst that contemporary society had to offer. Simultaneously, 'teenagers' were both Colin MacInnes's (1959) exhilarating and spirited 'absolute beginners' and Richard Hoggart's (1958) 'passive barbarians' whose culture was the most artificial nadir of the mass-produced 'candy floss world'—or, as Bryan Wilson put it in 1959:

> Today's high income receivers are without background, education and information necessary to the cultivation of stable tastes . . . They are exposed in innumerable ways to commercial exploitation, and induced to pay high prices for the merely novel and ephemeral . . . Consequently people, and especially young people,

become confused about their norms, values, tastes and standards. (Wilson, 1970, p. 23, originally published 1959)

In post-war Britain, therefore, youth, specifically the 'teenager', became a central pillar within dominant accounts of the changes taking place in culture and social relations. It is useful, here, to draw upon the work of the Russian philosopher Valentin Vološinov (1973) and his attempt to understand language within a comprehensive Marxist theory of ideology. According to Vološinov the sign should be conceived as a site of class tension, and language, rather than being 'a neutral horizon of fixed and given meanings' should be understood as 'part of a primary class-based struggle for the terms in which reality is to be signified' (Bennett, 1979, p. 192). From this viewpoint it is possible to see the term 'teenager', during the post-war era, as not simply a descriptive noun but as an ideological terrain upon which particular definitions of the nature of social change were constructed. So while it is perfectly legitimate to talk of 'youth subcultures' and a 'youth market' as existing before 1945, the application of the term 'teenager' prior to this date is inappropriate. The 'teenager' was an ideological construct generated within specific debates about culture and class at a particular historical juncture.

As an element within broader post-war 'ideologies of affluence', notions of the 'teenage' market misrepresented the reality of socio-economic reorganisation. While the 1950s and 1960s undoubtedly witnessed major changes in the structures of British society, politics and culture, the relations of capitalist production and its attendant inequalities were left essentially intact. Indeed, 'classless youth' was one of the greatest myths of the post-war era. Rather than transcending old barriers, the 'teenage' experience was, and continues to be, shaped and mediated by the structural constraints of a class-divided society. Even Abrams conceded that the cultural forms associated with 'teenage demand' were 'typical only of working class teenagers' and that the 'teenage market' was

> almost entirely working class. Its middle class members are either still at school and college or else only just beginning on their careers . . . it is highly probable, therefore, that not far short of 90 per cent of all teenage spending is conditioned by working class taste and values. (Abrams, 1959, p. 13)

Throughout the 1950s and early 1960s, therefore, the 'teenager' was essentially a working-class phenomenon, an ideological category employed within dominant accounts of the profound shifts taking place within the material structures and cultural practices of working-class life.

At the same time, however, middle-class youngsters were never completely excluded from the British youth 'spectacle' of the 1950s and early 1960s. The generic term 'beatnik' was applied to disparate groups of unconventional and radical middle-class youths who frequented a duffle-coated world of CND and trad jazz. In 1964, for example, a bearded 18-year-old student explained to the Brighton press:

> The way I dress is my means of self-expression and my comment on the legacy of the world . . . People who look at me and turn up their noses and say, 'God, isn't

he scruffy?' do so out of jealousy. They long for my freedom of dress and hate me because I break the rules by which society forces them to live . . . My pipe is a sign of my rebellion. (*Brighton and Hove Herald*, 28 December 1964)

Of course, the 1920s and 1930s had seen flappers, 'gay young things' and *Brideshead Revisited*-style student cliques, and Arthur Marwick (1970) has charted the rise of stridently political movements among militant university students during the same period. None of these groups, however, is commensurate with the post-war emergence of a highly visible counter-culture populated largely by disaffected middle-class youngsters. Indeed, if a major break in the continuity of twentieth-century youth culture is to be identified it is perhaps towards the 'beatniks' of the 1950s that we should look, though obviously it was only with the expansion of higher education in the mid-1960s that middle-class youngsters began to participate in the British youth experience at a level comparable with that of their working-class peers.

Conclusion: 'The times they are a changin' '

From this brief survey it is clear that British youth culture after the Second World War evidenced a number of striking continuities, cultural patterns and structures established in much earlier periods being maintained and extended. Spectacular subcultural groupings had long existed among sections of working-class youth and since the late nineteenth century many working youngsters had possessed a degree of disposable income. The first stirrings of a commercial youth market also occurred during this earlier period and then began to flourish between the wars. At the same time, however, important discontinuities are also detectable. The nature and scale of youth consumption during the 1950s and 1960s has often been exaggerated and distorted, yet there remain grounds for arguing that it surpassed by far that of previous generations. Also significantly augmented was the 'ideological' role of youth, the 'teenage consumer' emerging as an ideological vehicle in which discussions about broader patterns of social, economic and cultural change were embodied.

There are never any consummate breaks in the course of history and historical analysis is always, in some sense, a constructed narrative distilled by the historian from the seamless flow of events. Nevertheless, the post-Second World War era can, with some justification, be seen as an important turning-point in the nation's cultural life, a turning-point in which the 'youth debate' figured most prominently.

References

Abrams, M. (1959), *The Teenage Consumer*, London, Press Exchange.
Abrams, M. (1961), *Teenage Consumer Spending in 1959*, London, Press Exchange.
Bagot, J.H. (1941), *Juvenile Delinquency*, London, Cape.
Bennett, T. (1979), *Formalism and Marxism*, London, Methuen.
Blanch, M. (1979), 'Imperialism, nationalism and organized youth', in J. Clarke, C.

Critcher, and R. Johnson (eds), *Working Class Culture: Studies in History and Theory*, London, Hutchinson.

Brighton Education Committee (1959), *Report of the Commission of Enquiry into the Needs of Youth in Brighton*, Brighton.

British Medical Association (1961), *The Adolescent: Observations Arising from Discussion Among Members of the British Medical Association*, London, BMA.

Cashmore, E.E. (1984), *No Future*, London, Heinemann.

Chambers, I. (1985), *Urban Rhythms: Pop Music and Popular Culture*, London, Macmillan.

Clarke, J., Hall, S., Jefferson, T. and Roberts, B. (1976), 'Subcultures, cultures and class: a theoretical overview', in S. Hall and T. Jefferson (eds), *Resistance Through Rituals: Youth Subcultures in Post-war Britain*, London, Hutchinson.

Davis, J. (1990), *Youth and the Condition of Britain: Images of Adolescent Conflict*, London, Athlone.

Department of Employment (1971), *British Labour Statistics Historical Abstract, 1886–1968*, London, HMSO.

Doherty, J. (1988), *Teenagers and Teenpics: The Juvenilization of American Movies in the 1950s*, London, Unwin Hyman.

Dunning, E., Murphy, P. and Williams, J. (1988), *The Roots of Football Hooliganism: An Historical and Sociological Study*, London, Routledge & Kegan Paul.

Ferguson, K. and Ferguson, S. (1965), *Television Show Book*, London, Purnell.

Fowler, D. (forthcoming), 'Teenage consumers? Young wage earners and leisure in Manchester, 1919–39', in A. Davis and S. Fielding (eds), *Workers' Worlds: Cultures and Communities in Manchester and Salford, 1880–1914*, Manchester, Manchester University Press.

Fyvel, T.R. (1961), 'The Teddy boy international: unhappy hooligans', *Encounter*, vol. 15, no. 2, pp. 17–31.

Fyvel, T.R. (1963), *The Insecure Offenders: Rebellious Youth in the Welfare State*, Harmondsworth, Pelican.

Gillis, J. (1975), 'The evolution of juvenile delinquency in England 1890–1914', *Past and Present*, vol. 67, pp. 96–126.

Hawes, D. (1966), *Young People Today: An Account of Young People in Voluntary Youth Organisations*, London, National Council of Social Service.

Healey, B. (1980), *Hard Times and Easy Terms and Other Tales by a Queen's Park Cockney*, Brighton, QueenSpark.

Hill, J. (1991), 'Television and pop: the case of the 1950s', in J. Corner (ed.), *Popular Television in Britain: Studies in Cultural History*, London, BFI.

Hoggart, R. (1958), *The Uses of Literacy*, Harmondsworth, Penguin.

Humphries, S. (1981), *Hooligans or Rebels? An Oral History of Working Class Childhood and Youth, 1889–1939*, Oxford, Blackwell.

Jephcott, P. (1942), *Girls Growing Up*, London, Faber.

Jephcott, P. (1948), *Rising Twenty*, London, Faber.

Jephcott, P. (1967), *A Time of One's Own*, Edinburgh, Oliver & Boyd.

Labour Party Youth Commission (1959), *The Younger Generation*, London, Labour Party.

Laurie, P. (1965), *The Teenage Revolution*, London, Anthony Blond.

Lewis, P. (1978), *The Fifties*, London, Heinemann.

MacInnes, C. (1959), *Absolute Beginners*, London, MacGibbon & Kee.

Marwick, A. (1970), 'Youth in Britain, 1920–1960: detachment and commitment', *Journal of Contemporary History*, vol. 5, no. 1, pp. 37–51.

Melly, G. (1972), *Revolt into Style: The Pop Arts in Britain*, Harmondsworth, Penguin.

Ministry of Education (1947), *School Life: A First Enquiry into the Transition from School to Independent Life* (Clarke Report), London, HMSO.
Ministry of Education (1959), *15 to 18* (Crowther Report), London, HMSO.
Ministry of Education (1960), *The Youth Service in England and Wales* (Albermarle Report), London, HMSO.
Ministry of Education (1963), *Half Our Future* (Newsom Report), London, HMSO.
Ministry of Education (1963), *Higher Education: Report* (Robbins Report), Cmd. 2154, London, HMSO.
Pearson, G. (1983), *Hooligan: A History of Respectable Fears*, London, Macmillan.
Pearson, G. (1984), 'Falling standards: a short, sharp history of moral decline', in M. Barker (ed.), *The Video Nasties*, London, Pluto Press.
Pearson, G. (1987), 'Short memories: street violence in the past and in the present', in E. Moonman (ed.), *The Violent Society*, London, Cass.
Roberts, R. (1973), *The Classic Slum*, Harmondsworth, Penguin.
Smith, C. (1966), *Young People: A Report on Bury*, Manchester, University of Manchester.
Springhall, J. (1986), *Coming of Age: Adolescence in Britain 1860–1960*, Dublin, Gill & Macmillan.
Stevenson, J. and Cook, C. (1977), *The Slump: Society and Politics During the Depression*, London, Cape.
Vološinov, V. (1973), *Marxism and the Philosophy of Language*, New York, Seminar Press.
Weeks, J. (1989), *Sex, Politics and Society*, 2nd edn, London, Longman.
Wilkins, L.T. (1960), *Delinquent Generations*, London, HMSO.
Willcock, H.D. (1949), *Report on Juvenile Delinquency: A Mass-Observation Report*, London, Falcon Press.
Wilson, B. (1970), 'The trouble with teenagers', in *The Youth Culture and the Universities* (orig. pub. 1959), London, Faber.
Zweig, F. (1961), *The Worker in an Affluent Society*, London, Heinemann.

III

What difference did the war make to Britain's role in the world?

7 The impact of the Second World War upon British foreign policy

Geoffrey Warner

Before 1939 Britain was one of a number of great powers in a multipolar world. After 1945, it was, despite many of the trappings of great power status, much reduced in rank to what one Foreign Office official described as 'the position of Lepidus in the triumvirate with Mark Anthony and Augustus' in what had become essentially a bipolar world led by the United States and the Soviet Union.[1] The decline in Britain's position was particularly marked in relation to the United States. Although the fact that the latter overtook Britain as an industrial power in the last decade of the nineteenth century is so well known as to constitute almost a cliché of international history, it is not perhaps so widely appreciated that the decisive shift in the balance of power between the two countries did not occur until some fifty years later, as a direct result of the Second World War.

In economic terms, Britain's per capita national income in 1938 was still 90 per cent of that of the United States, whereas by 1948 it had fallen to only 51 per cent (Woytinsky, 1953, pp. 389, 392). This growing disparity was reflected in the output of the basic ingredients of industrial power. Thus, while the United States produced 2.75 times as much steel and 1.5 times as much coal as Britain in 1938, these ratios had increased to 5.25 times and 2.75 times as much ten years later. And while the British Empire's merchant fleet accounted for 36 per cent of the world's gross tonnage in 1939 compared to the United States' 15 per cent, the proportions in 1947 were 26 per cent and 57 per cent respectively (Mitchell, 1981, pp. 389, 422; 1983, pp. 401, 457; Milward, 1977, p. 346).

On the military side, the size of Britain's armed forces in 1938 was actually slightly larger than that of the United States: 381,000 to 323,000. Once the United States had entered the war at the end of 1941, however, its huge reserves of human resources enabled its armed forces rapidly to overtake those of Britain so that by 1945 the former totalled 12,123,000 while the latter had only reached 4,682,000 (US Department of Commerce, 1975, p. 1141; UK Central Statistical Office, 1950). It was a similar story with respect to naval and air strength. At the outbreak of the Second World War in September 1939, the British and American navies were roughly equal in terms of the number of fighting ships. The United States Navy had 15 battleships, 5 aircraft carriers, 37 cruisers, 214 destroyers and 95 submarines, whereas the Royal Navy had 15 battleships, 7 aircraft carriers, 64 cruisers, 192 destroyers and 59 submarines. By the end of the war in September 1945, however, a large gap had opened up between the two fleets. The United States then had 25 battleships, 99 aircraft carriers, 74 cruisers, 850 destroyers and 242 submarines, compared to Britain's 14 battleships, 52 aircraft carriers, 64 cruisers, 368 destroyers and 122 submarines (Bennet, 1975, pp. 37, 52). The gap was even wider in respect of air power. In 1939 the United States Army Air Force had 2,177 aircraft and the Royal Air Force 1,911. By 1945 the figures were 63,715 and 8,752 respectively (Mowrer, 1987, p. 352; Goldberg, 1959, p. 92).[2]

The crossover point between American and British military power came in 1943. On his way to the summit conferences at Cairo and Tehran in November–December of that year, President Roosevelt discussed with his chiefs of staff the relative military strengths of the two allies and was told that the United States was rapidly pulling ahead of Britain.[3] This fact made it inevitable that, despite its reservations, Britain would have to accept the American timetable for OVERLORD (the cross-Channel invasion), as well as an American commander-in-chief for the operation. Later on in the war, Britain was compelled to go along with American plans for an invasion of southern France (Operation ANVIL/DRAGOON) and to accept its exclusion from the negotiation of the Yalta agreement on Soviet entry into the war against Japan for essentially the same reason.

To this picture of declining economic and military power must be added Britain's dire financial plight at the end of the Second World War. Over a quarter of the country's national wealth had been sold off to pay for the war and, as Lord Keynes pointed out in a famous paper circulated to the Cabinet on 14 August 1945, Britain was living beyond its means to the tune of £2 billion a year, a situation made possible only by American Lend Lease, Canadian Mutual Aid and Sterling Area credits. Once the war was over, Keynes forecast a deficit of £1.7 billion on the balance of payments for the three years 1946–8. Without remedial action, this would result in what he called 'a financial Dunkirk', which he described in the following apocalyptic terms:

> Abroad it would require a sudden and humiliating withdrawal from our onerous responsibilities with great loss of prestige and an acceptance for the time being of the position of France. From the Dominions and elsewhere we should seek what charity we could obtain. At home a greater degree of austerity would be necessary than we have experienced at any time during the war. And there would have to be an indefinite postponement of the realisation of the best hopes of the new Government.

Keynes thought it would probably take five years to overcome these problems.[4]

The 'remedial action' which Keynes proposed was threefold: (1) an increase in exports; (2) a reduction in overseas commitments; and (3) American aid. Of these, the first two would take time. The third option was therefore the only short-term solution, and it was obtained by means of the American loan agreement, concluded on 6 December 1945. But this, when combined with the economic and military factors outlined above, created an enormous dependence of Britain upon the United States. As the US Ambassador to the Soviet Union, Averell Harriman, told his colleagues in the Moscow embassy at the beginning of 1946, 'England is so weak she must follow our leadership. She will do anything that we insist [upon] and she won't go out on a limb alone' (Harriman and Abel, 1975, p. 531).

British policy-makers were well aware of the decline in the position of their country, not only *vis-à-vis* the United States, but also the Soviet Union. In his 'Stocktaking after VE Day' memorandum of 11 July 1945, Sir Orme Sargent, who was to become the permanent under-secretary at the Foreign Office in February 1946, pointed out that Britain's role in dealing with the problems posed by the end of the Second World War would be very different from that at the end of the First. In 1918, Sargent wrote, 'we and France shared and disputed and eventually lost control of Europe', whereas in 1945 'the control is to a large degree in the hands of the Soviet Union and the United States, and neither of them is likely to consider British interests if they interfere with their own and unless we assert them.' The only way in which Britain could 'compel our two big partners to treat us as an equal', in Sargent's opinion, was 'by enrolling the Dominions and especially France, not to mention the lesser European powers, as collaborators with us in this tripartite system.'[5]

The Dominions, however, were soon to prove a broken reed. John Darwin has shown how the British government's attempt to push the idea of defence cooperation in the Commonwealth met with a less than enthusiastic response from most of the parties concerned. The unpalatable truth was that the Dominions were far more interested in obtaining security guarantees from the United States than in entering into entangling commitments with the mother country (Darwin, 1988, pp. 147–50).

A British-led 'western bloc' in Europe had been much discussed by the Foreign Office and the Chiefs of Staff during 1944, but the idea had been criticised and discouraged by the Prime Minister, Winston Churchill. This was not so much on account of his attachment to cooperation with the United States as to his conviction that the western European countries were so weak that they were not only unable to provide any worthwhile military assistance to Britain in the foreseeable future, but would actually sap its limited strength still further by creating an obligation to defend them.[6]

After the formation of the Labour government in July 1945, the new Foreign Secretary, Ernest Bevin, revived the notion of a 'western bloc'. Recent research has shown that, contrary to his reputation as a 'Eurosceptic' (to use today's jargon), Bevin took the idea of a European 'third force', independent of the United States and the Soviet Union and ideologically animated by a spirit of democratic socialism, very seriously indeed.[7]

The same research has also shown that there were a great many obstacles in the way of the realisation of Bevin's dream. There was the lukewarm attitude of many officials, especially in the economic departments of the Treasury and the Board of Trade. There was the weakness of many of the western European governments involved, which was compounded by what in British eyes was their inexplicable attachment to the unrealistic concept of federalism as opposed to the more practical procedure of intergovernmental coop-eration. But the greatest obstacle of all was the problem referred to by Sargent in his 'Stocktaking' memorandum, namely, the growth of Soviet power and the perceived threat therefrom. Despite earlier differences it is

clear that, by the beginning of 1946, the Foreign Office and the Chiefs of
Staff were agreed upon the nature and the extent of the Soviet threat to
British interests (Lewis, 1988, pp. 252–64). Even though ministers may not
have been in full agreement until some time later,[8] by the turn of 1947–8 such
events as the failure of the London Council of Foreign Ministers, the Czech
coup and the onset of the Berlin blockade had convinced all but the most
unshakeable optimists that the threat was real and had to be resisted.

Yet this was precisely the period during which Bevin launched his plan for
a European 'third force'.[9] Whatever his original intentions, it was clear that
in any confrontation—and especially in an armed confrontation—with the
Soviet Union, the only ally worth having was the United States, and if Bevin
had failed to realise that himself, the Chiefs of Staff would soon have
impressed it upon him. For a while, Bevin attempted to square the circle, by
simultaneously proceeding with negotiations for a 'Western Union' and for
an American military commitment to western Europe. But slowly and perhaps inevitably the notion of a European 'third force' began to shade into that
of an 'Atlantic Community'. In May 1949, one month after the signature of
the North Atlantic Treaty, the recently formed Permanent Under-Secretary's
Committee was arguing that a 'third force' was no longer viable,[10] while a
year later Bevin's deputy at the Foreign Office, Kenneth Younger, noted in
his diary:

> We and the Americans want to start building up an Atlantic Community which
> includes and transcends western Europe, while the French still hanker after a
> European solution in which the only American function is to produce military and
> other aid. This difference is important because it stems from two quite different
> conceptions. Ernie [Bevin] has no faith in the solidity of France or Belgium and
> believes western Europe will be a broken reed, and will not even attract the loyalty
> of Europeans or impress the Russians unless it is very solidly linked to North
> America.[11]

The wheel had indeed turned full circle, for Younger's description of the
French conception was not all that different from what we know of Bevin's
own ideas in 1948, while the Foreign Secretary's lack of faith in the solidity of
the western European countries closely paralleled that of Churchill in 1944.

In addition to these security considerations, which were of course greatly
reinforced by the outbreak of the Korean War in June 1950, and which
forced Britain to look across the Atlantic for its principal ally, there was
Britain's continuing economic dependence upon the United States. The
American loan was exhausted in 1947 as the Marshall Plan was being debated
in Congress. Sir 'Otto' Clarke's Treasury memorandum of 23 July 1947,
which spelled out the dire consequences for Britain of a failure to receive
Marshall Aid, bears comparison with Lord Keynes's jeremiad of two years
before (Cairncross, 1982, pp. 176–80). And officials from the Treasury, the
Board of Trade, the Foreign Office and the Dominions Office agreed on 5
January 1949 that 'there is no attraction for us in long-term economic
cooperation with Europe. At best, it will be a drain on our resources. At
worst, it can seriously damage our economy.' While not wishing to 'burn our
boats in Europe' the officials concluded that 'we must secure a de facto
special position with [the] USA' (Cairncross, 1982, pp. 208–10). This official

consensus was approved by ministers in the Cabinet's Economic Policy Committee later in the month and was reaffirmed in July 1949.[12] The devaluation of the pound in September 1949 was carried out in consultation with the United States, but not with western European countries.

Despite the attachment of British politicians of both major parties to the so-called 'special relationship' with the United States, the basis for it began to crumble almost as soon as it came into existence. This was due to the continuing decline of Britain's position in the world, not only in relation to the United States, but also to western Europe and later Japan.

Although a long way behind the United States in 1950, Britain was still unquestionably the second most powerful country in the western world. Its national income was twice that of the German Federal Republic and getting on for 2.5 times that of France, while its armed forces were larger and stronger than those of any other member of the North Atlantic Treaty apart from the United States. During the 1950s, however, West Germany's economic growth rate increased to almost three times that of Britain's and that of France almost double. This paved the way for both countries to overtake Britain as economic powers in the course of the 1960s. Moreover, after West Germany began to rearm in 1955 and Britain abolished conscription in 1960, both West Germany's and France's armed forces became larger than those of Britain, while Britain also ceased to be western Europe's only nuclear power with the explosion of the first French nuclear device in February 1960. By the end of the decade, too, it was manifest that what the British Prime Minister, Harold Macmillan, referred to as the 'wind of change' was leading to a marked decline in Britain's imperial presence, both formal and informal, of which the Suez fiasco of 1956 was only the most striking example.

The consequences were gradually to become clear. If Macmillan could tell his Foreign Secretary on 22 December 1959 that '[f]rom [the] Bermuda [conference of March 1957] I set myself to rebuild the Anglo-American alliance to its former strength [i.e. after the Suez crisis of 1956]. This has been achieved and must never be abandoned', he was wondering only seven months later, 'Shall we be caught between a hostile (or at least less and less friendly) America and a boastful, powerful "Empire of Charlemagne"—now under French, but later bound to come under German control[?] Is this the real reason for joining the Common Market . . .? It's a grim choice' (Macmillan, 1972, p. 112, 316).

Macmillan made his 'grim choice' in July 1961 and Britain applied for full membership of the European Economic Community. In a revealing speech to Commonwealth leaders in September 1961, he explained that one reason for the government's decision was that he thought it inevitable that, given the realities of power, the United States would attach growing importance to the views of the EEC and that there would be a growing tendency for the Americans and the EEC to 'concert policy on major issues without the same regard for our views and interests such as our present relationship with Washington affords' (Macmillan, 1973, p. 531).

By precipitating the decline in Britain's international position, the Second World War created the great post-war dilemma of British foreign policy: whether to adopt an American or European orientation. It did not, however, solve it. If the onset of the Cold War determined the outcome in the late 1940s, continuing changes in the balance of power modified that outcome in the 1960s and 1970s, while the ending of the Cold War in the 1990s may yet reverse it altogether.

Notes

1. Sargent minute, 1 October 1945, in Roger Bullen and M.E. Pelly (eds) (1986), *Documents on British Policy Overseas*, Series I, Vol. III, *Britain and America: Negotiation of the United States Loan 3 August–7 December 1945*, London, HMSO, p. 22.
2. Communication from Air Commodore Henry Probert, former head of the Air Historical Branch of the Ministry of Defence, 11 December 1991.
3. Minutes of the President's meeting with the Joint Chiefs of Staff, 19 November 1943, US Department of State, *Foreign Relations of the United States: Conferences at Cairo and Teheran 1943*, USGPO, Washington, 1961, p. 249.
4. Enclosure to Dalton Note, 14 August 1945, *Documents on British Policy Overseas*, Series I, Vol. III, pp. 28–37.
5. Sargent memorandum, 11 July 1945, Rohan Butler and M.E. Pelly (eds) (1984), *Documents on British Foreign Policy Overseas*, Series I, Vol. I, *The Conference at Potsdam 1945*, London, HMSO, pp. 181–7.
6. Eden minute, 6 November 1944, FO371/40722/U8165/G; Churchill minute, 25 November 1944, PREM 4/30/8; W. M. (44) 157th Conclusions; Confidential Annex, 27 November 1944, CAB 65/48; Churchill minute, 31 December 1944, PREM 4/30/8. All in the Public Record Office, Kew, London.
7. Geoffrey Warner (1984), 'The Labour governments and the unity of western Europe, 1945–51', in Ritchie Ovendale (ed.), *The Foreign Policy of the British Labour Governments 1945–51*, Leicester, Leicester University Press, pp. 61–82; *idem* (1986), 'Britain and Europe in 1948: the view from the Cabinet', in Josef Becker and Franz Knipping (eds), *Power in Europe? Great Britain, France, Italy and Germany in a Postwar World*, Berlin/New York, De Gruyter, pp. 27–46; John Kent (1989), 'Bevin's imperialism and the idea of Euro-Africa', in Michael Dockrill and John W. Young (eds), *British Foreign Policy 1945–56*, London, Macmillan pp. 47–76; John W. Young and John Kent (1991), 'British policy overseas: the "third force" and the origins of NATO—in search of a new perspective', in Beatrice Heuser and Robert O'Neill (eds), *Securing Peace in Europe, 1945–62*, London, Macmillan, pp. 41–64.
8. As late as January 1947 Bevin could say 'that danger still came from Germany rather than from Russia'. See Duff Cooper, *Old Men Forget*, London, Rupert Hart-Davis, 1953, p. 371.
9. See the literature cited in note 7 above.
10. See PRO FO 371/76384.
11. Kenneth Younger Diary, 14 May 1950 (transcript in the author's possession). This diary is quoted by kind permission of Lady Younger.
12. EPC (49) 5th Meeting, Minute 2, 26 January 1949; EPC (49). 27th Meeting, Minute 1, July 1949; PRO CAB 134/220.

References

Bennett, Geoffrey (1975), *Naval Battles of World War II*, London, Batsford.
Cairncross, Alec (ed.) (1982), *Anglo-American Economic Collaboration in War and Peace 1942–1949*, Oxford, Oxford University Press.

Darwin, John (1988), *Britain and Decolonisation: The Retreat from Empire in the Post-War World*, London, Macmillan.

Goldberg, Alfred (ed.) (1959), *A History of the US Air Force 1907–1957*, Princeton, Van Nostrand.

Harriman, W. Averell and Abel, Elie (1975), *Special Envoy to Churchill and Stalin*, New York, Random House.

Lewis, Julian (1988), *Changing Direction: British Military Planning for Post-war Strategic Defence*, London, Sherwood.

Macmillan, Harold (1972), *Pointing the Way 1959–61*, London, Macmillan.

Macmillan, Harold (1973), *At the End of the Day 1961–63*, London, Macmillan.

Milward, Alan S. (1977), *War, Economy and Society 1939–1945*, London, Allen Lane.

Mitchell, B.R. (1981), *European Historical Statistics*, 2nd edn, London, Macmillan.

Mitchell, B.R. (1983), *International Historical Statistics: The Americas and Australasia*, London, Macmillan.

Mowrer, Maurice (1987), *Aviation in the US Army 1919–1939*, Washington, DC, Office of Air Force History.

UK Central Statistical Office (1951), *Annual Abstract of Statistics 1938–1950*, London, HMSO.

US Department of Commerce, Bureau of the Census (1975), *Historical Statistics of the United States: Colonial Times to 1970*, Part 2, Washington, DC, USGPO.

Woytinsky, W.S. and E.S. (1953), *World Population and Production: Trends and Outlook*, New York, The Twentieth Century Fund.

8 War and Britain's political crisis in India

Nicholas Owen

One of the most striking features of the long encounter between the British raj and Indian nationalism is the mutual incomprehension of the participants. Wartime negotiations between Indian and British leaders were dogged by repeated accusations of bad faith, deceit and unreliability. The Viceroy, Archibald Wavell, regarded Gandhi as 'verbose, petty minded and quite devoid of constructive statesmanship' and Jinnah as an obstinate and vain prima donna.[1] Nehru accused Cripps of misleading Congress with insincere promises.[2] For his part Cripps could not see why Nehru, whom he thought of as a fellow socialist, could not bring the Indian National Congress to cooperate in an anti-fascist war effort.[3] Wavell's predecessor, the Marquess of Linlithgow, thought of the members of the Congress Working Committee as 'entirely ruthless politicians' quite incapable of 'running straight' and that Cripps himself was 'crooked'.[4] Cripps thought Linlithgow 'sphinx-like' and found it near-impossible to work out his intentions.[5] Comparison of what was said on public platforms with what was said in private produces further contradictions. According to Wavell, the Congress leaders on his Executive Council were 'outwardly very reasonable'. But in dealing with their followers, they had 'no balance or sense of proportion'. In particular, Nehru was 'unbalanced and unreliable'.[6] The moderate nationalist Tej Bahadur Sapru complained that 'the most sickening thing' about Congressmen and Congresswomen was their habit of talking 'quite sensibly in private', but adopting in public 'a different tone or language'.[7]

Why should this be? Of course, this is the stuff of politics, and in the protracted cross-fire of conferences, false starts and breakdowns that characterised the final years of British rule it is hardly surprising to find politicians speaking with forked tongues. Furthermore, wartime censorship and restrictions of movement fractured personal relationships between Indian nationalists and their sympathisers in Britain. After the end of the war, Nehru told Cripps:

> It is our misfortune that with all the goodwill in the world we fall out . . . and so somehow India and England drift further apart—they were far enough—till it becomes frightfully difficult for either to have any real conception of the other, much less understanding. [8]

Moreover, as George Orwell pointed out at the time, principles that had seemed uncomplicated before the war had become worryingly inadequate:

> In our time, political speech and writing are largely the defence of the indefensible. Things like the continuation of British rule in India . . . can . . . be defended, but only by arguments which are far too brutal for most people to face, and which do not square with the professed aims of political parties. Thus political language has to consist largely of euphemism, question-begging and sheer cloudy vagueness . . . When there is a gap between one's real and one's declared aims, one turns . . . instinctively to long words and exhausted idioms, like a cuttlefish squirting out ink. (Orwell and Angus, 1968, vol. 4, pp. 127–40)

But most importantly, each of the major participants was acutely conscious that it was addressing many and diverse audiences. Congress appealed to its much-divided supporters in India, and to sympathisers in Britain and the United States; Jinnah addressed Congress Muslims, Muslim minorities and Muslim majorities; and the raj spoke to potential supporters in India, to its wartime allies and to its political masters in the coalition. Despite strenuous claims to the contrary, neither the leaders of Congress, nor of the Muslim League, nor of the raj itself were free agents. Each was forced to pander to a broad range of constituents. The Congress claim to represent all India was, it now appears, simply wishful thinking. Congress was a prisoner of its environment, reacting to, rather than shaping events, a 'ramshackle coalition' of disparate interests: Gandhian utopians, trades unionists, peasant agitators, lawyers, businessmen and industrialists. Its 'national' agitations were often patchy affairs, in which the All-India leadership could only synchronise local disputes which ran according to their own clocks (Seal, 1973). Similarly, the claim of Jinnah's Muslim League to be the sole spokesman of India's Muslims had equally little substance before 1945. There were powerful independently minded Muslim premiers in the Punjab and Bengal whose allegiance to Jinnah and the League was at best fitful. Even the raj itself, for all its insistence on its imperial responsibilities, and on the dogma that constitutional progress must wait until the war's end, remained a vulnerable and rickety structure, held up as much by prestige as real power, its options heavily limited by wartime stringencies.

Jawaharlal Nehru was painfully aware of the constraints on leadership. His inability to lead the unwieldy Congress in new directions was a constant theme in his correspondence. In April 1937, he told Edward Thompson not to think India's problems could be solved by 'handfuls of people at the top imposing their will on others'.

> It seems to me that you forget or ignore the fact that Indian politics are more and more shaped by mass urges and by the conscious opinions of hundreds of thousands of persons . . . [Individuals] may be good or bad, intelligent or otherwise. But they have all ceased, or are progressively ceasing to represent vital forces in India. Therefore in the final analysis they do not count.[9]

Indeed, Nehru regularly found himself obliged to speak with more than one voice. On Easter Monday 1942, with the Cripps negotiations at their most vexed and with bombs falling on eastern India, Nehru addressed two meetings of journalists. The Indian journalists were told: 'It is a question of who is to be boss in Defence—Englishmen or Indians.' Their European colleagues were assured that Congress had no desire to question the authority of the British Commander-in-Chief, but only 'to be able to arouse a mass war effort' (Moore, 1979, p. 107). Sapru attempted to assure a British acquaintance that it would be 'a great mistake' to judge Nehru by his speeches. 'To know his own views, you must discuss things across the table from him.'[10]

The impact of global war upon these unstable alliances and fragile structures is an immense theme, and one to which an essay of this length can scarcely hope to do justice. R.J. Moore has already provided a comprehensive bibliography of the substantial range of literature that exists for each of the major players (Moore, 1986). Rather than provide a bald summary of this writing, the discussion that follows will focus instead on the theme identified above: the extent to which the war wrenched control from those who were supposedly in charge of Nehru's 'vital forces'. The war finally broke the hold of the leaders of Congress and the Muslim League over their respective followings, and weakened their ability to back up their hollow words with actions. The British, too, were deprived of the initiative and ability to control events which was the vital underpinning of their plans to advance India to the status of a Dominion. Accordingly, the wartime encounter between 'imperialism' and 'nationalism' looks much less like the clash of two competing ideologies, and more, as Anil Seal once characterised it, as the clash of two men of straw, sometimes wrestling, sometimes clinging unsteadily together. By the war's end, the 'elegant exchanges' between Gandhi's ashram, the Viceregal Lodge at Simla, Jinnah's home on Malabar Hill, and the India Office in London had begun to seem almost irrelevant.

I

On the outbreak of war in September 1939, the standing policy of the British government remained the pursuit of All-India Federation as enshrined in the 1935 Government of India Act. By gradual stages India was to reach independence as a self-governing Dominion within the Commonwealth, with continuing military, trading and financial links to Britain. India was to achieve such freedom as a Federation, in which the princes would act as a conservative brake on the demands of more radical nationalists. The Congressmen and Congresswomen elected to India's free Parliament would thus be forced to come to terms with the locally autocratic princes and hence, it was hoped, to moderate their programmes of reform. For the immediate future, the 1935 Act had provided for full responsible government in the provinces.

The 1935 Act was never intended as the first stage in the dissolution of the British Empire (Bridge, 1986). On the contrary, it was meant to direct potentially destabilising forces into channels which would permit the maintenance of the strategic and economic substance of the imperial connection. Many of the supporters of Federation believed Congress was an artificial coalition held together only by the ability of its leaders to stir up anti-British grievances. The more cynical of British observers believed the pressure of government would break Congress into parties on a class, regional or perhaps communal basis; the more optimistic that it would inject a much-needed sense of responsibility.

The success of the constitutional experiment depended crucially on five unwritten rules. Firstly, emergent nationalism should be weakened and divided less by repression, except in obvious cases of insurrection, than by the encouragement of moderate politicians to cooperate in government. Of course, coercion could not be dispensed with altogether, since the morale of the civil administration depended in large measure on its ability to maintain its authority in the face of nationalist challenges. But after Jallianwalla Bagh (the Amritsar massacre), senior British officials came increasingly to realise that displays of force were almost invariably counter-productive, likely to alienate moderate opinion, and put the loyalty of Indian troops and police under strain.

Secondly, the final advance to Dominion status should be the result of British initiative, not Indian pressure. This was important, because British interests had to be protected in whatever final settlement emerged. There were army and civil careers, investments and military bases to be considered.

Thirdly, nationalist aspirations and moderate opinion might also be satisfied by progressive Indianisation of the administration, and by the concession of tariff and fiscal autonomy to Delhi. The latter moves were well under way by 1939, with the government of India's right to set import duties firmly established, and the newly established Reserve Bank of India exercising its powers to control India's monetary policy. The introduction of Indians into the predominantly white British cadres of the Indian Civil Service (ICS) and the officer corps of the Indian Army was admittedly a slow process, but one designed to show that Indian political aspirations could be met within an imperial framework. Better still, the presence of a British-trained administration would ensure a close post-colonial relationship when the time came for India to make the final advance to Dominion status.

Fourthly, rapid social change should be avoided as far as possible, especially if it could be used by Congress to gain mass support. As Jack Gallagher put it, 'low taxation and salutary neglect [were] the keys to the political kingdom' (Gallagher, 1984). So that the burden of taxation was kept low, the Indian Empire should be run cheaply. There could, of course, be no question of allowing India to become a burden on the British tax-payer.

Finally, communal rivalries might be tolerated, or even useful, if they operated within the political frameworks devised by the British, but not if they became a threat to public order.

Of course, as had already become obvious by September 1939, this plan was by no means foolproof. It had provided the Indian Princes and their Tory die-hard supporters at Westminster with a dangerous veto over India's political emancipation, one which it was readily apparent they were prepared to use. In June 1939, a conference of India's princes finally rejected terms for participation in the Federation, a step which brought the constitutional experiment to a humiliating halt. Muslim fears that a Congress-dominated centre would be inimical to their interests had pushed them into demanding additional safeguards. Nevertheless, though government policy was in serious difficulties before the outbreak of war, there was little reason to believe that the problems were insoluble. Indeed, in so far as the reforms were intended to break the unnatural coalition of moderates and radicals that made up Congress, they had proved rather successful. Congress itself had become increasingly embarrassed by the dual role it was forced to play: as a party of government in the provinces, but a party of opposition at the centre. It had found insufficient funds in provincial treasuries to finance the reforms it had promised, and the ICS, with which its relations had often ranged from frostiness to outright hostility, seemingly unsympathetic to implementing them. No one believed that the collapse of Federation meant the end of constitutional progress in India, and Linlithgow was not alone in his confidence that the British would remain in India until a settlement was reached.[11] It was still widely expected that India would achieve independence without the loss of unity, that power would be transferred in an orderly fashion, and that Britain would continue to exercise a guiding influence over the new state, especially in the domain of foreign and defence policy. The assumptions underlying the constitutional experiment seemed to remain valid.

However, as Linlithgow recognised in his retirement, global war and the 'delicate process of constitutional adjustment . . . went ill together'.[12] The war forced the pace of Britain's plans, when precise matching of gears and speeds was essential to their success. Even before the end of 1939, the Secretary of State for India, the Marquess of Zetland, told the Prime Minister that he did

> not believe that the picture of India moving towards the goal which we have set before her by smooth, measured and leisurely stages—which is what we have hitherto had in mind—is likely to be realised. As in the case of Planck's quantum theory, so in the case of peoples, progress seems to proceed not smoothly but by jumps.[13]

Hitler, as Linlithgow observed to Baldwin, had 'rather overset our Indian politics'.[14]

In the first place, the war revealed the limits of Britain's willingness to concede Indian freedom. Under Britain's pre-war plan, defence and foreign affairs were to be the last matters to be delegated to Indians. Indeed, many British politicians believed that even after attaining Dominion status, India would still accept Britain's leadership in diplomatic and strategic matters. These assumptions were finely revealed in wartime. Just at the moment when the British were beginning to devolve power to Indians, albeit in a manner best calculated to further British interests, the war exposed the pragmatic nature of British intentions. In September 1939, Linlithgow declared war on India's behalf without consulting a single Indian, an action technically within the constitution, but sufficiently tactless to sting Congress. During the Cripps Mission, the British resolutely refused to transfer the Defence Department to Indian control. Even Stafford Cripps himself, despite long sympathy with Congress nationalism, was quite adamant that this could not be done during the war.[15] The Indian Army was deployed in imperial interests, not merely in those of India herself. Even in May 1942, at the height of the Japanese threat to India, seven well-equipped divisions were deployed in the Middle East (Gwyer and Butler, 1964).

Secondly, the war cut short Britain's attempt to remodel the raw material of Indian nationalism into forms with which she could work in the years to come. Even before Japan joined the war, India was considered to be a vital part of British defence, both as a supplier of men and of materials. Such mobilisation necessitated an alliance not with the ideal partners which the constitutional experiment had been designed to produce in a matter of decades, but with the flesh-and-blood Indian politicians of the day. Many of the Conservative members of the British Cabinet were simply unprepared for this. As Zetland told Linlithgow, the fires of 1935 were still smouldering, and the die-hards were still a significant force.[16] Indeed, an early effect of the war was to strengthen the diehard influence through the elevation of Churchill to the premiership, and the appointment of Leo Amery to the India Office. Churchill himself was personally determined to resist all concessions to Congress nationalism, regarding all Indians as 'a beastly people with a beastly religion'.[17] He was wholly convinced that negotiations with Congress would weaken India's defence effort. Amery, who recognised the inevitability of political progress in India, none the less saw the war as the ideal opportunity to break down the artificial Congress coalition.

The anti-fascist struggle also preoccupied the nationalists' traditional—if wary—allies in Britain: the British Labour Party. Although Churchill protested to Eden that he was being 'jostled by Socialists', the Labour Party remained anxious and uncertain of its views on India's future.[18] Many of its leaders still harboured mistrust of the bona fides of Congress which they saw as politically irresponsible, and disconcertingly supported by Indian big business. At the start of the war, Labour's relationship with Congress was initially good, but rapidly decayed as soon as Congress began to talk of civil disobedience. By the war's end, Nehru was barely on speaking terms with Attlee, whom he thought of as 'weak, pedestrian and singularly ineffective', and Cripps, whom he told Krishna Menon had 'injured Indo-British relations far more than any Englishman could have done'.[19]

Thus the two constitutional schemes drawn up in wartime London—the 'August Offer' of 1940 and the Cripps Mission of 1942—bear little similarity to the careful and detailed legislation created in the 1935 Government of India Act. They were contingency plans drawn up hastily amid much disagreement between senior ministers with the main aim of drawing Congress into cooperation with the war effort. There was barely any consultation of Parliament in their making. Gandhi's dismissive description—embellished by an imaginative journalist—of the Cripps offer as 'a postdated cheque on a crashing bank' captured much of the feeling that Britain had surrendered the initiative. As D.A. Low has pointed out, the crushing of Congress in 1942 showed that 'at moments of crisis, [the British] were being steadily pushed back upon their ultimate, military, bulwark' (Low, 1977, p. 9). By the end of the war, the British had seen each one of the self-imposed rules that underpinned their plans for India broken. The passage of events that led to the partition of the subcontinent, and its refusal to participate in Britain's Commonwealth defence system east of Suez amounted to a substan-

tial defeat of pre-war objectives, which only very careful political management by Attlee could disguise as a kind of triumph: the uncontroversial and
long-expected crowning stage of Britain's imperial mission.

II

Within Congress, the war upset the delicate balance between those who
demanded confrontation with the British administration and those who
favoured working constitutional reforms, and drove India's largest party into
open conflict with the raj. The Congress was already split at the outbreak of
war by its participation in provincial administration. It was at once a populist
nationalist movement dedicated to the overthrow of British rule, and a party
of government which felt an obligation to maintain law and order. In
opposition, it had managed to represent a broad coalition of interests. But
once Congress accepted office, it became increasingly difficult to balance the
diverse interests of communities and classes. Congress ministries 'had to
decide whether they would continue to tolerate or favour industrial strikers
and agrarian protesters, or, like the British before them, align state power
with the interests of property and the control of labour' (Arnold, 1986, p.
228). In most areas, ministers felt obliged to repress communal riots and
leftist peasant and worker movements. Nehru feared that Congress was in
severe danger of fragmenting under the pressures of provincialism and the
social divisions which governing inevitably produced.[20] Gandhi, too, had
been disappointed with the factionalism, place-seeking and corruption that
had apparently accompanied the taking up of office, and believed the
Congress must 'go into the wilderness again before it becomes strong and
pure enough to reach its objectives.'[21]

The war deepened these divisions. Although in 1927 Congress had declared that it could not be party to an imperialist war, it had developed no
common policy on questions of defence. Gandhi opposed war on principle,
and hoped that his philosophy of non-violence might render armed defence
unnecessary. In 1940, he threatened to start a fast if Congress joined a
national government and 'fostered a war-like spirit'. For his part, Nehru
wished to resist Japanese expansion not by means of the Indian Army, but
with a popular militia. Others, including Rajagopalachari, were prepared to
enter a national government in return for immediate independence. The
leadership was also divided over whether to exploit Britain's difficulties by
threatening civil disobedience. Subhas Chandra Bose, the President of
Congress at the time of the Munich crisis, favoured confronting Britain with
a wartime ultimatum: to hand over power or face open disorder. Though
Bose had been forced to resign by Gandhi and the Working Committee of
Congress in May 1939, he continued to lead a disaffected group of younger
Congressmen and Congresswomen who pressed for direct action. Other
Congress politicians had settled to the work of provincial government and
were loath to give up the spoils of office.

The collapse of Federation meant that the question of the centre was
thrown open once again. For the Congress leadership, it was vital above all

else to preserve unity until it gained control there. The strains occasioned by the outbreak of war could not be allowed to split the party. Accordingly, Congress embarked on a series of unstable compromises designed primarily to allow the agitators to let off steam without giving the British an excuse to crush the movement, and to provide limited support for the war effort without alienating the Gandhian wing.

Initially, in response to British unwillingness to countenance constitutional change in wartime, the leadership called upon the provincial ministries to resign. This was a move that Gandhi privately admitted was a way of 'cover[ing] the fact that we were crumbling to pieces'.[22] In seven of the eleven provinces of British India, the powers exercised by Congress ministers reverted to the governors. The resignations broke the links that were fast developing between provincial Congress politicians and British officials, and allowed the All-India politicians to recover ground lost during the period of cooperation. But this was no real substitute for a positive policy, and on this Congress was painfully divided.

Nevertheless, the war was still a distant affair, and was bringing healthy profits to farmers and industrialists. Before Pearl Harbor and the entry of the Japanese into the war, Congress leaders needed to offer the prospect of action to conciliate the radical and restive, while not provoking a conflict with the raj for which the organisation was unready. Accordingly, at Ramgarh in March 1940, civil disobedience was approved in principle, but its start deferred until Gandhi judged it necessary.

However, in the aftermath of the fall of France, the Congress Working Committee refused to adopt Gandhian non-violence as the guiding principle of national defence. Instead, it accepted Rajagopalachari's contention that 'the problem of the achievement of national freedom has now to be considered along with the one of its maintenance and the defence of the country against possible external and internal disorder' (Moore, 1979, p. 40). But the British response to Congress demands was so inadequate that the balance of Congress swung back towards non-cooperation. In October 1940, Gandhi persuaded the Working Committee to launch a campaign of individual civil disobedience. Prominent Congressmen were to court arrest by stating publicly their opposition to the British war effort. In later stages, the timing of which Gandhi kept under tight control, local party leaders and individual members were to make the same symbolic protest.

Gandhi's methods were accepted by a decisive section of the Indian leadership precisely because they attracted radical Congressmen and Congresswomen, while keeping their activities strictly pegged down to certain limited forms under the tight control of the leaders. Mass civil disobedience, the Congress leadership believed, would be difficult to control, and could easily tip over into communal unrest, especially in Bengal and the Punjab, where the struggle would be not against the British, but the non-Congress ministries.[23] Moreover, Gandhian civil disobedience of this peculiarly limited kind would not seriously hamper the war effort, yet provided a powerful demonstration of national feelings.

The civil disobedience was successful to the limited extent that it preserved Congress unity and never became a vehicle for more radical action, but it hardly troubled the British administration. Thus by the end of 1941, this compromise, too, had collapsed. With the apparently inexorable Japanese advance through South East Asia, the war was approaching India herself. The divisions between those who thought Gandhian methods put insufficient pressure on the British, and therefore favoured a quick push to drive the British out, and those like Rajagopalachari who favoured immediate cooperation with the British war effort, became acute (Brown, 1989, pp. 331–3). Meeting at Bardoli, the Working Committee was torn between Nehru's advocacy of a direct offer of cooperation in return for immediate independence, and Gandhi's refusal to countenance Congress association with the war effort. Although a majority favoured Nehru's position, it was again thought essential to preserve party unity, and the Bardoli resolution thus reaffirmed the uncompromising stance of September 1940 on national independence, while refusing to extend Gandhian principles to national defence, and hence opening the door to possible cooperation. Gandhi retired from active leadership of Congress, exhorting Congress to unite behind its new policy. Once again, as Sir Maurice Hallett told Linlithgow, Gandhi had cunningly 'welded Congress together with a formula which is capable of numerous interpretations'.[24]

Thus in early 1942, the fragile balance of opinion in the Congress Working Committee seemed to have tipped momentarily towards cooperation. Meanwhile, Japanese military successes culminating in the capture of Singapore and Rangoon persuaded the British Cabinet of the need for a fresh approach to India. On 22 March, Cripps arrived in India, armed with a new offer. Cripps proposed post-war Dominion status with the right to secede from the Commonwealth, a 'constitution-making body' elected by the provincial legislatures, with individual provinces given the right not to join it. Representative Indians would be invited to join the Viceroy's Executive immediately.

But far from providing a rallying point for the divided forces of Indian nationalism, the offer merely divided them more painfully than ever, and Cripps returned empty-handed. In explaining the failure of the mission, it has been argued that Cripps was tripped up by Churchill and Linlithgow, and forced to retract part of the offer (Moore, 1979). But it is instructive to consider the specific points upon which the talks broke down. Much to Cripps's surprise, they were not concerned with arrangements for the end of the war, but with the provisions made for wartime cooperation in government. In particular, Congress was anxious that the Viceroy's Executive would operate like a Cabinet, with collective responsibility, and that the portfolio of defence should be given to an Indian. These seemed relatively minor details to Cripps, but for Congress they constituted the essence of the wartime dilemma. There was little to be gained from a piecemeal participation in wartime government. As Japanese forces swept through Malaya, Singapore and Burma in the space of four months, Indian defeat seemed a strong possibility. Denied the right to negotiate peace, Congress leaders would be reduced to the impotence they had often felt in provincial government: held responsible for events it was beyond their power to control. Participation in Britain's war would almost certainly drive the Gandhian wing to break away. Not long after the outbreak of war, Nehru had confessed his difficulties to a long-standing correspondent, Edward Thompson. Cooperation in Britain's war effort would be 'an unknown and dangerous adventure':

> We shall have nothing to do with it even if the whole Viceroy's Council is offered to us, with the Viceroyalty thrown in . . . We could not do this even if we wanted it. The Congress would throw us overboard.

> It is a complete change in the outlook, the system, the structure, the objective that is an essential preliminary. If that does not take place we shall wait for a better day.[25]

Now Nehru told Rajagopalachari that nothing would be more dangerous for the Congress than to be 'saddled with responsibility without complete power'. It was 'inconceivable' to suppose that the British would part with complete power in wartime, and 'partial power will make our position worse'.[26] A successful Japanese assault now looked very likely, and Gandhi himself became convinced that the days of the raj were numbered. Accepting Cripps' offer would entail asking Indians to fight those 50,000 other Indians training in Malaya in support of the imminent Japanese invasion of the subcontinent. If Congress was to emerge intact from the crisis of invasion, it had to wrest full political control from the British. The half-measures offered by Cripps would deny Congress powers sufficient to organise national defence, and the freedom to negotiate a peace treaty. Moreover, Gandhi, Prasad and Patel remained convinced that support of Britain's war would entail abandoning the principle of non-violence. Short of an immediate and far-reaching transfer of power, nothing the British could offer Congress leaders was worth losing the precarious and intermittent hold they still enjoyed over the movement.[27]

The decision to resort once again to civil disobedience was itself the product of the same reasoning. Its policy of seeking accommodations with the British now discredited, the leadership now had to move quickly in the opposite direction to outflank the increasing numbers who favoured pushing the British out without delay. The belief that Japan might now successfully overrun India was now widespread, and shared by increasing numbers of the Congress leadership, including Nehru himself.[28] Even businessmen, who had hitherto benefited from the British connection through lucrative military contracts, began to have second thoughts. Scorched earth, bombing and invasion seemed too high a price to pay for cooperation with the British.[29] British prestige, always an important prop for British raj, was undermined not merely by military defeat at the hands of an Asiatic power, but by the conduct of military retreat to Bengal, in which the British soldiers burned what they did not commandeer. This included the destruction of all country boats, the only means of transport during the monsoon. Rumours of an apocalyptic end to British rule spread by means of returning evacuees and wounded soldiers from the Burmese front, and fuelled expectations of a violent outburst against British rule (Sarkar, 1983, pp. 391–2). The Inspector-General of the Bengal Police told Colonel Louis Johnson, Roosevelt's Personal Representative in India, that the invading Japanese would probably be garlanded by the police (Voight, 1987, p. 148).

On 8 August 1942, the All-India Congress Committee ratified the 'Quit India' resolution, which sanctioned 'a mass struggle on non-violent lines on the widest possible scale', and early the following morning, Gandhi, the Working Committee of Congress and numerous local leaders were arrested. The detention of the principal leaders of Congress marked the start of spontaneous and popular outbursts across India. The first phase consisted of a wave of industrial strikes in mills and steelworks, and a large number of street demonstrations led by the urban middle classes, especially students. However, this was short-lived. In the factories, the failure to win over the communists, who favoured cooperation in the 'People's War' against fascism, and, on the streets, the rapid use of British firepower against demonstrators weakened the urban movement. In later weeks, unrest spread to the country-side, with attacks on local officials and sabotage of communications and government buildings (Sarkar, 1983, pp. 394–6). To suppress the rising, the British were prepared to be ruthless, killing or wounding nearly 3,000 people and arresting over 90,000.[30] Although isolated incidents continued until the end of the war, the revolt was crushed by the end of September. The pattern of the disturbances and the relative ease of its suppression illustrated the absence of common goals in the nationalist movement (Henningham, 1983).

In fact, the Congress leadership had envisaged a much more limited campaign than actually occurred. Despite strenuous British efforts to prove otherwise, there was very little evidence that Congress *leaders* favoured violent confrontation. The 'Quit India' resolution drawn up in the Congress Working Committee in early July had demanded the termination of British rule and threatened non-violent civil disobedience if the demand was not met. But Gandhi's call for the withdrawal of Allied troops, made repeatedly in the weeks after Cripps's departure, had been set on one side. Provincial Congress committees proposed simply the traditional Gandhian methods of making salt, boycotting schools and courts, and picketing foreign products. Non-payment of rents and taxes was proposed, but only as a last resort, and only if landlords refused to support the movement. Above all, the Congress leadership hoped for a controlled renewal of civil disobedience, enough to hold the more militant elements of the movement within the fold, and enough to make it clear to all that Congress could not safely be ignored. The idea of a non-violent mass movement was a compromise: Gandhi's price for agreeing to Nehru's demand that Allied troops should remain on Indian soil. Nevertheless, Congress leaders had been pessimistic about the chances of controlling the movement once it was under way.[31]

Thus, by another of the cruel misunderstandings with which the end of empire seems replete, the British, by imprisoning the Congress leadership, made quite certain that the 'Quit India' movement was much harder to control than it would otherwise have been. Gandhi had intended to seek an audience with the Viceroy before launching the movement.[32] The precipitate arrests allowed the movement to pass rapidly into the hands of younger, less experienced and often more militant activists, often the very people the Congress leaders had been anxious to placate. Ironically, one unintended effect of the British propaganda effort, which portrayed the Congress leader-ship as rebels plotting violent insurrection, was to convince such young activists that this really had been the plan all along, and that the eruption of strikes and clashes that followed had indeed been sanctioned by the leaders. For the next three years, with many of the moderates interned and the Congress organisation driven underground, a substantial fillip was given to those who rejected the constitutional path to Indian freedom.

War not only made repression necessary for the British, it also made it feasible. Linlithgow had taken care to secure emergency wartime powers to use against Congress in the event of civil disobedience. On the same day as he had announced the August Offer, he had told his governors that 'the only possible answer to a declaration of war by any section of . . . Congress . . . must be a declared determination to crush the organisation as a whole' (Voight, 1987, p. 54). The heavy concentration of troops in the country made it possible to devote fifty-seven battalions to the task of crushing the revolt. Sweeping wartime powers of censorship made certain that news of British methods was kept from world opinion. The machine-gunning of saboteurs from the air, which Linlithgow personally approved, was unknown even to the British Cabinet. Even left-wing sympathy was guaranteed as long as 'Quit India' could be successfully represented as fifth-column activity.

The desperation of war thus forced the British to break the unwritten rule that coercion should be used only sparingly. After the release of Congress prisoners in 1945, there was widespread criticism of British ruthlessness in 1942. Ultimately, such methods had sapped British authority, and did much to discredit the raj in the eyes of international opinion. Worse still, the war forced Britain to upset the careful balance between attracting collaborators and coercing dissenters which had enabled her to survive earlier periods of civil disobedience. By 1945, according to one of Stafford Cripps's correspondents, there was 'not a single element in Indian public life on whose support the British Government [could] rely'.[33] In the suppression of 'Quit India' the subtleties of the constitutional experiment and the attempt to divert moderate Congress supporters from agitation to constructive participation in British institutions were lost.

III

War also placed unprecedented strain on the weakened administrative machinery of the raj. Under wartime pressure, Indianisation was accelerated far beyond the gentle pace set before the war. By January 1946, for the first time, the number of Indians in the ICS exceeded the number of Britons.[34] With little recruitment during the war, the total establishment fell to under a thousand, and the British component was set to decrease still further with long overdue post-war retirements. By 1946, in one province, there were only nineteen British civil servants available to fill the sixty-five senior executive posts. Moreover, new wartime tasks had stretched the overburdened civil administration: recruitment, the construction of roads, aerodromes and supply bases, requisitioning, the raising of war funds, propaganda, and air raid precautions (Hunt and Harrison, 1980, pp. 206–25).

But the manpower shortage alone is an insufficient explanation of the loss of administrative initiative. The crucial factor was the rapid decline of its prestige and authority. In the districts, overwork and delegation started to allow local politicians to supersede the raj almost by default, a quieter but no less decisive process than the shouting match of confrontational politics in Delhi. In some areas, British officials were simply bypassed, and the public began to turn to Congress officials as a parallel or alternative source of authority. The events of 1942 also undermined the effectiveness of the Civil Service. Congress threatened to put members of the services on trial for their wartime conduct, while many British officials, disgusted by the apparent treachery of 'Quit India' found themselves unable to cooperate with Indian politicians. By the end of the war, the administration was badly run down, and perhaps an unreliable agent of British interests. In particular, as Wavell and the Cabinet recognised, the confused loyalties of Indian officials would be stretched to breaking point in the event of civil unrest.[35] Once Britain had given notice to quit, Indian members of the ICS were forced increasingly to think of their futures (Potter, 1986). While during earlier periods of civil unrest, the Indian members of the civil service had remained aloof from the nationalist movement, they now began to split along communal lines, especially in Bihar and the United Provinces (Ewing, 1982). British hopes that the calming influence of a staunchly loyal administration would ease India's transition to Dominion status seemed increasingly optimistic.

But the ultimate bastion of British rule in the subcontinent was a military one. Even before the war, for every official in the Indian Civil Service, there were over 150 soldiers in the Indian Army. In wartime, the Army increased in size from about 166,000 men to 2,250,000 men by 1945.[36] The proportion of British to Indian officers fell from 10:1 to 4:1 (Low, 1977, p. 13). Of course, the unquestioning loyalty of the sepoys had never been taken for granted by the British. In the aftermath of the 1857 'Mutiny', complex strategies of recruitment and regimentation were developed to contain dissent and accommodate the religious sensibilities of the soldiery (Omissi, forthcoming). But under the pressure of the war, many of these practices became unsustainable. The Army, which had almost invariably recruited from catchment areas prized for their conservatism and loyalty, found itself forced to cast its net more widely (Gupta, 1987, pp. 5–6). The new recruits were predominantly drawn from the urban intelligentsia and entrepreneurial families, rather than the more traditionally minded landed classes (Voight, 1987, p. 66). In February 1946, the Commander-in Chief reported that 'every Indian officer worth his salt is a Nationalist' (Inder Singh, 1984, p. 196). More worryingly, communal rivalries began to spread into the regiments. There were also growing resentments of discrimination in pay, prospects and promotion (Gupta, 1987, p. 6). By April 1946, the Home Member of the government of India had serious doubts whether the three services, and especially the Royal Indian Navy and Royal Indian Air Force, would support the British in the event of renewed Congress civil disobedience. 'On the whole,' he 'doubt[ed] whether a Congress rebellion could be suppressed . . . At the worst there will be uncontrollable rebellion over the greater part of British India; at the best, I doubt whether orderly administration could be generally restored.'[37]

IV

War also forced the British to make demands on the colonised which in peacetime they avoided. Intervention in local economies was bound to produce losers as well as gainers. It was hazardous because the raj lacked the popular base to justify the sacrifices that its economic policies made necessary. As an alien and overstretched administration it had little capacity to resolve the conflicts that resulted from them. With Congress politicians refusing to cooperate in government, there were few mediatory institutions capable or willing to explain British intentions. Indeed, the failure of the raj to develop an effective wartime propaganda machine to put the British case was a constant worry to its political masters in London.[38]

At the heart of the problem were Britain's war debts. As a result of pre-war agreements, Britain was committed to pay for the modernisation and mechanisation of the Indian Army, and for its deployment outside India's borders. When these agreements had been drawn up, it had been intended that Britain's contribution would be partly financed by a reduction of some 25,000 men in the size of the army (Voight, 1987, pp. 61–2). The war made such cuts unthinkable, and the British Treasury was soon faced with a mounting bill. In the early years of the war, these liabilities could be met by cancelling out India's sterling debts in London. But after 1942, Britain was running on credit. The government of India, deprived of these revenues, and faced with the increasing burden of its own defence spending, was forced to expand the money supply against government securities. The effect of this was to increase local purchasing power just as the supply of consumer goods began to shrink with the contraction of imports and the placing of much Indian industry on a war footing. In short, it was inflationary (Tomlinson, 1979, pp. 92–100).

The most horrifying results of wartime inflation were felt in Bengal. Caught in an inflationary spiral, producers and merchants preferred hoarding to the purchase of meagre and overpriced consumer goods. British ministers considered that the war precluded any large-scale diversion of shipping to meet India's need for imports. Wavell was told that 'war is a gamble and . . . it is better to take the risk of . . . famine in India than to risk the failure of the Second Front.'[39] Convinced that the problem was one of supply rather than distribution, provincial governments confined their initial efforts to famine relief. But this did little to reach the roots of the problem, and procurement and price-fixing on an unprecedented scale became imperative. This entailed extensive government intervention in 'the most convoluted and sensitive areas of the internal economy'. At first, the provincial governments worked cautiously through systems of licensing, but these proved inadequate, and the direct purchase of grain and its sale to responsible merchants became commonplace. By 1944, requisitioning had become inevitable. District officials became involved in procurement, storage, transport, supply through rationing and 'fair-price' shops. By 1945, 'legitimate food-grain marketing was a government monopoly' (Tomlinson, 1979, pp. 98–9).

The Bengal famine, Wavell wrote, was 'one of the greatest disasters that has befallen any people under British rule . . . [D]amage to our reputation here both among Indians and foreigners in India . . . is incalculable.'[40] Moreover the measures taken to alleviate it did little to endear the British officials to farmers and traders. In the Punjab, intervention broke the alliance between the imperial administration and the prosperous landowners of the Punjab Unionist Party. Punjabi grain was requisitioned to feed Bengalis, and price controls held down the profits the farmers hoped to make from wartime shortages. As a result, the Muslim League, which had hitherto found it impossible to make much headway in the Punjab, began to win the support of those classes which had hitherto been the strongest supporters of British rule (Talbot, 1982).

While many Indian industrialists relished the opportunities war provided for rapid profit-making, their sympathies moved ever closer to Congress. The war revealed more clearly than ever British unwillingness to sponsor industrial growth in India. The needs of the war effort had prompted the government of India to take control of issues of fresh capital, the establishment of new plant, and the supply of capital goods from abroad. Even in wartime, British fears of post-war competition in the aircraft industry hampered local initiatives, such as that of Walchand Hirachand (Voight, 1987, pp. 75–6). British obstruction was motivated as much by strategic considerations and a simple inability to transfer scarce machinery and skilled manpower to India, as by purely selfish motives. But Congress made considerable political capital out of it, and the attractiveness of the British connection to Indian industrialists correspondingly diminished.[41]

V

But perhaps the most decisive wartime developments lay in the increased leverage gained by Jinnah and the Muslim League, and the escape of communal rivalries from the flimsy bonds with which the British had sought to contain them. Of all the major participants in these events, Jinnah has seemed to contemporaries and historians the most perverse. For Mountbatten, Jinnah was 'a psychopathic case' bent on the partition of India, a judgement from which historians have until recently seen little reason to dissent.[42] But at the outbreak of war, Jinnah's overriding concern was not to effect the partition of India, but in securing for the League the right to speak for all Muslims, and an equal say with Congress in India's future. To this end, the thoughts of many Muslim leaders had begun to turn to the 'two nations doctrine', the contention that Indian Muslims had a distinct national identity. Since nations, unlike communities, negotiate as equals, acceptance of the 'two nations doctrine' would give Jinnah the recognition he needed to gain concessions for the Muslim community within a united India. In March 1940, the doctrine found stark expression in the so-called 'Pakistan Demand', which insisted that Indian Muslim nationhood should be recognised in territorial form, and that those parts of India with Muslim majorities should be grouped to constitute sovereign independent states.

However, the 'two nations doctrine' logically required that India's Muslims speak with a single voice. The problem for Jinnah was that the

League had won fewer than a quarter of the Muslim seats in 1937, and powerful provincial Muslim groupings still existed in the Punjab (the Unionists under Sikander Hyat Khan) and in Bengal (Fazlul Huq's Krishnak Praja). Congress, too, had begun a 'mass contact' programme aimed at securing Muslim votes. Moreover, Jinnah's strategy was complicated by the differing demands of Muslims in those provinces in which they formed a substantial majority (Sind, the North-West Frontier Province and Baluchistan); those in which they held a bare majority (Bengal and the Punjab); and those in which they remained in a minority (especially the United Provinces, where they numbered 8 million, but only 14.5 per cent of the population). In the firm majority provinces, there was some support for the 'solid gains of national status'. But for Muslim leaders in Bengal and the Punjab, Pakistan would almost inevitably entail partition of their provinces, and the collapse of the intercommunal alliances that they had been operating with considerable success under the 1935 Act. For Muslims in the minority provinces, it had nothing to offer but the prospect of being a permanent minority in Hindustan, or the upheaval of migration. They accordingly favoured safeguards, minority rights and negotiations with Congress rather than outright secession (Jalal, 1985; Roy, 1990).

Thus Jinnah needed an appeal which would unite all Muslims *as Muslims* behind his banner, but which would also give him equal status with the Congress in the fresh negotiations for the reform of the centre which would inevitably follow the collapse of Federation. The Pakistan Demand served these ends well enough, provided Jinnah took care not to define it too precisely. In early 1942, the Reforms Commissioner, H.V. Hodson, reported to Linlithgow that among the Muslim Leaguers in the provinces he had visited 'there was no genuine enthusiasm for Pakistan'. Rather, they reluctantly supported it:

> not only for fear of incurring the wrath of Mr Jinnah or impairing the Muslim solidarity which they feel to be vitally necessary at the present time, but also . . . because the policy . . . extreme and unpalatable as it may seem to them, expresses however crudely some inarticulate but vital theme in the Muslim mind.[43]

The war complicated matters still further. Jinnah pursued a complex strategy, steering an independent course between outright cooperation with the British, which would have laid him open to charges of complicity with imperialism, and meekly following Congress into non-cooperation, which would compromise the League's independence and its oft-repeated claim to be the sole spokesman of India's Muslims. Again, the Pakistan Demand served this purpose admirably. It enabled Jinnah to maintain his nationalist credentials while making a distinctive appeal to those of India's Muslims who might otherwise be tempted into the Congress camp. Jinnah gambled that Britain would never countenance the destruction of Indian unity, so vital to her strategic and economic interests. Nor did it seem likely that Gandhi or Congress would be prepared to accept the loss of India's Muslim provinces. Thus the Pakistan Demand began as a bargaining counter, which Jinnah was prepared to trade away later once the principle of an equal say at the centre was accepted.

The effect of the war was to turn this bargaining counter into the central plank of Jinnah's political strategy. While the British had little sympathy for Pakistan, the war demanded that they retain Muslim goodwill. Muslims occupied a position in the Army out of all proportion to their share of the population, and the possibility of war with the Soviet Union in the early months of 1940 made it vital that the Muslim north-west of India be contented with British rule.[44] Moreover, the demand for Pakistan ensured that the alliance between Congress and India's Muslims which had developed during the First World War would not be repeated. Jinnah was a useful figure in this strategy since his weakness in the Punjab, the main recruiting ground for the Army, and Bengal, the eastern front against Japan, made it unlikely he could seriously disrupt the war effort, while his claims of separate nationhood were a useful riposte to the claims of Congress. In the absence of Congress cooperation, the British gave encouragement to the Muslim League, and credibility to its claim to be treated as the sole spokesman of India's Muslims. In August 1940, they assured the League that it could not countenance a settlement in India which it opposed. Jinnah was henceforward provided with a dangerous veto over any revision of the constitution. Furthermore, the arrests of popular Congress leaders allowed the League to establish a truly popular base, and to take power from the Congress in North West Frontier Province and Assam.

But there were already dangerous signs that the frequently reiterated 'Pakistan Demand' was starting to acquire its own momentum. In the Punjab, the concept of Pakistan began to serve as a unifying influence for the disparate interests of the Muslim communities of the countryside and the cities. The British administration had nurtured Muslim institutions without providing the central Islamic authority that had existed under Muslim rule. The failure of the colonial state to foster the notion of an Islamic community had troubled many Muslim scholars, who came to see Pakistan as 'a new symbolic foundation for the political order', a powerful slogan which religious leaders took to the countryside (Gilmartin, 1988).

VI

By October 1944, it had already become obvious to Wavell that the resumption of normal political life after the war would place immense strains on Britain's ability to influence events. The end of the war would bring demobilisation, the dispersal of labour from war factories, and the winding up of vast wartime clerical establishments. He warned Churchill and Amery:

> All this will cause unemployment and discontent . . . We can hope for no quick improvement in the food situation and the other economic troubles caused by the war. Our political prisoners . . . will have to be released, and will find explosive material ready to their hands.

The civil service was in no position to handle such events. It 'might almost be described as moribund, the senior members are tired and disheartened, and it will be extremely difficult after the war to secure good recruits.'[45]

There was little chance of reinforcing the British presence in India. At the war's end, Britain faced, in J.M. Keynes's words, 'a financial Dunkirk'. The wartime multiplication of foreign debts had created a shortfall in her balance of payments which neither her depleted stocks of foreign exchange nor her crippled export trade were in any position to make good. Although an early collapse was to be averted by an American loan, there was consistent pressure from the Treasury for Britain to cut back her overseas commitments: a ripe target for economy since they were not only a burden on the balance of payments, but also kept some 18 per cent of the working population away from the tasks of domestic reconstruction—either directly in the armed forces, or indirectly in supplying them. Faced with the necessity of new commitments to resist Soviet expansion, Britain could not undertake the burden of sending fresh troops to India (Tinker 1988).

Above all, however, British control in India by the autumn of 1945 had become *politically* fragile. Shortage of fresh officials alone was not the problem. As D.A. Low has pointed out, 'the British went on recruiting public schoolboys for their colonial empire for another fifteen years' (Low, 1977, p. 39). Even in 1947, Ernest Bevin pleadingly asked Attlee 'if we were able to move into Germany and other occupied countries and find administrators among the young men from the Services, as we had to do, why can't we find them from the forces in India and at home?'[46] But as Attlee observed in his reply, the effectiveness of new recruits had become as much a matter of politics as one of logistics. Coercion was no longer practical 'against the active opposition of the whole of the politically-minded of the population': 'If you proposed to govern by . . . force, you would be driven into shootings and the like for which you would find very little support in this country.'[47]

Moreover, post-war reorganisation of the Army had left the task of controlling internal disorder largely in the lap of the Indian Police. The Army was only to be called upon in the last resort. Under the 1935 Government of India Act, control of the police was vested in the elected provincial governments. Their instructions could only be overridden by the governor in the exceptional circumstances laid down under Section 93. This meant that the majority party in control of the administration in a province could, if it wished, connive at breaches of law and order. In Bengal, the Muslim League ministry was repeatedly charged with connivance at communal rioting; in Bihar, where a Congress ministry was in power, similar charges were made. In each case, the governor was largely powerless to intervene.[48] To declare Section 93 was not a step to be taken lightly. After serious rioting in Calcutta, R.G. Casey, the Governor of Bengal, told Auchinleck that he 'had Dyer and Amritsar constantly in my mind in the last few days'.

> I think that the principal lesson of the last few days has been that the Army is a weapon that is not of much value in support of the civil power—in that one is afraid to use it for fear that the long range consequences may be worse than the immediate good that it can do . . . I had the most potent weapon of several battalions of armed and disciplined troops—but I was afraid to use them.[49]

The Congress leadership emerged from prison as the unlikely heroes of

1942, thoroughly mistrustful of British intentions. But despite their haloes of patriotic self-sacrifice, the Congress leaders found it as difficult as ever to control the actions of their followers. Nehru observed that 'the past three years have affected our people very deeply, and, I think, changed them considerably. Intense passion has been aroused and iron has entered the soul of large numbers of the people.'[50] The trials for war crimes of members of the Indian National Army, which had fought alongside the Japanese during the war, aroused widespread outrage, and Nehru, who had hitherto criticised their activities as misguided, was forced to appear in court to defend them (Mahajan, 1987).

As Wavell had predicted, the aftermath of war saw high rates of unemployment, famine and distress in the countryside, and rising prices in the towns. With the restored Congress ministries bearing the brunt of unpopularity, the communists began successfully to stage general strikes in major cities. Congress leaders spoke out against industrial and political agitation, fearful that the long-expected transfer of power would be delayed by a premature upsurge of nationalist feeling. The Karachi and Bombay mutinies of the Royal Indian Navy in February 1946 were brought to an end with the help of Congress leaders, for, as Patel wrote in confidence, 'discipline in the Army cannot be tampered with . . . We will want [the] Army even in free India.'[51] Privately, they were becoming convinced that only a swift transfer of power would allow them to prevent a chaotic breakdown of order. After meeting Congress leaders privately, Cripps wrote in his diary that

> the right wing of Congress, which is now in power, is very alarmed indeed at the prospect of left wing movements creating serious disturbances or worse. The Bombay incidents have greatly impressed them and they are most anxious to avoid trouble in any way they can. This means they want a very rapid settlement and will go to great lengths to get it quickly.

The President of Congress, Maulana Azad confirmed this impression. The Congress leadership was 'very anxious about the dangers to India from Russia and also internally from their own left wing and other subversive movements.'[52]

But more than anything else it was mounting communal unrest that frightened Congress. The Muslim League emerged from the war determined to enforce its newly strengthened claim to be the sole spokesman of India's Muslims. With elections in the offing, fierce competition for Muslim votes between Congress and the League forced Jinnah to play on communal differences. Sir Bertrand Glancy, Governor of the Punjab, told Wavell that the uninformed Muslim voter 'will be told that the question he is called to answer at the polls is—Are you a true believer or an infidel and a traitor?' Pakistan might be 'quite illogical, undefinable and ruinous to India and in particular to Muslims', but there was no denying its potency as a political slogan.[53] Resistance to Jinnah's demand for Pakistan was a rare point of unity for Congress, and Nehru launched a series of bitter attacks on the League. This in turn convinced wavering Muslim voters that they could expect little sympathy under Congress rule.

But the remarkable success of the League had made Jinnah the prisoner of the Pakistan demand. Nicholas Mansergh has drawn attention to the way in which conceptual imperatives like 'Pakistan', once formulated and popularised, 'impose . . . rigorous constraints on the freedom of action even of the most powerful of political leaders' (Mansergh, 1976). When Jinnah began to tack back towards his real aim—the securing of concessions within a united India—his supporters were outspoken in criticism. Jamil-ud-Din Ahmed told him it was scarcely possible to retreat 'after having sworn on the Quran to fight and die for undiluted sovereign Pakistan.'[54] Jinnah did his best to ensure that the League's Day of Action called for August 16 would pass off peacefully, but by now his control over the forces he had conjured was minimal: '[Jinnah] had much in common with King Canute: the spirits of Calcutta's underworld were minded to pay as much heed to his ineffectual commands as the tides of the North Sea' (Jalal, 1985, p. 216). The Governor of Sind was told by his Chief Minister that 'if Jinnah had not agreed to something of this sort, feeling was so strong that he would have been swept away.'[55] In Calcutta communal riots left 4,000 dead and 15,000 injured. As waves of communal unrest spread to the Punjab, the raj, and the leaders of Congress and the League were reduced to the role of impotent spectators.

The crucial solvent in the final phase of British rule in India was mass disorder. The Labour government was deprived of both of the traditional methods of imperial rule: coercion, which became impractical, and collaboration, which was unforthcoming. It was keen to get Congress into office as soon as possible in order to restore order, and to forestall Conservative cries of 'scuttle' (Owen, 1991). Congress, too, was keen to inherit the raj before its own authority was irretrievably broken. Moreover, while accommodation of the Muslims within a united India would mean the surrender of much power to the provinces, partition provided Nehru with a strong central authority capable of curbing civil and communal unrest and planning the economy. 'Imperialism' and 'nationalism' thus came together in a manner which neither side could have foreseen. Mountbatten's much-acclaimed 'solution' of the Indian problem thus owed much to good fortune. Only once Nehru and Jinnah had finally lost control of their own movements were they prepared to compromise, and make an agreed settlement feasible. To the last, as Nehru had told Cripps in 1945: 'On both sides, whatever our personal feelings in the matter, we have become the agents of powerful forces which we may influence somewhat but cannot control.'[56]

Notes

All references to Nicholas Mansergh *et al.* (1970–83), *India: The Transfer of Power 1942–47* (HMSO, 12 volumes) are indicated in the notes by the initials *TP*, followed by the volume and document numbers.

1. Wavell's *Journal* entries for 19 June 1944, 11 July 1944, reprinted in Moon (1973, pp. 75, 77–9).
2. J. Nehru to V.K.K. Menon, 13 April 1942, National Archives of India New Delhi (hereafter NAI), Home Political File 225/42-Poll(I).

3. R.G. Coupland, *Indian Diary*, 1941–42, entry for 10 April 1942, Coupland Papers, Rhodes House Library, Oxford.
4. Marquess of Linlithgow to L.S. Amery, 21 April 1942, *TP* I 23; Linlithgow's marginal notes to Amery to Linlithgow, 3 April 1942, *TP* I 517; Wavell's *Journal* entry for 19 October 1943, reprinted in Moon (1973, pp. 32–4).
5. R.S. Cripps to J. Nehru, 24 December 1939, Jawaharlal Nehru Correspondence, vol. 14, Nehru Memorial Museum and Library, New Delhi (hereafter NMML).
6. Wavell to Pethick-Lawrence, 12 August 1945, *TP* VI 20.
7. T.B. Sapru to B. Shiva Rao, 15 May 1941, B.Shiva Rao Papers, NMML.
8. J. Nehru to R.S. Cripps, 1 November 1945, Public Record Office, Kew (hereafter PRO), Cripps Papers, CAB 127/143.
9. J. Nehru, to E. Thompson 22 April 1937, Edward Thompson Papers, in possession of E.P. Thompson.
10. T.B. Sapru to G. Pole, 25 February 1946, copy in Cripps Papers, PRO CAB 127/149.
11. Linlithgow to Zetland, 3 January 1939, Linlithgow Papers, MSS Eur F 125/7, India Office Library and Records, London (hereafter IOLR).
12. Linlithgow, *Speech at Edinburgh*, October 1944, cited in Voight (1987, p. 200).
13. Zetland to N. Chamberlain, 1 December 1939, Private Office Papers, L/PO/251 IOLR.
14. Linlithgow to Baldwin, 22 March 1940, cited in John Darwin (1984), 'British decolonization since 1945: a pattern or a puzzle?' *Journal of Imperial and Commonwealth History*, vol. XII, no. 2, pp. 187–209.
15. A. Harrison circulars for India Conciliation Group, 28 February 1942, 8 April 1942; A. Harrison to C. Heath, 2 February (?March) 1942, ICG Collection TEMP MSS, Box 47, Cripps File, Friends House, London.
16. Zetland to Linlithgow, 18 January 1940, 28 February 1940, Linlithgow Papers, MSS Eur F 125/8 IOLR.
17. L.S. Amery, *Diary* entry for 9 September 1942, reprinted in J. Barnes and D. Nicholson (1988) *The Empire at Bay: The Leo Amery Diaries 1929–1945*, London, Hutchinson, p. 382.
18. A. Eden, *Diary* entry for 7 March 1942, Avon Papers, AP 20/1/22, Birmingham University Library; Nicholas Owen (1991), 'Labour and the "Quit India" Movement', unpublished paper given at Oxford University Commonwealth History Seminar.
19. J. Nehru, 'Reply to Stafford Cripps: statement to the press', 27 July 1942, reprinted in S. Gopal (1972–82), vol. 10, p. 419, *Prison Diary* entry for 17 December 1943, ibid., vol. 13, p. 311.
20. J. Nehru to S. Mahmud, 12 December 1939, Syed Mahmud Papers, NMML; V. Patel to R. Prasad, 17 July 1939, 14 October 1939, Rajendra Prasad Papers, File 3-C/39; File 3-RP/PSF(I)-1939 NAI, cited in J.M. Brown (1989, p. 325).
21. M.K. Gandhi, 'Addresses to the Ramgarh Congress', 18 and 20 March 1940, reprinted in *The Collected Works of Mahatma Gandhi*, Government of India, 1958–84 (hereafter *CWMG*), vol. 71, pp. 348–54, 357–60. 'Statement to the press, 18 October 1939, *CWMG*, vol. 70, pp. 267–8.
22. J. Nehru's notes of a lecture by Gandhi 'W[orking] C[ommittee] Wardha, Bapu, June 18 1940', Jawaharlal Nehru Papers Misc. Draft Resolutions I, NMML.
23. Congress Working Committee, 16–19 April 1940, Papers of the All-India Congress Committee, AICC G32/1940, NMML, quoted in part in Moore (1979,

pp. 38–39).
24. M. Hallett to Linlithgow, 19 January 1942, *TP* I 20.
25. E. Thompson to J. Nehru, 11 November 1939, Jawaharlal Nehru Correspondence, NMML.
26. J. Nehru to C. Rajagopalachari, 26 January 1942, Jawaharlal Nehru Correspondence, NMML.
27. Home Department Intelligence Bureau, 'Report of Working Committee meeting of April 1 1942', Home Political 221/42-Poll(I), NAI.
28. J.Nehru's comment at the secret session of the Allahabad Working Committee session of 27 April–1 May 1942, reported in R. Tottenham *Congress Responsibility for the Disturbances*, Government of India, 1943, Appendix I; and Home Department Intelligence Bureau report of his speech of 21 May 1942, Home Political 4/1/42-Poll(I), NAI.
29. H. Twynam to Linlithgow, 25 May 1942, *TP* II 83.
30. 'Evidence of the regional incidence of the "Quit India" movement and its suppression, for the period ending 31 December 1943', Home Political File 3/52/43(I), cited in F.G. Hutchins (1973, pp. 230–1).
31. J. Nehru, 'Note: instructions for workers and talking points', 24 July 1942, Jawaharlal Nehru Papers, Writings and Speeches, NMML; M.K. Gandhi to Mira Ben, 22 May 1942; Gandhi to Chiang Kai-Shek, 14 June 1942; conversation with young volunteers, 28 May 1942; *Harijan* 28 June, 5 July 1942, *CWMG*, vol. 76, pp. 136,159–60, 225, 237, 253.
32. M.K. Gandhi speech to AICC, 8 August 1942, *CWMG*, vol. 76, p. 394; Gandhi to Linlithgow, 14 August 1942, *TP* II 553.
33. B. Shiva Rao to R.S. Cripps, 20 November 1945, PRO CAB 127/147.
34. Home Establishments File, 30 November 1946, cited in Inder Singh (1984, p. 195).
35. Cabinet India and Burma Committee Meeting, IB(46)8, 11 December 1946, *TP* IX 186.
36. Annual Returns showing the composition of the Indian Army, Military Section Records, L/MIL/14/234-6 IOLR, cited in Voight (1987, p. 66).
37. Appreciation by J. Thorne, 5 April 1946, *TP* VII 60.
38. L.S. Amery to Linlithgow, 5 October and 14 October 1940, Linlithgow Papers, MSS Eur F 125/8; Note on Discussion of India at Chequers, 27 November 1945, PRO PREM 8/58.
39. L.S. Amery to Wavell,17 February 1944, *TP* IV 389.
40. Wavell to L.S. Amery, 9 February 1944, *TP* IV 364.
41. R. Prasad speech made on 21 June 1941, Rajendra Prasad Papers, 3-S/41 NAI.
42. Viceroy's Staff Meetings: Uncirculated Record of Discussion no. 6, 11 April 1947, *TP* X 119.
43. 'Note on the tour of the Reforms Commissioner from 8 November to 7 December 1941 to Madras, Orissa, Assam, Bengal and Bihar', undated, *TP* I 30 (Annex).
44. War Cabinet Meetings, 2 February 1940 and 12 March 1940, PRO CAB 30(40)4 and 66(40)2.
45. Wavell to L.S. Amery, September 1944, *TP* V 19; Wavell to W.S. Churchill, 24 October 1944, *TP* V 64.
46. E. Bevin to C.R. Attlee, 1 January 1947, *TP* IX 236.
47. C.R. Attlee to E. Bevin, 2 January 1947, *TP* IX 243.
48. S. Ghosh to R.S. Cripps, 31 October 1946, Cripps Papers, PRO CAB 127/129.
49. R.G. Casey, *Diary* entry for 24 November 1945, Photo. Eur 48/4 IOLR, extracts reprinted in *TP* VI 235.
50. J. Nehru to V. Pandit, 26 July 1945, reprinted in S. Gopal (1972–82), vol. 14, p. 61; see also his speech at Patna, 24 December 1945, ibid., p. 280.

51. V. Patel to Viswanathan, 1 March 1946, reprinted in Nandurkar (1977, vol. 1, p. 168).
52. R.S. Cripps, *Diary of the Cabinet Mission*, copies in the possession of Sir Maurice Shock and Nicholas Owen, entry for 30 March 1946; 3 April 1946, pp. 11, 17. On the 'Bombay incidents', see Sarkar (1983, pp. 423–5).
53. B. Glancy to Wavell, 16 August 1945, *TP* VI 29; Banning Richardson to C.R. Attlee, 25 March 1946, Attlee Papers, MSS Attlee dep. 34/132-4, Bodleian Library, Oxford.
54. Jamil-ud-Din Ahmed to M.A. Jinnah, 29 May 1946, Jinnah Papers, QAP/10/ 1092, p. 429, cited in Jalal (1985, p. 208).
55. Note by F. Mudie, undated, *TP* VIII 213.
56. J. Nehru to R.S. Cripps, 3 December 1945, Cripps Papers, PRO CAB 127/143.

References

Arnold, David (1986), *Police Power and Colonial Control: Madras 1859–1947*, Oxford, Oxford University Press.
Bridge, C.R. (1986), *Holding India to the Empire*, London, Oriental University Press.
Brown, J.M. (1989), *Gandhi: Prisoner of Hope*, Oxford, Oxford University Press.
Ewing, Ann (1982), 'Administering India: the Indian Civil Service', *History Today*, vol. 32, no. vi, pp. 43–8.
Gallagher, J.A. (1984), *The Decline, Revival and Fall of the British Empire*, Cambridge, Cambridge University Press.
Gilmartin, David (1988), *Empire and Islam: Punjab and the Making of Pakistan*, Oxford, Oxford University Press.
Gopal, S. (1972–82), *Selected Works of Jawaharlal Nehru*, First Series, Hyderabad, Orient Longman.
Gupta, P.S. (1987), 'Imperial strategy and the transfer of power, 1939–51', in A.K. Gupta (ed.), *Myth and Reality: The Indian Freedom Movement 1945–47*, pp. 1–53, New Delhi, Nehru Memorial Museum and Library/Manohar Publishing.
Gwyer, J.M.A. and Butler, J.R.M. (1964), *Grand Strategy*, vol. 3 (June 1941–August 1942), London, HMSO.
Henningham, Stephen (1983), 'Quit India in Bihar and the Eastern United Provinces: the Dual revolt', in Ranajit Guha (ed.), *Subaltern Studies*, vol. II, pp. 130–79.
Hunt, Roland and Harrison, John (1980), *The District Officer in India 1930–1947*, London, Scolar Press.
Hutchins, F.G. (1973), *Spontaneous Revolution: Gandhi and the Quit India Movement*, Cambridge, Mass., Harvard University Press.
Inder Singh, Anita (1984), 'Decolonization in India: the Statement of 20 February 1947', *The International History Review*, vol. VI, no. 2, pp. 191–209.
Jalal, Ayesha (1985), *The Sole Spokesman: Jinnah, the Muslim League and the Demand for Pakistan*, Cambridge, Cambridge University Press.
Low, D.A. (1977), *Congress and the Raj: Facets of the Indian Struggle 1917–1947*, London, Heinemann.
Mahajan, Sucheta (1987), 'British policy, nationalist strategy, and popular national upsurge, 1945–46', in A.K. Gupta (ed.), *Myth and Reality: The Indian Freedom Movement 1945–47*, pp.54–98, New Delhi, Nehru Memorial Museum and Library/ Manohar Publishing.
Mansergh, Nicholas (1976), *The Prelude to Partition: Concepts and Aims in Ireland and India* (The 1976 Commonwealth Lecture), Cambridge, Cambridge University Press.

Moon, E.P. (1973), *Wavell: The Viceroy's Journal*, Oxford, Oxford University Press.

Moore, R.J. (1979), *Churchill, Cripps and India*, Oxford, Clarendon Press.

Moore, R.J. (1986), 'The transfer of power: an historiographical survey', *South Asia*, vol. IX, no. 1, June, pp. 83–95.

Nandurkar, G.M. (1977), *Sardar's Letters: Mostly Unknown*, Ahmedabad, Navajivan Publishing.

Orwell, Sonia and Angus, Ian (1968), *The Collected Essays, Journalism and Letters of George Orwell*, Harmondsworth, Penguin Books.

Omissi, David E. (forthcoming), *The Sepoy and the Raj: The Indian Army 1860–1940*, London, Macmillan.

Owen, Nicholas (1991), 'Responsibility without power: the Attlee governments and the end of British rule in India', in N. Tiratsoo (ed.), *The Attlee Years*, pp. 167–89, London, Pinter Publishers.

Potter, D.C. (1986), *India's Political Administrators*, Oxford, Clarendon Press.

Roy, Asim (1990), 'The high politics of India's partition: the revisionist perspective', *Modern Asian Studies*, vol. 24, no. 2, pp. 385–415.

Sarkar, Sumit (1983), *Modern India*, Bangalore, Macmillan (India).

Seal, Anil (1973), 'Imperialism and nationalism in India', *Modern Asian Studies*, vol. 7, no. 3, pp. 321–47.

Talbot, I.A. (1982), 'Deserted collaborators: the political background to the rise and fall of the Punjab Unionist Party 1923–1947', *Journal of Imperial and Commonwealth History*, vol. XI, no. 1, pp. 73–93.

Tinker, Hugh (1988), 'The contraction of empire in Asia 1945–8: the military dimension', *Journal of Imperial and Commonwealth History*, vol. XVI, no. 2, pp. 218–33.

Tomlinson, B.R. (1979), *The Political Economy of the Raj 1914–1947*, London, Macmillan.

Voight, J.H. (1987), *India in the Second World War*, New Delhi, Arnold-Heinemann (India).

9 The rise and fall of a 'special relationship'?: Britain and Czechoslovakia, 1930–48

Mark Cornwall

In 1944, Edvard Beneš, President-in-exile of Czechoslovakia, celebrated his 60th birthday at his home in the village of Aston Abbotts in Buckinghamshire. To mark the occasion his friends decided to produce a small book of eulogistic articles, edited by the historian and close adviser of Beneš, Jan Opočenský. When published in early 1945, the book included contributions from William Temple, late Archbishop of Canterbury, from senior statesmen such as Robert Cecil and Eric Drummond, and from prominent British and American historians of Eastern Europe: R.W. Seton-Watson, A.J.P. Taylor, Robert J. Kerner and S. Harrison Thomson. It also contained an article entitled 'Czechoslovak–British Relations' by Richard Law, Minister of State at the Foreign Office (Opočenský, 1945, pp. 33ff.).

This chapter of the book was in fact written entirely by the Foreign Office, and therefore, not surprisingly, Opočenský viewed it as the most important contribution of them all. In February 1944, Richard Law had received an invitation from Jan Masaryk, Beneš's Foreign Minister, to contribute something on Anglo-Czech relations. Law himself had had few personal contacts with Beneš, so he passed the letter on to the Foreign Office. A discussion then took place there in the Central Department over the pitfalls of any study of Anglo-Czech relations: most notable, of course, was the subject of Munich, which Opočenský himself realized would be 'a bit tricky' to handle. The Central Department dealt with it by largely omitting any discussion of 1938 from the final draft. Frank Roberts, who felt the whole tone of the article was a bit too apologetic anyway, wanted a paragraph inserted about why Britain had agreed to the Munich settlement. But he was overruled by Oliver Harvey: 'this is not the time or the place to try and justify Munich to the Czechs'. As a result, the final version, while admitting that Munich was 'the low-watermark of British–Czechoslovak relations', merely noted that 'it would be superfluous, untimely and ill-judged to recall, at this stage, the detailed development of this unhappy episode'.[1]

The article sent off to Opočenský under Law's name was a brief survey of Anglo-Czechoslovak relations from 1918 to 1944. It summed up their relationship with the word 'healthy'. If in the 1920s it had been one 'of rather formal goodwill', with Britain genuinely benevolent but also disinterested in Czechoslovakia, the political and commercial contacts established had still begun at that time to 'weave themselves into a substantial durable fabric'. It was a friendship which had 'progressed and deepened' after Locarno, as more British businessmen than ever began to visit the country. And in the following years, the article asserted, the few differences of opinion over economic issues and reparations had been

> insufficient to upset seriously the development of fundamental goodwill between Czechoslovakia and Great Britain; the Czechoslovak people and press continued to express their high esteem for British institutions and for the high standard of integrity in British public and commercial life.

After 'the tragedy of Munich' and the creation of the Protectorate, there was born 'a feeling of remorse and profound sympathy for the Czechoslovak nation'. Now in 1944 Czechoslovakia was 'a trusted and respected ally'; British and Czech airmen were fighting shoulder to shoulder, Czechoslovak workers were engaged in British industry, the British government had finally renounced the Munich settlement and recognised President Beneš's government on British soil. Above all, 'ordinary Czechoslovak and British people have had the opportunity of seeing one another at close quarters, of getting beneath the crust of formal relationship and knowing one another as people with much in common.' Thus, according to the article, there had been slow but steadily upward progress in the relationship, a progress which was 'solidly based and essentially sound and there are good grounds for hoping that on such a foundation the existing friendship will deepen and endure.'

About four years later, on the eve of the communist *coup d'état* in Czechoslovakia, these sentiments could still seem quite realistic. One Czech newspaper—the Social Democrat *Právo Lidu*—actually wrote in January 1948 of there being a 'special relationship' between Britain and Czechoslovakia.[2] This idea had some foundation. It could be argued that for both of them Munich had been a fatal turning-point; then in the war years Britain had become the main seat of Czechoslovak resistance. It was also true that in post-war Europe, despite his alliance with the Soviet Union, Edvard Beneš envisaged his country as a bridge between East and West, with France and Great Britain as the chief western links. Moreover, for the British, if in 1938 the Sudeten question was the prime test for the policy of appeasement, in 1948 the events in Czechoslovakia seemed to close a period in post-war history: Soviet intentions were now laid bare and, in the Labour Party at least, attitudes towards Czechoslovakia became the touchstone of members' commitment to the principles of democratic socialism. The communist *coup d'état* caused the 'special relationship' to be abruptly cut off and replaced by 'frigid but correct relations' for the next forty years.

In the rest of this essay the three most significant aspects of Anglo-Czechoslovak relations in the 1930s and 1940s are surveyed: namely, British attitudes towards the Sudeten problem, the contacts made during the war years, and the nature of the relationship in the immediate post-war period. Can one really speak of a 'special relationship'? And how far can relations during these years of crisis be justifiably described, as in Richard Law's article, as 'healthy . . . climbing steadily towards the level of mutual respect and genuine friendship'? Certainly the contacts were to be enhanced rather artificially by the Sudeten crisis and the war years. But many of the criteria governing British and Czechoslovak foreign policy remained the same after 1945, severely limiting the plans of those in Prague or London who wished to reinforce the wartime links.

To begin in 1930 is no accident. For it was in that year that a new British envoy, Sir Joseph Addison, took up residence in the Thun Palace in Prague. Much has been written in the past twenty years about Britain and the Sudeten question in its international context; much less is known about the evolution of Britain's perception of the domestic Sudeten problem itself. The fact that the British Foreign Office and many other influential circles came to view Czechoslovakia's German minority as morally in the right, while the Czechs were the real nuisance for not solving the minority's justifiable grievances—this fact substantially aided Neville Chamberlain's approach to the crisis in 1938. Indeed, the moral argument, that one should support the oppressed Sudeten Germans, was the appeasers' counterweight to those who argued that the real moral dilemma was whether Hitler should be appeased anyway. As Sir Nevile Henderson (ambassador in Berlin) observed at the height of the Sudeten crisis in 1938: 'One may hate to see Germany encouraged: yet the moral principle is in the end of far far greater importance . . . The truest British interest is to come down on the side of the highest moral principle. And the only lastingly right moral principle is self-determination'.[3]

Sir Joseph Addison, who was British minister to Czechoslovakia from 1930 to 1936, was very much responsible for cultivating a negative view of the Czechs and their country in British official circles. In this he was markedly different from his predecessors of the 1920s, who had generally adopted a 'benevolent but disinterested' attitude, viewing the country largely through the spectacles of the 'Castle circle' around Masaryk and Beneš (Cornwall, 1991, pp. 314–21). Addison's appointment was to make 1930 something of a watershed in inter-war Anglo-Czechoslovak relations.[4] It was, of course, in that year that the economic crisis first began to affect Czechoslovakia more noticeably, reawakening Czech–German tensions: thus it was not surprising if any new British minister was more pessimistic than his predecessor. However, Addison brought to his post new prejudices as well as a new perspective. Some at the Foreign Office had long recognised him as an acute and well-informed observer, whose reports, often peppered with apt literary quotations, seemed full of amusing and perceptive asides (he was a brilliant mimic specialising in Japanese diplomats). Yet by 1930 Addison had become notorious for his pessimism and his habit of belittling the country in which he resided. Much of his outlook—especially his tendency from very early on to question the viability of the Czechoslovak state and to view the Czechs as inferior Slavs—undoubtedly stemmed from his career in the 1920s, when he had served seven years at the Berlin Embassy and two as the minister accredited to the Baltic states. In both of these appointments he had sensed the fragility of the Versailles peace. From Berlin he had detected a widespread German dislike of the Weimar Republic; from Riga he had predicted that it was only a matter of time before Latvia and Estonia were reincorporated into Russia.

The same outlook was soon to be found in his reports from Prague. According to the French envoy, Léon Noël, 'he could have played a useful and beneficial rôle in Prague . . . but he did not dream of doing so for a moment. For him the Czech lands were simply a myth' (Noël, 1982, pp. 134–5). In early 1932 Addison reported to the Foreign Office that Czechoslovakia was 'an artificial country' which could not be defended: 'You will have no peace, no confidence and no economic cooperation [in Central Europe] until the frontiers of 1914 are, more or less, restored.' In late 1933 he hinted again that the Republic in its present form might not be able to survive; it was, he wrote, like a patchwork quilt sewn together by an impatient *Hausfrau* and the slightest rent might ruin the whole fabric. Thus, four years before Munich, the British minster at Prague was suggesting to London that Czechoslovak frontiers might have to be adjusted in order to preserve peace. His arguments clearly acted as extra grist to the mill of those in London who favoured appeasement, all the more so because he went much further than his predecessors in underestimating the significance of Czechoslovakia on the European stage. She could, he wrote, 'only be a pawn in the game, dependent for [her] existence on the moves of the more important pieces' (Cornwall, 1991, p. 322).

Addison's pessimism about Czechoslovakia's future was based largely upon his pejorative assessment of the Czech authorities and what he felt to be their unjust treatment of the German minority. Instead of trying to create a purely Czech state by discriminatory and oppressive treatment of the minorities, the Czechs—who, he regularly stressed, were the real minority in the Republic—ought to be conciliatory on all sides. 'Czechification' could not even be justified on the grounds of revenge against former German oppressors, for Addison even went so far as to deny that they had been badly treated before 1918; they had, he admitted, been regarded as inferior by the Germans, but that inferiority was, and remained a fact.

Addison's racial prejudices were deep-rooted. While Bruce Lockhart, Commercial Secretary in the 1920s, felt that Czechs resembled 'the best type of Lowland Scot' (Opočenský, 1945, p. 83), Addison wrote to the Foreign Office that 'order, method, punctuality, honesty in dealing with one's fellow human beings are as alien to the Slav character as water to a cat'; he joked to the French minister in Prague that he would go out for a walk in the city only when Czechs had ceased to live there. He saw no reason to be diplomatic in his language: when Elizabeth Wiskemann lunched with him in 1935 she noted how he 'seemed obsessed with the traditional German view that Germans were gentlemen and Czechs were not' (Wiskemann, 1968, p. 77). Four years later at a dinner party in London he informed his fellow-guests 'that he [had] succeeded that day in preventing his Club from electing as a member "a dirty little Czech Jew" by threatening to resign.' Sir Stephen Spender, who was present on this occasion, thought of retorting, 'I thought we were fighting this war against people who hold views like yours, Sir Joseph' (*Weekend Guardian*, 11 February 1989, p. 3).

In 1931, in his first annual report to the Foreign Office, Addison pointed out that Czechoslovakia's minority problems had in no way been solved. There was subtle discrimination: the state's whole machinery was run exclusively in the Czech interest, with the aim of furthering Czech predominance. While his predecessors would have accepted this with the proviso that, to a large extent, 'Czechification' was necessary in order to consolidate the Republic and integrate a troublesome German minority, Addison himself, partly because of his anti-Slav prejudices, painted the whole picture from a difficult angle. The Foreign Office was encouraged to believe that Czech authorities had always been needlessly provoking the German population and that therefore it was the Czechs above all who should be blamed for any German grievances or any increase in Czech–German tension. Since Addison wrote very little about the German activists (those who cooperated with the government) and dwelt instead on the signs of Czech–German conflict, his pessimistic and anti-Czech outlook was quickly accepted by the Foreign Office. Even when he reported the growth of Nazism in Czechoslovakia in 1932, he described Czech chauvinism as an equally dangerous if not greater evil, so that London concluded that the *Volksport* trial and other actions to pre-empt Nazism were simply more evidence of unnecessary Czech 'petty persecution'.

The standard legation argument in the following years was that the Sudeten movement under Konrad Henlein was not fostered by the German Reich but was a natural reaction to unjustifiable Czech behaviour. In this way Addison, and his faithful deputy Robert Hadow, paved the way for those at the Foreign Office and elsewhere who, whether real appeasers or not, could argue that it was the Czech regime which was the real culprit in providing Nazi Germany with an excuse to intervene in Czechoslovakia's affairs. The legation consistently played down the influence of Berlin, emphasising instead that the economic crisis was at the root of the problem, a crisis exacerbated by the Czechs through their preference for agrarian interests and their increasingly discriminatory behaviour; it was the Czechs who had stimulated the dormant racial antagonism and produced a logical closing of German ranks in Henlein's *Sudetendeutsche Partei* (SdP).

Some at the Foreign Office shared Edvard Beneš's view that Henlein from the start was simply a camouflaged Nazi. Others—who mattered more, like Robert Vansittart and Orme Sargent—soon disagreed. By mid-1935, Sargent, for instance, was convinced not only that the SdP was not Nazi, but that it was a moderate movement which, as a result of Henlein's stunning victory in the May elections, was thoroughly representative of the German minority. Both conclusions placed the Czechs in a bad light: they could now be seen as overreacting, needlessly provoking a major section of their population, facilitating rather than thwarting Germany's ambitions and thereby endangering European peace. With Addison constantly portraying the SdP as the 'Cinderella of the Czechoslovak household', the stage was set for the Foreign Office to be very receptive to overtures from the Sudeten leaders.

After the May elections the SdP proceeded with a clear goal of internationalising the Sudeten problem. It turned particularly to Britain which, in contrast to France, preserved a positive image among the moderate Sudeten leaders. Here must be mentioned the contacts, begun in 1934, between

Colonel Graham Christie, former air attaché in Berlin and member of the Intelligence Service, and Heinrich Rutha, Henlein's principal adviser on foreign issues and a prominent activist in several European minority and nationality organisations. Christie, through his contacts in high places, was largely responsible for organising Konrad Henlein's four visits to Britain between 1935 and 1939 and certainly contributed to that trust of Henlein which permeated much of British officialdom. Even in May 1938 Sir Archibald Sinclair told a newspaper that 'Herr Henlein is a mutual friend of Mr Churchill and myself' (Luh, 1991, p. 368).

However, the role of the British legation in Prague also needs to be emphasised as crucial in moulding the British outlook. In December 1935, for example, the Foreign Office hastened to get confirmation from Addison that the SdP had, as Henlein said, no links to the Nazis but that it could easily fall under dangerous radical influences if his moderate demands were not met in the near future. Not surprisingly, Addison did not dissent. Henlein seemed to be 'moderate, a man of his word', who in the face of Czech persecution had finally turned to the British for support. Addison continued, in typically vivid language: 'On these barley loaves and small fishes Herr Henlein's disciples are now endeavouring to feed their hungry multitudes. But the winter is upon them and the age of miracles is, in Czech estimation, already past.' Britain, Addison emphasised, should respond to the plea from this modern Moses, for otherwise the Sudeten Germans would appeal to Germany with disturbing consequences (Cornwall, 1991, p. 326).

As a result of this advice, the British began to press President Beneš to settle the Sudeten problem and at the same time directed the British press to publish Henlein's complaints. The Foreign Office was, nevertheless, aware of the perils of Britain interfering in an essentially Czechoslovak affair. There was the danger that too much British interest in the question might, as Addison warned, implicate Britain too far in an area of Europe where her vital interests were not directly affected. There was also the danger that too much British interest would simply play into Hitler's hands by further internationalising what would best be solved as a domestic Czechoslovak concern. On this point one might well argue that the Foreign Office had been doing just that, and doing so long before 1938 when the Sudeten question first really came to the attention of the British press and public. The official assurances of sympathy made to Henlein on his visits, even if they were made off the record, clearly encouraged him and they also had their effect on the outlook of the Nazi leaders; they thereby contributed to that internationalising of the Sudeten problem which the Foreign Office was expressly trying to avoid.

Admittedly, the Foreign Office was not the only receptive audience in Britain, nor were Henlein's visits the only examples of Sudeten propaganda successes in these years. In the summer of 1936, for example, Heinrich Rutha headed a Sudeten delegation to Britain to attend, amongst other things, the European Nationalities Congress in London. He reported enthusiastically back to Henlein that he had had very successful contacts with the Foreign Office, with some knowledgeable academics like R.W. Seton-Watson, C.A. Macartney and Elizabeth Wiskemann, with a host of MPs—including

Archibald Sinclair, Harold Nicolson and Duncan Sandys—and with several British newspapers: the ground, he concluded, had been thoroughly prepared for England to resume an active interest in minority issues.[5] If from the British point of view such contacts threw new light on a possible powder keg of the future, from Henlein's point of view they emboldened him in two ways: firstly, they gave him a weapon to use against radicals in his own party who wanted to rely wholly on Germany, and secondly they encouraged him to hold out against Czech intransigeance.

They also, of course, made the Czech authorities, including Beneš himself, both more suspicious of Sudeten disloyalty and more wary of any official advice being proffered by the British. But here in any case the Foreign Office soon faced considerable difficulties. By July 1936 they were aware that there were few ways by which they could influence the Czechs. Most significantly, Addison, because of his constant criticism of the Czechs, was resented in Prague and totally ineffectual as a counsellor. A few years earlier Beneš had complained about him to Sir John Simon in Geneva (Noël, 1982, p. 136). By October 1936 Vansittart himself was afraid 'that Sir J. Addison has never had much influence at Prague; indeed, to be plain, he has had none, probably because he is too penetrating in mind—and word' (Cornwall, 1991, p. 328).

In contrast, Addison had exercised considerable influence in moulding the Foreign Office view of the Sudeten question. Although he retired in late 1936 his view survived, perpetuated in 1937 by his deputy Robert Hadow who regularly stressed the need for British pressure on President Beneš. In March 1937 Sir Basil Newton became the new minister, a man described by Bruce Lockhart as having 'an almost judicial impartiality, a quality . . . unfortunately not possessed by all previous British Ministers in Prague' (Lockhart, 1938, p. 264). However, one may question whether Newton was or could be really impartial when dealing with the Sudeten problem. He was plunged into an environment where most of his colleagues in Prague and London had already convinced themselves that the Czechs were morally in the wrong. He himself was indeed a staunch anti-Nazi, but he had read and accepted much of what Addison had written about Czechoslovakia's German minority. It can, of course, be argued that many of Addison's reports about Czech discrimination, were wholly accurate and that he showed remarkable foresight of the potential international dangers of Czech–German tension. But this 'penetrating' outlook—as Vansittart termed it—was always mixed up with a good deal of racial prejudice, a tendency to make exaggerated and pessimistic judgements, and an inclination, as a result, to appease the Sudeten Germans and Germany herself. Not surprisingly, when the Foreign Office was considering personnel to take part in the Runciman mission to Czechoslovakia in 1938, Addison's name (suggested by Sir Nevile Henderson) was rejected, for it was bound to provoke Czech hostility.[6]

Despite Addison's views, the Foreign Office, as long as Eden and Vansittart were in control, stopped short of actively suggesting to Hitler that Germany had any legitimate interest in Czechoslovak affairs. British action until 1938 was confined to urging the Czechs to alter their 'immoral behaviour'. Thus Newton was told to counsel moderation in Prague 'not because that will make [a Czech] agreement with Germany possible, but because it will put Czechoslovakia right in the eyes of the world, and at the same time strengthen her internally in case of trouble ahead' (Cornwall, 1991, p. 331). The idea that Beneš and the Czechs were dragging their feet while the Sudeten Germans had legitimate grievances was well established by December 1937 when the British Cabinet discussed the Sudeten problem for the first time. It was a view accepted without question by Chamberlain—for much of his information about Czechoslovakia at the start of the crisis stemmed from the Foreign Office or directly from Addison's reports (Wheeler-Bennett, 1966, p. 51)—and it provided him in the months ahead with a fundamental moral argument to support his policy towards Hitler. Where Chamberlain's outlook differed from that of Eden and Vansittart was not on the point of how the Czechs treated their German minority, but on the wider question of how the problem should be solved in order to preserve European peace.

Here Chamberlain took the internationalisation of the Sudeten question a stage further. The dispatch of Lord Runciman to try to mediate a settlement in August 1938 has interesting parallels with Britain's previous contacts with Konrad Henlein. In both cases the British were ostensibly posing as impartial neutrals; but in both cases their sympathies, because of the Nazi threat, were very much in the Sudeten camp; and in both cases British intervention tended to make the interested parties (in Prague, Berlin and the SdP) more intransigeant, thereby heightening tension and playing Hitler's game. Lord Runciman on his arrival in Prague announced that he came 'as an independent person, acting with no instructions, and free from prejudice'. In fact he was in regular touch with the Foreign Office and, most importantly, he was viewed on all sides as a British official representative. He himself could not ignore the Nazi shadow hanging over his mission. It convinced him that since a settlement depended on Hitler's aims, it was hardly likely that any agreement satisfactory to the Czechs would produce peace. Indeed, Runciman undoubtedly knew Lord Halifax's opinion, that Britain would find it 'very embarrassing' if his mission ended by blaming the SdP for the lack of settlement.[7] His own role as mediator was circumscribed by the international situation. It was bound to be the Czechs—a 'pig-headed race' as Henderson called them[8]—who needed to be seen to back down in the face of German demands. And the very fact that Runciman was dealing with the Czech government and the SdP as equal parties in the dispute was clear evidence in itself as to where British interests really lay.

Edvard Beneš had certainly been aware of this danger as soon as Newton proposed the Runciman mission to him; for as he told Newton at the end of July, 'if the [*Sudetendeutsche*] party were to be put on an equal footing with [the] Government it would mean that [the] Government were no longer sovereign' (Luh, 1991, p. 357). However, now as later, Beneš bowed to British pressure: he believed, wrongly, that his own cooperation would favourably impress the British and, even more wrongly, that it was to Czechoslovakia's advantage if Britain took responsibility for the negotiations and their outcome.[9] He ordered that Runciman—'distinguished foreigner', as he termed him—should be received with complete openness; his secretary Jaromír Smutný was to meet him at the railway station and flowers were to be left at the hotel for Lady Runciman. On 3 August Smutný noted down a description of his first sight of Runciman at Prague's Wilson station:

> An old gentleman [who] appears rather like a grandfather . . . represents a type of clever Englishman, a kind of educated man of the street. And one part of his mission is indeed to gain for all English men of the street a view on the question which is worrying them. According to this view, Runciman will then find a way to a solution, especially a way along which English policy can proceed in this matter.[10]

The Runciman mission was perhaps the high point of the special contacts which had developed in 1938 if not earlier between Britain and Czechoslovakia. But these could hardly be said to constitute a 'healthy relationship'. Beneš himself continued to be optimistic about Britain's attitude, feeling that she would not permit Germany to dominate Europe from Berlin to Baghdad; in fact, it was partly his own strong commitment to the western powers which resulted in his overestimating the degree of British support for Czechoslovakia in the months after the *Anschluß* (see Wallace, 1960). Jan Masaryk, the affable Czechoslovak minister in London, was a bit more realistic. Sensing that Czechoslovakia's position had worsened with Eden's resignation, he painted a gloomy picture of those controlling British policy. 'The English', he wrote on 4 June 1938, 'dislike us intensely. We are only dead-weight for them and they curse the day on which we were founded [as a state]. Hence our worth for England is completely negative (nuisance value).' As for the British leaders:

> conversation with Chamberlain is very difficult—he is narrow-minded, and his ignorance is stupendous [*velkolepá*]. With Halifax I have personally managed quite well, but he too is a peculiar type of combination of Albion and mystic.[11]

For most 'men in the street' in Czechoslovakia who had never met an Englishman, 1938 was the year when Britain came to their attention. Yet it is important to note that before this, in several fields, the ties had been steadily growing. Anglo-Czech economic contacts were not at all insignificant; by 1937 they were on the increase, Czechoslovakia exporting over 700 million crowns of goods to Britain which was her third largest trading partner.[12] Culturally, too, great strides forward had been made as French prestige diminished. Whereas in 1919 few people knew English, by 1938, according to one observer, many young Czechs in Prague spoke English and more than 50 per cent of foreign books were in English (Lockhart, 1938, pp. 291–2). From the time of the *Anschluß*, the British connection acquired a more political dimension, with educated Czechs adopting a hopeful or resentful attitude to Chamberlain's efforts to keep the peace.

Similarly, it was only in 1938 that Czechoslovakia really received attention in Britain. From the 1920s the works of Karel Čapek had appeared increasingly on the British book market (Polišenský, 1968, p. 71), but had clearly reached a very limited audience. Only in 1938 did the Sudeten problem become important for the British Cabinet, let alone for the British press or public. For most people, their attitude towards Hitler and peace were the touchstones of their attitude towards the Czechoslovak state; those who were for or against Chamberlain's behaviour could both justify their position in terms of British state interests and on moral grounds. And the moral thread, as we have seen, ran through the Sudeten question itself as well, lending weight to both positions. Thus while R.W. Seton-Watson's wife, visiting the Czechoslovak Sokol festival in July 1938, could observe *'liberté, égalité, fraternité* in action' (Seton-Watson, 1991, p. 341), others who had also had direct experience of Czechoslovakia had an entirely different perception: Sir Joseph Addison at this time was even writing anonymous letters to *The Times* protesting at Czechoslovakia's existing borders.[13] Some, like the historian Arnold Toynbee, would put their faith in Henlein after seeing the economic distress of the Sudetenland at first hand;[14] others, like Richard Crossman, visiting the country in May 1938 as a correspondent of the *Daily Herald*, ended up speaking on German Social Democrat platforms in the local election campaign.[15]

Indeed, the issue of Czechoslovakia cut through the British political scene, dividing those who had no direct experience of the Sudeten problem. The divisions were clearly evident in the House of Commons debate on Hitler's invasion of Prague on 15 March 1939. A number of Conservatives described Czechoslovakia as 'an unfortunate country cobbled together by the Treaty of Versailles' whose frontiers 'bore as little relation to justice as the act of the German Government now under discussion'. For Labour, however, Hugh Dalton—to Conservative jeers—spoke of 'that once free and happy model democracy in Central Europe', while Ellen Wilkenson claimed that the Sudeten Germans and the Slovaks had been Europe's 'best treated minorities' (*Hansard*, vol. 345, cols. 478, 481, 503, 536). The arguments of neither side in the debate were strictly accurate, for the Sudeten question had never been a clear-cut issue for British policy-makers. But by 1939 Czechoslovakia had secured a unique and sensitive place in the evolution of British appeasement policy, one which critics now exploited while British officialdom was anxious to push the whole subject under the carpet.

Britain continued to recognise the rump state of Czecho-Slovakia and, after March 1939, gave *de facto* recognition to independent Slovakia, allowing a Slovak consul to reside in London for a few months in the summer. But it was during the war that the British link resumed a special significance: firstly, because Britain became the main refuge for those fleeing from Czechoslovakia; secondly, because she became the principal centre for Czechoslovak resistance abroad, centred around Edvard Beneš's government-in-exile.

Peter Heumos has calculated, in his comprehensive study of Czechoslovak emigration, that out of 42,000 'Czechoslovak' émigrés about one-third eventually ended up in Britain. While 10,000 of these were civilians, 4,000 were members of the armed forces, most of whom were evacuated to Britain after the fall of France. Perhaps most interesting is Heumos's ethnic breakdown of the emigration: over 80 per cent of the civilians were Sudeten Germans or German Jews. This undermines any claim by Beneš to represent

the majority of émigrés for, even if Czechs dominated both the Czechoslovak
Brigade and the air squadron, they numbered at most only 2,000 civilians
(Heumos, 1989, pp. 207–8).

Immediately after Munich it was clear that Britain, because of its relatively
liberal immigration policies, would be the main destination for refugees.
While a number of charities—the Lord Mayor's Czech Refugee Fund, Save
the Children, etc.—as well as the Labour Party and the TUC began to
organise refugee work in Prague, the British government—though not the
legation in Prague—also assumed some responsibility for the situation. It
agreed to grant asylum to 350 Sudeten Germans who were in 'immediate
danger' and negotiated a loan to Czecho-Slovakia of £12 million, £4 million of
which was to be spent on financing emigration. By March 1939 about 1,100
'Czechoslovak' citizens, mostly Sudeten Germans, had arrived in Britain.
The refugee organizations, however, faced increasing obstacles. Apart from
the difficulty in 1939 of organising large-scale emigration from a new base in
Poland, the work was constantly in financial straits as well as coming up
against restrictions from the Home Office. The Home Office, for example,
hoped for some time that Britain would be only a transit station for refugees
who were hoping, in its words, to 'dig themselves in in British territory'; it
continued to resist attempts by the Czech Refugee Trust Fund to extend its
work to cover Czechoslovak refugees in all parts of Europe. The Trust Fund
therefore devoted most of its time to aiding the refugees in Britain itself,
finding work or housing for them and financing its activities from the £4
million of the loan originally intended for the Prague government.

A large number of the refugees appear to have enjoyed a happy existence in
Britain. True, Jewish émigrés regularly encountered anti-semitism, communists were interned for two years and many Sudeten Germans, already viewed
with some suspicion, were increasingly worried about Britain's support for a
transfer of German minorities out of East Central Europe. The Czechs, too,
even if most of them found work, felt awkward in the new cultural environment and proceeded to establish their own cultural outlets, separate from the
Sudeten Germans but occasionally in harmony with their hosts—the
Czechoslovak–British Friendship Club, for example, had 1,500 members.
Indeed, many Czechs, if wary at first, seem to have viewed the British with
some admiration, especially after June 1940. Eduard Táborský, arriving in
England in April 1939, marvelled at the English discipline with litter and at
the 'typical "English countryside", resembling a cleanly-washed park'.
Although he deeply mistrusted the Chamberlain government, he soon noted
in his diary:

> Here then, on these islands is the key to our freedom. But England must hold firm
> so that we don't get another Munich. That must be our aim. And at the moment
> the signs for it do appear auspicious. (Táborský, 1947, pp. 131, 145, 155).

The same optimism was expressed by Beneš's Finance Minister, Ladislav
Feierabend, who received a typical British welcome on disembarking at
Falmouth in June 1940. 'The cool English phlegmatic atmosphere blew over
us': he and his fellow-Czechs were treated to a vigorous examination of their
papers while enjoying a cup of tea in a local golf club. There he read in *The*

Times of Churchill's determination to fight on. And after being transported to a pleasant quarantine camp in London, patrolled by friendly 'bobbies', he learned that President Beneš, too, had echoed Churchill's optimism in a radio broadcast to the home resistance. Beneš, Feierabend wrote in his memoirs, 'believed firmly from the beginning that we would win our struggle if we joined forces with the struggle of Great Britain' (Feierabend, 1986, pp. 135ff., 194).

From his arrival in Britain in mid-1939, Beneš worked methodically with typically precise aims: firstly, to gain British recognition for a Czechoslovak government-in-exile; secondly, to win assurances that the Munich agreement was invalid and that the British would support a Czechoslovak state within its old borders but with some transfer of the Sudeten German population. The first aim was achieved by the time that Germany attacked the Soviet Union: in December 1939 Britain had recognised Beneš's Czechoslovak National Committee as the representative of 'Czechoslovak peoples'; in July 1940 a provisional government was recognised; in July 1941 full recognition was granted. The second aim was believed by Beneš to have been secured in 1942: for by August the British Cabinet had agreed both to the principle of transferring German populations and that the Munich settlement was invalid; Beneš naturally trumpeted these statements as evidence of a commitment to Czechoslovakia's old borders. In fact the British were always hedging their bets, never prepared as long as the war lasted to be too precise about territorial details. Beneš's success depended on a whole range of favourable circumstances, some of which were outside his control. It was perhaps vital in securing full recognition that both Chamberlain and Halifax were removed from office; both refused to use the word 'Czechoslovakia' (Chamberlain had only ventured to restore 'Czechia' as a state). In contrast, Churchill and Eden were immediately more amenable. Equally valuable for Beneš was the fall of France: it meant the evacuation and concentration of the Czech armed forces in Britain and a much publicized participation of Czech airmen in the Battle of Britain (see Bohuš Beneš, 1942). In April 1941, when Churchill reviewed the Czech army in Warwickshire, Beneš used the opportunity to press the Prime Minister for full recognition; to lend added weight to the occasion the soldiers suddenly belted out 'Rule Britannia'. Bruce Lockhart, the official British liaison to the Czech President, noted that the lusty singing 'stirred the emotions of all present' and 'loosed the heart-strings of Mr Churchill. He descended from his car. He sang with them. His eyes welled with tears' (Lockhart, 1947, p. 115).

It was not the only leverage which Beneš used to push his case. Even more important was the information which he had been gaining for British Intelligence from his contacts with Prague; most notably there was the Wehrmacht agent Paul Thümmel (A-54) who, according to the British official history, supplied SIS 'with first class political and military intelligence during the first two years of the war' (Hinsley, 1979, p. 58). Beneš made much of his close relationship with the Hácha government in Prague, something to which the Foreign Office attached special weight when considering the possibility of full recognition for Beneš's government in 1941. At that time, Lockhart put Beneš's case to the Foreign Office, arguing that the

Czech people might be 'the spear-head of the revolt against Germany'. He went on:

> Since August 1940, Czech faith in Britain has risen steadily until today it embraces almost the whole nation . . . We have to recognize that during the seven years before the war British prestige declined in Europe, and nowhere more sharply than in Czechoslovakia. We have recovered much of the lost ground, but we must consider if we can afford to neglect an area which is exposed unceasingly to the propaganda of the enemy.[16]

For the Foreign Office these arguments, coupled with pressure from Eden and the news of imminent Soviet recognition, were enough to outweigh the scepticism—from the Dominions in particular—about any further recognition for Beneš's government. As for Beneš, he was thoroughly satisfied and turned his attention immediately to badgering the Allies about the Sudeten question and about the future international position of Czechoslovakia.

Many at the Foreign Office were always irritated by Beneš's methods of diplomacy and by his cocksureness. Frank Roberts, who remembered Beneš's behaviour in 1938, observed with grudging admiration on one occasion: 'Not only is Dr. Beneš convinced that he is and always has been right but he constantly proclaims this in his speeches.'[17] The irritation certainly increased when Beneš insisted on travelling to Moscow in December 1943 to sign an alliance with Stalin; not only did the treaty appear to Eden to violate the Anglo-Soviet 'self-denying ordinance' and to exacerbate the position of the Polish exiles in Britain, but it ostentatiously tied Czechoslovakia closely into the Russian sphere of influence.

Nevertheless, in the last year of the war there was still ample evidence that Beneš planned to keep a special link with Britain. It was perhaps significant that when he visited Coventry on 12 March 1944, while mentioning the pleasant Warwickshire experiences of Czech soldiers, he also pointed out the common experience of the towns of Coventry, Lidice and Stalingrad.[18] Elsewhere he was more specific, warning his new British liaison, Sir Philip Nichols, that he wished Czechoslovakia's liberation to come from both East and West and hoped for increased cultural and economic contacts with Britain in the post-war period. Nichols, like Lockhart before him, came to admire the President's tireless determination. He wrote to Eden on Beneš's 60th birthday that 'no other Allied statesman living and active today . . . has a comparable record'; Beneš was 'a convinced friend of the British Commonwealth and can be relied on to pursue doggedly what he terms a policy of balance between the east and west.'[19]

While this was undoubtedly true—and Beneš was undoubtedly sincere in declaring on the BBC that he was 'proud to have lived in Great Britain during her darkest and most glorious hour'[20]—the Foreign Office was justifiably worried about the President's ability to preserve such a delicate balance in the circumstances of 1945. The Czech government's Košice programme of April 1945 sounded some alarm bells for the country's future domestic and foreign orientation. Not only did it announce the suppression of the pre-war Agrarian party, something which Orme Sargent viewed as a 'first essay in totalitarianism', but it emphasized that the Soviet alliance would be the guiding light of Czechoslovakia's foreign policy. In contrast, there would be an 'especially close friendship' with France and only 'friendly relations' with Britain. Britain, in Nichols' words, received 'a somewhat perfunctory word of gratitude for her help during the war'.[21] Thus Beneš's vision of Czechoslovakia as a bridge between East and West was already being sabotaged by the Czech Communists in favour of the slogan, 'Alliance with the East, Friendship with the West' (see Kaminski, 1987). In the last weeks of the war Churchill himself realised the danger of acting too passively in dealings with Stalin over any 'shared occupation' of Czechoslovakia. As he noted to the Foreign Office, when Moscow refused to allow Nichols to join Beneš in Košice:

> What happens if the Americans get to Prague first as they seem very likely to do? Will the Russians then tell them whether the American Ambassador may take a toothbrush with him or not, or will it be the western Allies who will determine the character of the United Nations representation in the capital?

In fact it was already too late. Eisenhower was leaving it to Soviet troops to liberate most of Czechoslovakia and, as Churchill feared, this was to make all the difference to the post-war situation in the country (Gilbert, 1986, p. 1322).[22]

Czechoslovakia was now once again moving outside the British sphere of direct influence. The British could only hope to make use of their wartime solidarity to reinforce the western end of the Czechoslovak bridge. This was the aim of Sir Philip Nichols, who now continued as the British ambassador to Czechoslovakia. He pointed out on the eve of his departure for Prague that, because of Czechoslovakia's 'vital strategic position in Europe', Britain should try to prevent her falling wholly into the Russian orbit. This might partly be achieved through helping to re-establish the Czech air force: 'a great spirit of camaraderie has been built up between Czechoslovaks and the Royal Air Force during the war and it would be a great pity if we were not able to nourish and maintain these feelings.' But secondly, Nichols felt, Britain should try to improve on her pre-war commercial links with the Czechs. And thirdly, by ousting France, she should try to assume 'a pre-eminent position as cultural guide in Czechoslovakia'.[23] The Foreign Office remained slightly sceptical of all this, but Nichols' plan was generally approved. A small loan of £5 million was already being negotiated as compensation for winding up various Czech financial claims from the post-Munich period. It now remained to be seen how far Britain could use the other few cards in her hand to counter Soviet influence.

There was a certain basic continuity in Britain's policy towards Czechoslovakia in the pre-war and post-war periods. At both times she was a country outside Britain's direct sphere of influence, too distant geographically. At both times she was viewed as a bastion of western democracy, but one seriously tainted from within, which might soon fall victim to an aggressive neighbour. At both times, because of this set of circumstances, Britain did not feel able to save the victim, but tried to alter a perhaps inevitable development. Most interestingly, as we will see, in 1947 as in 1938, though for different reasons, Britain tried to restrain the French from tying themselves too closely to Czechoslovakia.

But in other ways the Anglo-Czech relationship was bound to have changed. As with its attitude towards Poland (Rothwell, 1990, p. 159), the Foreign Office from 1945 accepted to a large extent the political and military realities stemming from Czechoslovakia's close ties to the Soviet Union. Starting from this basis, however, it still hoped to influence the country both culturally and economically, and believed it might be able to rely on President Beneš to keep Czechoslovakia balanced between East and West. After all, in his first speech in liberated Prague, Beneš made a point of coupling praise for the Red army with thanks to Britain for 'so much gallantry and perseverance'.[24] If British policy was now partly motivated by Ernest Bevin's desire to keep communism at bay, it also owed much to the special British–Czechoslovak relationship cultivated during the war—and now nurtured by Sir Philip Nichols in Prague.

Nichols was a highly popular ambassador, especially among those who had been exiled in Britain (Ripka, 1950, p. 36). He regularly pressed for more western interest in Czechoslovakia. 'It was clear', he wrote at the end of 1945, 'that the majority of the public, while subscribing to the pro-Soviet line on political and strategical grounds, felt themselves more closely linked with the west in all other respects. Contact with the Red army troops . . . reinforced this preference for western culture, habits and standards.'[25] Culturally, the British were not slow off the mark. While at the end of the war only Russian films were showing in Prague, British and American films soon began to dominate, aided by a British film festival in 1947. The British Council ensured that over a hundred British commercial and documentary films were shown in Czechoslovakia by May 1946 (*Hansard*, vol. 422, col. 1469). As for the printed word, the number of British newspapers sent out was daily 1,400 by the end of 1945. By June 1947, when Britain and Czechoslovakia signed a cultural convention, British periodicals were commonplace in Prague and the country had acquired the translation rights to about 150 English books (ibid., vol. 417, col. 1115).[26]

Economically, too, the prospects for British penetration were bright. In 1945 trade was almost non-existent, but by June 1947 Britain was overtaking the United States to become the leading source of imports—chiefly raw materials—to Czechoslovakia.[27] Admittedly, as the Board of Trade had warned early on, Britain was less able to buy the Czech semi-luxury export goods (she was ranked sixth in this regard), so that there was a considerable imbalance in their commercial relations. This in fact was a reversal of the slight imbalance in Czechoslovakia's favour, in the pre-war period. The postwar imbalance, however, was increased due to a number of British loans: following the state loan of £5 million in 1945, Hambros Bank supplied another million and £2.5 million was granted for Czechoslovakia to purchase surplus war materials.

While these credits underlined British interest, it was equally clear that commercial relations were constantly endangered by the growing East–West tensions. The Foreign Office in the face of these realities remained cool and objective. Thus, when Czechoslovakia was forced by Stalin to withdraw from the Marshall aid talks in July 1947, and both the British Treasury and Hambros Bank became jittery, Robin Hankey calmly pointed out that it was entirely understandable that Czechoslovakia had been bound to follow Russia's lead. He explained to the Treasury:

> The object of our kindly attitude towards the Czechs is to encourage all those who look westward for economic, commercial, cultural and other reasons to continue to do so and to preserve the strongest possible links between the Czechs and this country and thereby to weaken the success of Communist penetration there . . . I think this policy has yielded good results so far and we should like to continue it.[28]

This indeed was also the view of President Beneš and those around him who despaired of losing the western link. Writing in the *Financial Times* in December 1946, Hubert Ripka, the Minister for Foreign Trade, praised Anglo-Czech trade relations as 'a demonstration of sympathy by Great Britain's Labour Government with our own socialist economy', relations 'founded on our mutual endeavours during the war'. A year later in Moscow, Ripka buttonholed Harold Wilson, President of the Board of Trade, and secured an informal invitation to visit Britain in the New Year. By early 1948, for both Ripka and Beneš, a trade agreement with Britain was viewed as one of the last possibilities of keeping a window open on the western world.[29]

Yet cultural and commercial links were not a sufficient means of maintaining the western end of the 'bridge' so desired by Beneš. Indeed, it can be argued that this bridge was always illusory because of the amount of communist political control in the new Czechoslovakia. The British Foreign Office was well aware of this reality. But—most significantly—the Foreign Office itself was opposed to making any political alliance with Czechoslovakia. In other words, Britain was really not prepared to help Czechoslovakia act as a proper bridge between East and West.

There were several reasons for this. One was the nature of domestic conditions in Czechoslovakia. Churchill's fear, that Soviet liberation of the country would prejudice its post-war character, had become a reality. Nichols consistently pointed out from 1945 that the communists were the best organised and most influential of the political parties, something confirmed by their victory in the May 1946 elections. Communist domination could be blamed both for the extreme nationalisation measures, which injured British interests by giving no compensation, and for the harsh and rapid expulsion of the German population. The latter found a number of maverick defenders in the British Labour Party—for example, Fenner Brockway, and Richard Crossman who wrote personally to President Beneš on the subject. Admittedly, Nichols felt in 1947 that the Czech Social Democratic Party was showing some independence from the communists. But, on the whole he painted a picture of a rather unstable and communist-dominated country domestically, while in foreign affairs it definitely 'remained a satellite of the Soviet Union'.[30] In these circumstances it was hardly surprising that although Britain might seek to bolster her cultural and commercial influence in Prague, she remained very wary of any political commitment.

Nichols pressed for Britain to lend more support to western-orientated politicians, especially the Social Democrats. Many of the non-communists, perhaps including Beneš, were hoping that a Labour government would be particularly sympathetic to their brand of socialism. But Bevin argued that the Czech government should be treated with 'great tact' so as not to alienate the 'crypto-communist majority' (Barker, 1983, pp. 47–8). Instead he left it to the Labour Party to influence the Social Democrats. They were included in Labour plans for a new International—a rival to Soviet international influence. And when Denis Healey, as secretary of the Labour's International section, visited the Social Democrat congress in Brno in November 1947, he observed with satisfaction how a majority voted against fusion with the Communist Party (Healey, 1990, p. 87). Until the last, the Foreign Office prayed that these Social Democrats would not lose heart.

But Britain was unable or unwilling to do more than exercise indirect pressure. This had become clear in 1946. Ever since Beneš had signed an agreement with de Gaulle in August 1944, the assumption had been that it would eventually lead to a new political treaty between Czechoslovakia and France: hence the Košice programme had spoken of an 'especially close friendship' with the French. Klement Gottwald's communists were prepared to go along with this in 1946, but only because of the real possibility of aligning Czechoslovakia with a French government heavily influenced by communists. On 19 July he publicly announced that an alliance with France would soon be negotiated. At the same time, however, the Czech People's Party took the initiative. A young journalist Pavel Tigrid proposed, in a newspaper article approved by his party, that the alliance with France should be followed by one with Britain: thereby Czechoslovakia would indeed be balanced politically between East and West. Nichols himself sympathized with Tigrid, for a western alliance would emphasize Czechoslovakia's position outside the 'Iron Curtain'. But at the Foreign Office Sargent and Hankey were opposed, feeling that Britain would be drawn into a complicated situation if she had to fulfil her obligations as an ally. Moreover, the Foreign Office also quickly turned against the idea of a Franco-Czech alliance and worked against it throughout 1947; Bevin feared that, instead of Czechoslovakia being drawn into the western orbit, France was in danger of being lost to the East. Such an alliance might also thwart the possibility of a Four Power treaty on German disarmament. As a result, the British were themselves sabotaging the remains of Beneš's bridge to the West. Members of the Czech People's Party continued in mid-1947 to urge that an alliance was the logical outcome for Britain's close cultural and economic ties. But London was not to be drawn. As Sargent advised Nichols on 8 July, Britain would not be able to aid Czechoslovakia anyway because of her geographical location; and Czechoslovakia's withdrawal from the Marshall Plan made a British commitment in that part of Europe seem even less likely (Kaminski, 1987, pp. 445–63).

Despite this, British policy towards Czechoslovakia remained consistent until the communist *coup d'état*: its aim was, in Clement Attlee's words, 'to keep her from slipping behind the Curtain'.[31] By the end of 1947 Ernest Bevin was afraid that Prague was next on the Soviet menu, and decided to send his parliamentary private secretary Pierson Dixon to replace Sir Philip

Nichols (Bullock, 1983, p. 500). In preparation for his mission, Dixon on 16 January attended a meeting at the Foreign Office convened by Orme Sargent. Those present agreed that Czechoslovakia did indeed have a special role to play as a bridge between East and West and that Britain had to prevent her slipping further east. But, as in 1945, the means available to them were limited: they simply agreed that Britain should maintain as many contacts as possible, preserving the strong cultural ties, preparing for Ripka's visit and a new trade agreement and seeking, for example through Labour Party contacts, to boost the morale of non-communist parties. If the Czechs could be induced to stay independent for another few years, then the pull of a revived Western Europe might be even greater to them than at present.[32]

It was with these instructions, and a personal message of support from Bevin to Beneš, that Dixon arrived in Prague. The precariousness of the situation was immediately apparent to him. 'It looks to me', he wrote to Sargent, 'as if the edifice would collapse under a serious puff, but the Russians aren't really puffing yet.'[33] True, Beneš and most other non-communist politicians still pressed Dixon for the trade agreement and seemed fairly confident that democracy could be preserved as communist support was apparently waning. But Dixon was alarmed by the shakiness of the Social Democrats, and could also sense Klement Gottwald's sensitivity over the idea of contacts with the West. When he told Gottwald that Attlee, Bevin and Cripps had always been interested in Czechoslovakia, Gottwald replied sarcastically that 'this was a change from the attitude of Mr Chamberlain to whom Czechoslovakia was a remote little country.'[34] A few weeks later, a week before the *coup*, Dixon was convinced that Czechoslovakia would not be able to withstand any serious pressure from the Soviet Union. The reason lay partly in Czech defeatism after the Nazi occupation, when there had been a reflex swing towards communism. But it also lay in typical Czech resignation in the face of basic geographical and military realities. As Dixon observed.

> They are half-encircled by Russia and . . . they realize that Great Britain is ill-placed to give them effective help . . . The memory of Munich plays its part. The indignation once felt seems to have been erased or blurred by the comradeship in arms and the hospitality of our shores in the war: what remains is the reminder of our impotence to help them against a European aggressor and the knowledge that it would be still harder for us to help them now.[35]

This was, of course, the case. When the *coup d'état* occurred, Britain, in contrast to 1938, was not willing or able to interfere in Czechoslovakia's domestic situation. It could do nothing except cold-shoulder Gottwald's new government, preserving, as Bevin informed the Cabinet, 'frigid but correct relations'. Even the Three Power Declaration of 26 February, condemning 'the disguised dictatorship of a single party', was issued more as a warning to Austria and Italy than as a rebuke to Czechoslovakia. Yet the *coup* in Czechoslovakia in 1948, as in 1939, was something of a turning-point for the British policy-makers. It finally settled the arguments about Soviet intentions, and particularly within the Labour Party. True, there were a few extremists like Koni Zilliacus or John Platt-Mills who proclaimed the *coup* as a triumph for the working classes. But most of the party now rallied behind

Bevin's foreign policy, agreeing with the National Executive that 'the seizure of power by the Communist faction in Czechoslovakia closes a period in post-war history' (Bullock, 1983, pp. 531, 552).[36]

It also put an end to any special relationship between Britain and Czechoslovakia, for the period of 'frigid but correct relations' was to last for forty years, alleviated only slightly by fluctuating economic and cultural contacts. Certainly in the years after 1945 it had been an endangered relationship anyway, but the British, while realizing their limitations on the international stage, had still vainly hoped that their cultural and economic ties might keep them a foothold in the country. This was surely an illusion: their end of the Czechoslovak bridge was simply not strong enough. It was an illusion which derived partly from short-lived and sentimental Anglo-Czech contacts during the war. Indeed, if one can speak of a 'special relationship' between Britain and Czechoslovakia in these years, it was one which was bred by the crisis of 1938 and then artificially sustained during the uncertainties of the 1940s. In short, it was something of a 'brief encounter': it was always conditioned by the international situation, and enhanced but also limited by Czechoslovakia's geographical position.

Notes

1. See PRO FO 371/38951 for the relevant documents.
2. PRO FO 371/71302, Dixon to Bevin, tel. 39, 26 January 1948.
3. DBFP nos. 590 and 613.
4. Here I would query Gregory Campbell's view (1975, p. 348) that after the Franco-Czechoslovak alliance of 1924 'tension mounted in relations between London and Prague'. The reports of Sir George Clerk and Sir Ronald Macleay do not justify such an assertion; Clerk, after all, had recognised even in 1921 the reality that 'our interest in Czechoslovakia is more academic and benevolent than that of France' (Hanak, 1991, p. 62).
5. AKPR, T56/38, book B/16.
6. PRO FO 371/21729/7502.
7. DBFP nos. 583 and 587.
8. ibid., no. 551.
9. AKPR, T1627 38, notes by Přemysl Šamal, 26 July 1938.
10. ANM, Beneš Papers, 1938.
11. ANM, Mastný Papers, letter to Mastný.
12. PRO FO 371/65789/11256.
13. PRO FO 371/21729/7502.
14. PRO FO 371/21129/4023.
15. AKPR, D2981/47, File D, R791/47.
16. PRO FO 371/26394/4078.
17. PRO FO 371/38931, Nichols to Eden, no. 80, 14 June 1944, Roberts minute.
18. PRO FO 371/38931, Nichols to Eden, no. 32, 13 March 1944.
19. PRO FO 371/38931, no. 80, 14 June 1944.
20. PRO FO 371/47076/1973.
21. PRO FO 371/47121, Nichols to Eden, no. 68, 20 April 1945.
22. PRO FO 371/47121, Churchill to FO, no. M344/5, 16 April 1945.
23. PRO FO 371/41707/2839.

24. PRO FO 371/47076/5804.
25. PRO FO 371/56085, Annual Political Review for 1945.
26. PRO FO 371/65785/9430.
27. PRO FO 371/65789/11256.
28. PRO FO 371/65789, 19 July 1947.
29. See PRO FO 371/71283, Dixon to Bevin, tel. 81, 11 February 1948.
30. PRO FO 371/65785/7317.
31. PRO FO 371/71302/732, Dixon minute.
32. PRO FO 371/71302/732.
33. PRO FO 371/71283, Dixon to Sargent, private, 23 January 1948.
34. PRO FO 371/71302, Dixon to Hankey, no. 69/10/48, 29 January 1948.
35. PRO FO 371/71285, Dixon to Hankey, private secret, 13 February 1948.
36. PRO FO 371/71302, Dixon to FO, tel. 170, 28 February 1948; FO 371/71285/2547.

References

1. Archives and documents

Archive of the Chancellory of the President of the Republic, Prague (Archív Kanceláře Presidenta Republika—AKPR).
Archive of the National Museum, Prague (Archív Národního Muzea—ANM).
Documents on British Foreign Policy 1919–1939, Third Series, vol. II (DBFP), Woodward, E.L., and Butler, Rohan (eds), London, 1949.
Hansard, Parliamentary Debates.
Public Records Office, London (PRO): Foreign Office files.

2. Secondary works

Barker, Elisabeth (1983), *The British Between the Superpowers 1945–50*, London, Macmillan.
Beneš, Bohuš (ed.) (1942), *Wings in Exile*, London, The Czechoslovak Independent Weekly.
Bullock, Alan (1983), *Ernest Bevin: Foreign Secretary 1945–1951*, London, Heinemann.
Campbell, F.G. (1975), *Confrontation in Central Europe: Weimar Germany and Czechoslovakia*, Chicago, University of Chicago Press.
Cornwall, Mark (1991), 'A fluctuating barometer: British diplomatic views of the Czech–German relationship in Czechoslovakia 1918–1938', in Eva Schmidt-Hartmann and Stanley Winters (eds), *Great Britain, the United States and the Bohemian Lands*, Munich, Oldenbourg.
Feierabend, Ladislav (1986), *Soumrak Československé demokracie*, London, Rozmluvy.
Gilbert, Martin (1986), *Road to Victory: Winston S. Churchill 1941–1945*, London, Heinemann.
Hanak, Harry (1991), 'British views of the Czechoslovaks from 1914 to 1924', in Schmidt-Hartmann and Winters, op. cit.
Healey, Denis (1990), *The Time of My Life*, Harmondsworth, Penguin.
Heumos, Peter (1989), *Die Emigration aus der Tschechoslowakei nach Westeuropa und dem nahen Osten 1938–1945*, Munich, Oldenbourg.
Hinsley, F.H. (1979), *British Intelligence in the Second World War*, Vol. I, London.

Kaminski, Marek K. (1987), 'Velká Británie a československé pokusy o "most mezi Východem a Západem" 1945–1948', *Svĕdectví* Vol. 82.

Lockhart, R.H. Bruce (1938), *Guns or Butter*, London, Putnam.

Lockhart, R.H. Bruce (1947), *Comes the Reckoning*, London, Putnam.

Luh, Andreas (1991), 'Großbritannien, die sudetendeutsche Partei und das dritte Reich', in Schmidt-Hartmann and Winters, op. cit.

Noël, Léon (1982), *La Tchéchoslovaquie d'avant Munich*, Paris, La Sorbonne.

Opočenský, Jan (ed.) (1945), *Edward Beneš: Essays and Reflections Presented on the Occasion of His Sixtieth Birthday*, London, George Allen and Unwin.

Polišenský, J.V. (1968), *Britain and Czechoslovakia: A Study in Contacts*, Prague, Orbis.

Ripka, Hubert (1950), *Czechoslovakia Enslaved: The Story of the Communist Coup d'État*, London, Gollancz.

Rothwell, Victor (1990), 'Robin Hankey', in John Zametica (ed.), *British Officials and British Foreign Policy 1945–50*, Leicester, Leicester University Press.

Seton-Watson, Christopher (1991), 'R.W. Seton-Watson and the Czechoslovaks 1935–1939', in Schmidt-Hartmann and Winters, op. cit.

Táborský, Eduard (1947), *Pravda zvítězila*, Prague, Vydavatelstvo družstvení práce.

Wallace, William (1960), 'The foreign policy of President Beneš in the approach to Munich', *Slavonic and East European Review*, Vol. 38, no. 92.

Wheeler-Bennett, John W. (1966), *Munich: Prologue to Tragedy*, London, Macmillan.

Wiskemann, Elizabeth (1968), *The Europe I Saw*, London, Collins.

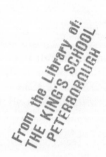

10 Change and continuity in British foreign policy towards Italy, 1939–48

E.G.H. Pedaliu

Italy's geopolitical position made it a major concern for British strategy and foreign policy in the inter-war, war and post-war periods. This essay will attempt to evaluate how far the war changed British policy towards Italy between September 1939 and 10 June 1940, resuming the story again in 1946 with the reunification of Italy under an Italian government, and continuing until the end of 1948 when Italy's pro-western orientation had been firmly established. These two periods have been chosen because they offer a clear picture of the themes of continuity and change in British policy towards Italy.

During both periods Britain was attempting to keep Italy away from an enemy: in the pre-war period from Nazi Germany, and in the post-war period from communism. In the first period, Hitler's fatal attraction proved to be too much for Mussolini to resist. However, in the post-war period, Italy was not lost to the enemy but to Britain's major ally, the United States. The war resulted in a change in the framework through which the two countries interacted. In the pre-war period, relations were based on the fact that the two countries were great powers, though Italy was so in name only, and that Britain was the major international player on the inter-war stage. In the post-war period, Britain found herself unable to match American power, as the United States adopted an interventionist policy in pursuing its anti-communist objectives.

Italy remained extremely important for Britain in both chronological periods, because of her geographical position and the significance this had for British strategy, namely the defence of the Middle East, the Mediterranean lines of imperial communication and the protection of traditional markets. These were traditional concerns and remained unchanged both under the pre-war governments and under the post-war Labour government: only the means of pursuing them changed. In the 1930s these concerns came under threat from Mussolini's increasingly rash behaviour over issues like Abyssinia and the Spanish Civil War, and in the post-war period once again seemed to come under threat from a different totalitarianism, in the guise of the perceived Soviet threat and the strength of the Italian Communist Party (PCI).

In September 1939, Britain and France declared war on Germany. After much dithering Italy found herself in the embarrassing position of declaring 'non-belligerency', a form of malevolent neutrality. Britain's strategy to defeat Germany was based on the concept of 'economic warfare'. This term was a new one but the concept behind it was the old and tried weapon of the English—the blockade (Medlicott, 1952, p. xi). The Ministry of Economic Warfare (MEW) was founded on 3 September 1939. Its main objective was to expose the vulnerabilities of the German economy and to cause such disruption to German imports that its industry would be unable to function smoothly, thus fomenting civil unrest (Medlicott, 1952, pp. 1–3). Only when economically weakened would Germany be given the *coup de grâce*, thus ending the war simply and without much bloodshed (Medlicott, 1952, p. 47). It is evident that British strategists were planning a kind of warfare based on the experience of the First World War. The blockade's potential to win the war 'by itself' depended upon how 'watertight' its application could be. The existence of the Nazi–Soviet pact, the neutrals who depended heavily on Germany, and Italy made such application problematic and rendered the blockade likely to leak 'like a sieve' (Einzig, 1941, pp. 19–28).

British policy towards Italy itself during this period was based on two principles. Having declared 'non-belligerency', Italy was to be treated as a neutral in relation to the blockade. Secondly, Britain strove to mitigate the strains caused by the blockade and to keep Italy out of the war through economic appeasement. It is extremely important to understand here the reasons why Italy did not enter the war on the side of Germany in September 1939, before trying to analyse the effect this two-pronged British policy had on Anglo-Italian relations during the 'phoney war' period. At this stage, Mussolini was still fettered by the Italian establishment (Knox, 1982) and fascism's inability to transform the 'race of sheep' into a martial people.[1] Italy remained non-belligerent because her armed forces were in no fit state to achieve the designs of fascist foreign policy. Mussolini was painfully aware of this. The foreign exchange reserves and fuel stocks were extremely low and completely inadequate for sustaining the country in a major war effort. To compound this, Mussolini and the King were aware, from police reports, that public opinion was strongly anti-German (Quarone, 1974, pp. 209–20). Throughout the last days of peace, Mussolini vacillated between pragmatism, which required neutrality, and opportunism, which meant belligerency. Realism and strong pressure from the Italian establishment led him to declare 'non-belligerency' and postpone, but by no means abandon, his plans for war until a more opportune moment (Knox, 1982). This would arise after a period of 'fat neutrality' as Ciano, the Italian Foreign Minister, called the 'conscious period of war preparation'. Thus Italy's declaration of non-belligerency in September 1939 must be interpreted as an attempt by Mussolini to gain time to prepare for war.

Italy's non-belligerency helped the British Chiefs of Staff to conserve their resources for a war with Germany. In the early days of the war the immediate objectives of British and Allied strategy were to keep the Western Front quiet for as long as possible, secondly to localise the war effort, and finally through the blockade to bleed away Germany's capability for aggression. Both the

CID (Committee for Imperial Defence) and the Chiefs of Staff Committee were determined to avoid the much talked-about worst-case scenario, namely the possibility of having to face the combined strength of Italy and Germany and the disruption Italy could create in the Mediterranean. However, Italian neutrality was taken to be of paramount importance for economic reasons. Both the Treasury and the Board of Trade were anxious to keep the Mediterranean open to maintain earnings from Britain's traditional markets.[2] The War Cabinet decided on 4 September 1939 that the overriding concern of Allied strategy towards Italy was to avoid provoking her (hence the decision not to press for clarification on what was meant by 'non-belligerency'; despite this, the blockade proved to be a major irritant in Anglo-Italian relations) and the British government bent over backwards in attempting to appease Italy.

By 5 September the Ministry of Economic Warfare, in conjunction with the Foreign Office, had decided that Italy's ships 'should be treated with the utmost courtesy and expedition'.[3] Britain intimated that she did not contemplate stopping Italy's seaborne coal purchases from Germany. Furthermore, it was decided that forcible rationing should not be imposed on Italy even at the risk of allowing supplies to go on to Germany.[4] The British blockade was thus imposed selectively at the beginning of the war, affecting only German imports.

Despite Britain's restraint, for Mussolini the whole idea of a British blockade was repugnant. It reminded him of encirclement, sanctions over Ethiopia and, even more disturbingly, the supremacy of the Royal Navy in the Mediterranean. Basic to his foreign policy ambitions were the concepts of '*mare nostrum*' and empire-building, and the determination to cease being Britain's prisoner in the Mediterranean. For Mussolini, 'the task of Italian policy [was] to first break the bars of the prison' and to expel the 'parasite' from the Mediterranean (Knox, 1982, pp. 39–40). The imposition of a British blockade meant that the Royal Navy was far from expelled as yet. However, he was willing to tolerate the situation as long as neutrality paid the dividends he needed. At the beginning, 'non-belligerency' seemed to bear fruit. The stock market boomed as did orders for Italian industrial and financial stock.[5] This idyllic period ended sharply in November when the stock exchange peaked and Italian foreign reserves plummeted once again (Toynbee and Toynbee, 1945, p. 218). Italy reawakened to the harsh reality that she was a net importer of foodstuffs and raw materials, and that she was heavily dependent for most of these, especially coal, on Germany.

By November 1939, Germany had started applying pressure on Italy to abandon its equivocal attitude towards the blockade. Hitler had expected Mussolini to oppose the blockade openly, allowing Italy to 'act as a funnel' for contraband to Germany. Germany also decided to make the blockade less damaging to its economy and restricted its exports of vital raw materials to Italy.[6] Such a policy filled the Italians with alarm as it might prove to have devastating consequences for the Italian economy. The Germans let the Italians stew for a month and then intimated that they could increase overland supplies substantially if Italy publicly denounced the blockade (Lowe and Marzari, 1975, p. 361).

Mussolini was not a man who took orders gladly, nor was he ready to precipitate a showdown with Britain, so he declined to bow to German pressure. However, from mid-October onwards, Italy's attitude towards the blockade stiffened; as for Italy acting as a funnel for contraband, it was widely known that she had done so from day one of the blockade.

As early as September 1939, Italy began to order large quantities of petroleum products, metals and cargoes of bauxite and foodstuffs she could supply from her own sources.[7] In October, further information arrived at MEW revealing that six cargoes of aviation spirit, aviation lubricant and about 42,000 tons of hemp were finding their way from Italy to Germany.[8] The French and British strategy to curb Italian re-exports to Germany was to buy up excess supply themselves.[9] From October, the British press began reporting such acts of Italian mischief, arousing the anger and consternation of the British public and back-benchers, led by official propaganda to believe that the blockade was 'watertight' (Einzig, 1941, pp. 19–26). The Foreign Office and MEW, however, decided to turn a blind eye to these reports and seek reassurances to the open and secret assurances from Giannini (Director General for Commercial Affairs) that Italy entirely prohibited any exports of petroleum and other re-exports to Germany.[10] Every time the Italians were approached about the leakage of contraband to Germany, Ciano and other officials pointed out that Mussolini was 'near boiling point'.[11] Faced with this situation, the British tried to appease Mussolini. Their objectives were first to minimise the problems the blockade was causing to the Italian economy and secondly to create the conditions which would render it politically and economically advantageous for Italy to remain neutral,[12] or, even better, prompt her to join the Allied bloc. The suggestion by Sir Percy Loraine (the British Ambassador to Rome) that trade might be a good way to achieve this goal fell on receptive ears.[13] Francis Rodd of MEW and Edward Playfair of the Treasury were sent on an unofficial visit to Rome to explore the possibilities of concluding a new trade agreement between the two countries to replace that of March 1938 (Medlicott, 1952, p. 284). When Rodd came back he reported that Britain should place large enough orders with Italian industries, and be prepared to import large enough quantities of Italian produce, to enable Italy to overcome her economic dependence on Germany.[14] This, it should be said, was an extremely tall order. In 1938, Italy imported from Germany 8 million tons of coal, nearly 75 per cent of its annual requirement; 67 per cent of its total imports of machinery; 48 per cent of its wool needs; 27 per cent of its iron and steel, and 22 per cent of its chemical pulp. Thus in 1938, Germany provided 27 per cent of total Italian imports. Germany in turn absorbed nearly 22 per cent of all Italian exports. By comparison, Britain and France provided only 19 per cent of Italy's total imports, while taking only 14 per cent of Italy's exports in return. Undeterred by this, Britain initiated trade negotiations with Italy in October 1939 (Knox, 1982, pp. 70–1; Medlicott, 1952, p. 283).

The bait for Italy was the prospect of obtaining essential British and French supplies.[15] On 6 December 1939, the War Cabinet approved a plan drawn up by Halifax and Cross for a comprehensive economic agreement with Italy.[16] This bold and Machiavellian plan meant that Britain would offer

8.5 million tons of coal in 1940, and, to make it easier for Italy to meet the cost, Britain would buy L20 million worth of Italian goods, including fruit, ornaments and munitions. As McGregor Knox put it, the plan was attempting nothing less than the 'economic conquest of Germany's ally' (Knox, 1982, p. 72). The draft was handed to Ciano by Sir Percy. Ciano raised no objections and on 17 December Mussolini announced that he accepted it as a 'basis' for further negotiations.[17]

By now it can be seen that Anglo-Italian relations were conducted on two levels during this period. Mussolini rarely met the British ambassador who came in touch only with Ciano, Giannini and other Germanophobes, and thus the British were led to believe that Mussolini could be swayed and become more amenable to their plans. In reality, nothing could be further from the truth. Ciano himself confided in his diary on 31 December 1939 that

> a war on the side of Germany would be a crime and a folly. Mussolini's point of view is exactly the opposite. He would never have war against Germany and when we are ready he would fight on the side of Germany against the democracies.

To compound matters even further, on 18 December the *Duce* instructed Italian aircraft manufacturers not to sell any combat aircraft or anti-aircraft guns 'at least for the moment,'[18] an order which totally undermined the basis of the British trade plan. Apparently London was playing a losing game and Mussolini let them continue playing for as long as it suited him.

The war trade negotiations had been devised as an appeasing mechanism for the ill effects of the blockade. These effects, however, could not simply be wished away. On 27 November, Britain decided to extend the blockade to cover German exports, too, because the Germans had broken international law through the indiscriminate planting of magnetic mines (Butler, 1957). This created serious anxiety in certain Italian circles as 6.5 million tons of Italy's German coal imports were sea-borne. If Britain were to stop German sea-borne coal deliveries Italian industry would face the probability of stoppage and her economy would collapse. Mussolini perceived this decision as another show of naval power in the 'sea of Rome'.[19] The British, aware of the feelings such a decision would arouse in Italy, decided to delay its imposition until the trade agreement that guaranteed Italy with the necessary coal was signed.[20] As the negotiations regarding the war trade agreement were running aground over the sale of aircraft and horticultural produce, the *Duce* was the only Italian who viewed the possibility of English coal not reaching Italy with relish. On 18 January, he said that when British coal no longer arrived in Italy it would be a good lash of the whip for the Italians so that they would learn to depend only on their own resources.[21] The British ambassador and delegation, however, were kept in the dark.

On 29 January 1940, the War Cabinet decided that further appeasement was needed. The British negotiators were instructed to go back to Rome and add to the £20 million already on the table £5 million for the purchase of horticultural produce. The offer, however, was conditional on the supply to His Majesty's government of the aircraft, guns and other equipment that had been under discussion since November.[22]

Mussolini turned down these proposals point-blank. On 7 February, he announced to Ciano that 'he refused to sell arms to Britain because he did not want to reduce the armaments that were at his disposal' and that he intended to fulfil his recently confirmed obligations to Germany. When Ciano tried to alert him to the dangers such a decision held for Italian industry and the Italian people, he bitterly replied: 'We must keep them disciplined and in uniform morning till night. Beat them and beat them, and beat them.'[23] On 8 February, Ciano communicated the *Duce*'s decision to Sir Percy.

Meanwhile, Mussolini had negotiated a far less advantageous agreement with the Germans (Lowe and Marzari, 1975, p. 363). Germany, despite her willingness to supply Italy with her annual coal requirements, declined to supply more than 500,000 tons per month by rail, exactly half of what Italy needed (Knox, 1982, p. 80). On 1 March, Britain began implementing her decision to seize German sea-borne coal exports. This produced angry official protests from the Italians.[24]

The downward spiral which Anglo-Italian relations had entered now seemed unstoppable. The final phase of the phoney war period was to be determined by Mussolini's increasing hostility towards Britain and his desire to intervene in the war (Lowe and Marzari, 1975, p. 363). Italian industrialists still keen to reach accommodation with Britain succeeded in convincing the British to send Playfair to salvage something from the trade agreement negotiations.[25] This time, British objectives were limited, but the chances of success were negligible. On 18 March, at the Brenner meeting, Mussolini reaffirmed to Hitler his intention that Italy would intervene, but at a convenient moment.[26] From this point onwards, Italian intervention could be only a matter of time.

The blockade had been a mere irritant and Britain's attempts to appease Mussolini had further compounded his opinion that Britain 'had become a hippopotamus, slow, fat, heavy, somnolent, weak in eyesight and even weaker in nerve' (Knox, 1982, p. 34). 'As soon as I am ready', he said, 'I shall make Britain repent. My intervention will be their defeat.'[27] It was not: it was fascism's destruction and Mussolini's end.

In 1946, Britain's position in relation to Italy was totally different from that in 1939. The war had ended the twilight of a multipolar world and given rise to an emergent bipolar world with the United States and the Soviet Union as the main international powers and ideological adversaries. Italy emerged from the Second World War a defeated, demoralised and almost totally destroyed country.

Britain had urged the Mediterranean campaign and the invasion of Italy on their American allies. In spite of the fact that the liberation/occupation of Italy was nominally a joint venture, Britain wished to be, and for a while was, the 'senior' partner in the post-armistice administration of Italy (Ellwood, 1985, pp. 1–3; Miller, 1986, pp. 50, 52, 77–8). In 1944, Britain had been forced to acknowledge that she could no longer maintain her status as senior partner in matters concerning Italy (Varsori, 1976), and from 1945 she realised that she could not even aspire to hold on to parity with the United States (Miller, 1986, p. 157; Ellwood, 1985). Hitherto, such an eventuality had not greatly concerned British foreign policy-makers. They had actively encouraged the United States to take an interest in Italian reconstruction, but had never intended that Britain's economic interests and political involvement in Italian affairs should suffer as a result. While painfully aware that their standing would have to be propped up by the United States, they saw no contradiction in still pursuing their global aspirations.[28]

Italy had been assessed to be important to British defence, strategic, colonial, economic and political concerns. As a Chiefs of Staff Committee memorandum of December 1946 put it:

> Italy's strategic position in the Mediterranean makes it important that SHE COULD NOT [*sic*] come under the influence of a potential enemy. Our Mediterranean communications could be seriously threatened from Metropolitan Italy . . . It is therefore to our military interests to have a friendly Italy who would look to Britain and Western Europe for support.[29]

The premises of this memorandum had been accepted by Bevin and the Foreign Office.[30] If Italy were not within the western orbit, safe passage through Suez would be threatened, British communications impeded and British interests in the Middle East undermined. Easy access to Middle Eastern oil was absolutely essential to Britain. Moreover, Italy had a population of 40 million people, which meant a potentially lucrative consumer market which Britain could ill afford to lose if she were to recover economically.

Thus during the period 1946–8 the twin primary objectives of British policy were to ensure that Italy would look to the West for its political orientation and to ensure that Britain would be able to maintain influence over Italian political and military affairs. All the areas of Italian reconstruction that Britain became involved in were intended to secure either one or both objectives. British policy towards Italy will be examined here in relation to two issues: the reconstruction of the Italian armed forces and Italy's place in the concept of a British-led Western Union.

Italy's need for cash aid and financial investment to keep it from collapse and to avert any serious domestic unrest which might play into the hands of the communists meant that only the United States was able to furnish the economic means for Italian reconstruction. The United States saw its influence in the area grow rapidly to the detriment of Britain's (Miller, 1986). Britain, unable to compete with the attraction of the dollar, decided that she could carve out an area of influence by maintaining and pursuing a strong interest in the reconstruction of the Italian military and police forces, and she was extremely well placed to do so. The majority of what was left of the Italian Navy, Air Force, Army and *Carabinieria* was under British control and supplied by British stores.[31] Furthermore, the Americans initially viewed this as a British sphere and up until the second half of 1946 did not pose a serious threat to British involvement.

The Foreign Office and the Service Departments — responsible for drafting a plan for the reconstruction and equipment of the Italian armed forces — based their hopes upon attaching a military mission to each of these forces.[32] These missions would train and provide part of the equipment for the Italian Army and also had the long-term objective of inducing Italy to become a client state for the British arms industry. This, it was hoped, would have the dual effect of improving the efficiency of the Italian Army and assisting the British export drive. The missions would also help Britain to maintain her hold over Italian affairs by consolidating the 'goodwill and influence' she possessed in Italian military circles.[33]

The idea of attaching missions to the Italian armed forces was not a new one: it originated in the wartime government, and it was endorsed by the Labour government soon after it was voted into office in July 1945. Bevin and the Foreign Office were extremely attracted to the idea.[34] When the Service Departments were approached on the plan, their response was uniformly favourable. However, each had reservations about the feasibility and practicability of such a plan under existing circumstances. Their reservations revolved around several complex issues. First, would Britain be able to overcome the bitter feelings the military clauses of the draft Peace Treaty had generated in Italian political and military circles? Secondly, would the Italian government be prepared to accept these missions, especially since British plans envisaged the missions being financed by the Italians themselves? Finally, how would the Soviet Union and the Italian communists interpret the attachment of such missions to the Italian armed forces and how would they react?[35]

In order to make the idea of military missions attractive to the Italian government, Britain planned to establish small missions with purely advisory and non-executive functions.[36] These missions would be worthwhile for Britain only if they could remain after the Peace Treaty was signed. According to the Peace Treaty, all foreign military forces would have to evacuate Italy within ninety days of its ratification.[37] Thus the British missions had a future only if the Italian government openly asked Britain to furnish such assistance. This was the main problem: having already once suffered the firm refusal of the Parri government on the grounds that acceptance of such missions would lead to the downfall of his government, Britain decided to try again with the new Italian Prime Minister, de Gasperi (Miller, 1986, p. 192). Throughout 1946, and for the greater part of 1947, the British hopefully awaited an invitation, basing their optimism on the fact that de Gasperi, a much stronger and wilful personality than Parri, was now in power and his conservative ideology was thought to favour British thinking.[38] Furthermore, this time the British were more aware of Italian sensibilities. The difficulties put forward by Parri in 1945 still existed in 1946. Italy was still governed by an extremely heterogeneous coalition, ranging from the conservative Christian Democrats to the communist PCI, whose foreign policy aspirations aimed for neutrality. The shape which the Peace Treaty was to take, and the fact that it was not to be a negotiated treaty, had generated much adverse feeling in the Italian government and in military circles, mainly directed against Britain.[39] With the Peace Treaty not yet signed, an astute politician like de Gasperi was neither going to jeopardise the existence of his government, nor to antagonise the Soviets. Even if all these obstacles could be overcome, the fact remained that the British plan envisaged that the Italian government would assume the financial burden of maintaining the missions.[40]

Initially, the Foreign Office aimed to sound out Italian feelings. Count

Carandini, the Italian envoy to Great Britain, favoured the idea. The Rome embassy was instructed to approach the Italians and to make it absolutely clear that the missions would have a purely advisory and technical role, and that 'they would have no intention to dictate policy'.[41] Throughout 1946 and up to June 1947, the Italians remained encouraging, but equivocal and uncommitted. While the Italian government kept the British waiting and guessing, Britain felt that she could eventually extract Italian acquiescence, as the Italian Army was generally standardised along British lines, and that in the final analysis the Italians would need, at the very least, training and technical assistance.

By 1947, the Foreign Office planners were becoming doubtful of ever persuading the Italians to request such missions. In March 1947, Sforza communicated the decision that the Ministry of Defence and the Italian government had decided not to accept the military missions. Nevertheless, the Foreign Office did not abandon the plan since the Italians had disguised their refusal as being dictated by fears as to how the PCI would react.[42] After the May 1947 exclusion crisis, and with the Peace Treaty signed, the Foreign Office hoped that the Italians would be more amenable, and produced new plans which it hoped Italy would find more attractive.[43]

Thereafter, however, the Foreign Office began to accept that the Italians were never going to invite the military missions, and it turned to the idea of training Italian officers in Britain.[44] The War Office was slower in adjusting to the changing circumstances, and as late as November 1947 still considered that the missions 'would also strengthen our means of retaining the Italians in the British orbit and prevent the Russians from supplanting us.' In their anxiety to keep the Soviet Union away from Italy, the British failed to see that they had already been supplanted by the Americans.[45]

From the moment that the United States adopted a more committed policy concerning the Italian armed forces, Britain could not sustain her influence without financing the reconstruction of the Italian Army, and this she was unable to do. Throughout the first half of 1946, the State Department had been at odds with the US military on how far they should intervene in reconstructing the Italian armed forces. The State Department was determined to reduce British influence in Italy, especially in military and police affairs. As late as August 1946, the US Chiefs of Staff had maintained that 'the American role in the Mediterranean theatre has always been that of a supporting one to the British' and that it was 'undesirable to disturb the present relationship'. The rapid deterioration of the internal security situation in the second half of 1946, fuelled by economic stagnation, food shortages and unemployment, helped the State Department line to become dominant, with the result that the United States decided to take over the reconstruction of the Italian armed and police forces.[46] It was under US tutelage and with US aid and equipment that the Italian armed forces were rebuilt and rearmed after 1948 (Cerquetti, 1975).

The turning-point for Anglo-Italian relations was in 1948. This was the year that Britain began to come to terms with the fact that American hegemony over Italy was nearly complete, but it was also the year Bevin launched publicly his Third Force idea, in which he envisaged a role for

Italy.[47] As John Kent has argued, Third Force, or the 'Euro-Africa' concept, was intended to overcome Britain's temporary weakness by enrolling France and the lesser Western European states as collaborators with the British Empire. The aim of such a policy was to aid Britain to regain a position of equality with the United States and the Soviet Union (Kent, 1989).

This year was also one of the most significant years in post-war Italian history. A general election was scheduled for 18 April 1948. This particular election would decide the future political orientation of Italy. Bevin was extremely concerned about the outcome of the election. If the PCI–PSI pact were to win, this would be disastrous from the British point of view. Foreign Office planners were alarmed at the prospect but they had realised that they had limited options in helping de Gasperi. However, with American hegemony over Italian affairs, they had little to worry about. The aid the United States afforded to the Christian Democrats and the Saragat Socialists was decisive and secured the victory of the anti-communist forces in Italy (Miller, 1986; Smith, 1983). Notwithstanding this, Britain continued to try to aid de Gasperi and his government to win and thus consolidate Italy's position in the West.

When Bevin met Sforza and the discussion came around to the Western Union and the development of African raw material resources, Bevin stressed the importance of the scheme 'not only for ourselves but even for America'. The programme would extend over at least twenty years, and he assured Sforza that 'in such a scheme there would be a place for Italy'.[48] Italian inclusion was viewed as a means of ensuring Italian political stability and its consolidation within the western sphere of influence. It would also draw Italy closer to Britain, safeguarding and preserving what remained of the waning British influence over Italian affairs. However, as Bevin had indicated, the scheme needed time to reach its maturity. As he told the Italian ambassador in London on 24 January 1948:

> There was not yet a cut and dried plan for Western Europe. [We] had to proceed step by step and if [we] had to put the Low Countries before the Mediterranean, this was a question of method and it did not indicate any ill-will towards Italy . . . [when the time was right, Italy] would be invited to participate on exactly the same level as other countries.[49]

Bevin was a shrewd politician and one could interpret the above statements as rhetoric. In this instance, however, this is not the case. There is no doubt that Bevin had hoped to build this British-led Third Force, but he needed time to put the scheme together. This was both because of Britain's weakness at the time and because of Italy's special and entrenched problems.

Italy's accession to the Brussels Treaty was obstructed by myriad complex problems. Until April 1948, the political situation in Italy had been charged and delicate. Italian public opinion was in favour of neutrality and remained so.[50] The PCI and PSI were active in advocating neutrality.[51] This made the Italian and British governments apprehensive since they believed that by pushing ahead with Italian inclusion in the Brussels Treaty, which was after all a military pact, they would play into the communists' and

Socialists' hands. Nenni (leader of the PSI), in a speech in Milan on 15 March 1948, likened the 'plan for a Western Union' to the Anti-Comintern Pact which had brought Italy into war in 1940. Sforza and de Gasperi also warned the British government that they could not commit themselves to the idea before the election.[52] Even after the Christian Democrats' election victory, de Gasperi told Victor Mallet (British ambassador to Rome) on 4 May 1948 that a 'future relationship of Italy to the Western European powers was a matter of great delicacy and needed most careful handling', as 'when the parliament met there would certainly be strong opposition to any form of entanglement.'[53] It was only after Sforza's speech at Perugia on 18 July 1948 that Italy became keen openly to associate itself with the Western Union, which by this time was in the process of being transformed into NATO.[54] The change in policy can be traced to A. Tarchiani, the Italian ambassador to Washington. He campaigned ceaselessly and indefatigably for Italian participation in the defensive alliance the Washington Exploratory Talks would give birth to. Tarchiani succeeded in convincing Sforza and de Gasperi that only by participating in the emerging alliance could Italy secure her territorial integrity and economic needs (Miller, 1986, pp. 266–8; Tarchiani, 1955).

Accession to the Brussels Treaty meant that Italy would have to share some of the military responsibilities for the defence of Europe.[55] The military clauses of the Peace Treaty and the state of the Italian Army rendered this almost impossible.[56] The Italian government, Britain feared, could use this opportunity to put forward more forcefully its case for wholesale revision of the Peace Treaty, and make it more insistent in requesting the return of the former Italian Colonies.[57] Thus Italy would not only be a military liability but also a nuisance.

The war brought great changes, but at the same time did not alter fundamentally the principal tenets of British policy towards Italy. Before the war, Britain and Italy interacted as sovereign states and powers. Their relationship was complicated by Britain's need to preserve her Empire and her communications through the Mediterranean, and by fascist Italy's need to build a Mediterranean Empire. Each believed that the other could influence critically its international strategic interests, hence Britain's attempt to appease Italy economically in the 1930s, and Italy's rejection of these overtures. Sir Percy Loraine's aphorism that 'if anything lost [Britain] the chance of keeping Italy out of the war it was the MEW and the Contraband Committee' is not borne out by the facts. What drove Italy and Britain apart were their inimical objectives.

The war brought the defeat of Italy and the victory of Britain, but also the supremacy of the United States and the Soviet Union in the world scene and the emergence of the Cold War. Britain and Italy found themselves entangled once again despite their reduced circumstances in the post-war world. Britain still viewed Italy as a vital factor in her foreign policy, defence and colonial interests. The war exposed British vulnerabilities and reactivated the United States on the international stage. As the United States became more interested in combating communism it simultaneously marginalised British influence in Italy. Britain's efforts to check this trend by becoming involved in projects such as the reorganisation of the Italian Army and the inclusion of

Italy in a British-led Third Force were in vain. By 1949, she had to reverse her policy towards Italy from one of involvement to one of detachment, under the aegis of the superpower in the West, the United States.

The war had changed the relationship of the two great powers from one of interdependence to one of Italian dependence on Britain initially, and the United States subsequently. However, during both periods under discussion, and despite differences in the international system, British policy showed remarkable continuity in attempting to coax Italy and keep it friendly or at least not actively hostile towards Britain. Britain failed in both instances to keep Italy within her orbit because of other international actors and circumstances. In the pre-war period, Hitler seemed to offer the *Duce* the best chance of attaining his dream of Empire. Later, it was the United States, with its milder behaviour and its enormous financial resources which could provide the means for the post-war Italian economic miracle and the basis of a pluralistic democratic regime.

Notes

1. PRO FO 371, R3835/86/22, 4 May 1939; see also Ciano (1947, 7 February 1940) and Mack Smith (1979).
2. PRO FO 837/5, MEW memorandum, 16 September 1939.
3. PRO FO 837/492, minute by Rodd, 7 September 1939.
4. ibid.; see also Medlicott (1952, p. 282).
5. Ciano, 5 September 1939.
6. PRO FO 387/491, tel. no. 937, Sir Percy Loraine to FO, 23 September 1939; see also Hildebrand (1973).
7. PRO FO 837/493, 3 October 1939, 12 October 1939.
8. PRO FO 837/493, tel. no. 4 from Sir P. Loraine, 14 October 1939.
9. PRO FO 837/492, minute by Rodd, 7 September 1939; FO 837/494, tel. secret, Sir P. Loraine, 23 October 1939, 26 December 1939.
10. PRO FO 837/493, Interdepartmental Committee Meeting at MEW, 17 October 1939.
11. Ciano, 10 December 1939; I.S.O. Playfair (1954, p. 40).
12. PRO FO 371/23818, memorandum, 1 September 1939.
13. PRO FO 371/23819, Loraine to FO, tel.
14. PRO FO 371/23798, report by Rodd, Rome 20 October 1939; PRO FO 837/492, ibid.
15. F0 837/492, 4 September 1939, 5 September 1939.
16. PRO CAB 65/4 War Cabinet Meeting, 6 December 1939; PRO FO 371/23866, R8860 Halifax memorandum, 4 December 1939.
17. PRO FO 837/496, Sir P. Loraine to FO, tel. no. 131 secret, 15 February 1940; PRO FO 837/495, Sir P. Loraine to FO, tel. no. 89, 8 February 1940.
18. *Documenti Diplomatici Italiani* (1952), 9th Series, vol. III, no. 146.
19. Ciano, 10 December 1939.
20. PRO FO 837/496 tel. no. 137, Sir P. Loraine to FO, 18 February 1940.
21. Ciano, 18 January 1940; *Documenti Diplomatici Italiani* (1952), 9th Series, vol. III, no. 146.
22. PRO FO 837/495, joint memorandum by Halifax and Cross, 22 January 1940; see also Medlicott (1952, p. 299).

23. Ciano, 7 December 1940.
24. Ciano, 3 March 1940; see also Knox (1982, p. 81) and Medlicott (1952, p. 304).
25. PRO CAB 65/6, WM 81(40), 4 April 1940.
26. Ciano, 12 March 1940, 17 March 1940, 18 March 1940.
27. Ciano, 6 March 1940.
28. PRO FO 371/66546, 'Stocktaking Memorandum' prepared by O. Sargent; see also Jebb, 1972.
29. PRO PREM 8/515, COS(46)43(0), 13 February 1946.
30. PRO PREM 8/66, ORC(45)23; PREM 8/515, 13 February 1946.
31. PRO FO 371/60622/ZM315/187/22, 24 Februay 1946; see also Miller (1986, p. 192) and *FRUS* (Foreign Relations of the United States) (1946), vol. 5, pp. 917–18, 940–1, 950.
32. PRO PREM 8/66, ORC(45)18, Revise 25 August 1945; CM14(45) 12 July 1945; CAB 66/67, CP(45)64.
33. PRO FO 371/60604/ZM3774/89/22, 11 November 1946.
34. PRO FO 371/60622/ZM619/187/22, 21 February 1946, ZM315/187/22, 24 February 1946.
35. PRO FO 371/60604/ZM3612/89/22, 22 October 1946, ZM3774/89/22, 15 November 1946; FO 371/60603/ZM264/89/22, 18 October 1946; FO 371/67731/ZM238/135/22, 28 February 1947.
36. PRO FO 371/60604/ZM3774/89/22, 11 November 1946.
37. Cmd.7026, *Treaty of Peace with Italy*, xx–xxiv, 1946–7; see also Wheeler-Bennett and Nicholls (1972).
38. ibid.
39. PRO FO 371/60604/ZM3162/89/22, 1 November 1946.
40. PRO FO 371/60603/ZM2883/89/22, 22 August 1946.
41. PRO FO 371/60604/ZM3162/89/22, 1 November 1946.
42. PRO FO 371/67792/Z4523/135/22, 13 March 1947.
43. PRO FO 371/67793/Z8558/135/22, 28 August 1947, Z7453/135/22, 15 August 1947.
44. PRO FO 371/67792/25735/135/22, 9 June 1947.
45. PRO FO 371/67793/28817/135/22, 8 October 1947.
46. PRO FO 371/60563/ZM2639, 3 August 1946; see also *FRUS* (Foreign Relations of the United States (1946), p. 940; Miller (1986, pp. 39–40).
47. PRO CAB 129/23 CM(48)6, CM(48)7.
48. PRO FO 371/73199, Z2308/1392/22, 17 March 1948.
49. PRO FO 371/73191/Z637/637/637/22, 24 January 1948.
50. PRO FO 371/73192/Z8985/637/22, 29 October 1948.
51. PRO FO 371/73192/Z9863/637/22, 6 December 1948.
52. PRO FO 371/73191/Z2454/637/22, 22 March 1948.
53. PRO FO 371/73191/Z8329/637/22, 18 October 1948; Z7354/637/22, 4 May 1948.
54. PRO FO 371/73191/Z6059/637/22, 26 July 1948.
55. PRO FO 371/73191/Z637/22, 26 January 1948.
56. The Italian Peace Treaty limited Italy's armed forces to 300,000 men and set total reparations of $360 million. The independence of Albania and Ethiopia were confirmed. Italy had to return the Dodecanese Islands to Greece and to cede a small amount of territory to France. Trieste became a Free Territory and the Italians surrendered most of their fleet to the victorious powers. Finally, Italy renounced its rights to all its colonies.
57. PRO FO 371/73191/Z4057/637/22, 13 May 1948, Z3464/637/22, 26 April 1948, Z3675/637/22, 1 May 1948.

References

Butler, J.R.M. (1957), *Grand Strategy*, Vol. II, London, HMSO
Cerquetti, E. (1975), *Le Forze Armate Italiene dal 1945 al 1975*, Milan, Feltrinelli.
Ciano, G. (1947), *Diary 1939–43*, London, Heinemann.
Einzig, P. (1941), *Economic Warfare 1939–1940*, London, Macmillan.
Ellwood, D. (1985), *Italy 1943–1945*, Leicester, Leicester University Press.
Hildebrand, K. (1973), *The Foreign Policy of the Third Reich*, London, Batsford.
Jebb, H.M.G. (1972), *The Memoirs of Lord Gladwyn*, London, Weidenfield & Nicolson.
Kent, J. (1989), 'Bevin's imperialism and the idea of EuroAfrica, 1945–49', in M. Dockrill and J. Young (eds), *British Foreign Policy, 1945–56*, Basingstoke, Macmillan.
Knox, M. (1982), *Mussolini Unleashed 1939–41: Politics and Strategy in Fascist Italy's Last War*, Cambridge, Cambridge University Press.
Lowe, C.J. and Marzari, F. (1975), *Italian Foreign Policy 1870–1940*, London, Routledge & Kegan Paul.
Medlicott, W.N. (1952), *The Economic Blockade*, Vol. I, London, HMSO.
Miller, J.E. (1983), 'Taking off the Gloves: the United States and the Italian Elections of 1948', in *Diplomatic History*, vol. VII, 1983, pp. 33–55.
Miller, J.E. (1986), *The United States and Italy 1940–1950*, Chapel Hill, University of North Carolina Press.
Pisano, (1987), 'The Italian armed forces', in Gann, D. (ed.), *The Defence of Western Europe*, London, Croom Helm.
Playfair, I.S.O. (1954), *The Mediterranean and the Middle East*, Vol. I, London, HMSO.
Quarone, A. (1974), 'Public opinion in Italy before the outbreak of World War II', in R. Sarti (ed.), *The Axe Within: Italian Fascism in Action*, New York, New Viewpoints.
Smith, E.T. (1983) 'The Fear of Subversion; the United States and the Inclusion of Italy in the North Atlantic Treaty', in *Diplomatic History*, vol. VII, pp. 139–55.
Smith, D. Mack (1979), *Mussolini's Roman Empire*, Harmondsworth, Penguin.
Tarchiani, A. (1955), *Dieci Anni tra Roma e Washington*, Milan, Mondadori.
Toynbee, A. and Toynbee, V. (1945), *Survey of International Affairs*, Oxford, Oxford University Press.
Varsori, A. (1976), ' "Senior" o "Equal" Partner', *Rivista di Studi Politici Internazionali*, vol. 43.
Varsori, A. (1982), 'La Gran Bretagna e le Elezione Politiche Italiane del Aprile 1948', *Storia Contemporanea*, vol. XIII, pp. 5–7.
Wheeler-Bennett, J. and Nichols, A.J. (1972), *The Semblance of Peace with Italy*, London, Macmillan.

Index